Genes and Behavior

Nature–Nurture Interplay Explained

D0017804

Michael Rutter

Blackwell
Publishing

BLACKWELL PUBLISHING
350 Main Street, Malden, MA 02148-5020, USA
9600 Garsington Road, Oxford OX4 2DQ, UK
550 Swanston Street, Carlton, Victoria 3053, Australia

First published 2006 by Blackwell Publishing Ltd

3   2008

Library of Congress Cataloging-in-Publication Data

Rutter, Michael.
Genes and behavior : nature/nurture interplay explained / Michael Rutter.
p. cm.
Includes bibliographical references and index.
ISBN 978-1-4051-1062-4 (hardcover) — ISBN 978-1-4051-1061-7 (pbk.)
1. Behavior genetics.   I. Title.

QH457 R88 2006
155.7—dc22
2005024530

A catalogue record for this title is available from the British Library.

Set in 10.5/12.5pt Dante
by Graphicraft Limited, Hong Kong
Printed and bound Singapore
by Fabulous Printers Pte Ltd

The publisher's policy is to use permanent paper from mills that operate
a sustainable forestry policy, and which has been manufactured from pulp
processed using acid-free and elementary chlorine-free practices. Furthermore,
the publisher ensures that the text paper and cover board used have met
acceptable environmental accreditation standards.

For further information on
Blackwell Publishing, visit our website:
www.blackwellpublishing.com

Contents

Preface

For far too long, behavioral genetics and socialization theory have been viewed as necessarily in opposition to one another. Researchers in both "camps" have very rarely referred to studies from the other "camp," other than to attack their concepts and findings. The result has been much fruitless dispute and serious misunderstandings of what each body of research has to contribute. My main aim in writing this book has been to provide a readable, non-technical account of what is involved in the possible various ways in which genetic influences on behavior may be important. That involves conveying something of how genes operate but, in making this clear, it will be very evident that genes do not operate in isolation. Hence, there will have to be a discussion of what is known about environmental influences and how the interplay between nature and nurture "works" over the course of development. "Nurture" is often used to refer only to patterns of upbringing in the family, but as used in the title of this book it is intended to cover a broader range of environmental experiences.

I am not trained as a geneticist but I have been a user of behavioral genetics for some 30 years[1] and I have made myself informed about genetic mechanisms and genetic issues. However, I have also been a developmental and psychosocial researcher over this same period of time.[2] The bringing together of these backgrounds has meant that I have ended up being both a strong supporter of behavioral genetics[3] and, to some extent, a critic of the excesses of behavioral genetics[4]. Accordingly, I am hopefully well positioned to be a "translator" of specialist genetic concepts and findings. In addition, I have been much involved in ethical considerations with respect to genetic research ethics.[5] This, too, helps to provide a good background for bringing about the integration that I want to achieve.

The first chapter outlines the major accomplishments of genetics and then goes on to consider why the topic of genes and behavior has proved to be so surprisingly controversial. In part, this arose through misunderstandings and misleading claims, but also it has to be accepted that genetics has been misused in the past and could be misused again in the future if it is not dealt with properly. Critics of genetics have attacked what they viewed as a damaging biological reductionism. Accordingly, the meaning of this concept is discussed, noting both the positive and negative aspects of reductionist approaches.

As is apparent throughout the book, genetic influences operate in a probabilistic, not deterministic, fashion. In order to indicate what this means, the second chapter discusses the concepts of risk and protective factors as they apply to both genetic and environmental influences. The evidence shows that it is usually necessary to think in dimensional as well as categorical terms with respect to both influences that contribute to causation and to behavior. Traditionally, people have tended to make a sharp distinction between abnormal disorders or conditions and normal variations as they occur in the general population. Modern research has shown that with respect to somatic conditions such as coronary artery disease, or mental disorders such as depression, there is much continuity between the two. That is so even with severe disorders, such as schizophrenia and autism.

Against that backcloth, Chapter 3 provides an account of how twin, family, and adoptee studies can be used to determine the relative strength of genetic and environmental influences on individual differences in behavior (both normal and abnormal) within particular populations. Chapter 4 then summarizes what has been found in relation to a selection of important mental disorders and normal traits or characteristics. Chapter 5 does the same with respect to environmental influences.

Chapter 6 serves a bridging role between the first group of chapters, concerned with quantifying the strength of genetic and environmental influences, and the second group of chapters, concerned with specific identified genes or with how genes work. Thus, Chapter 6 outlines what is known about different patterns of inheritance. Chapter 7 then provides an account of what genes actually do. Although written in a simplified way using non-technical language, Chapters 6 and 7 are likely to involve concepts and approaches that are least familiar to non-geneticists. Readers who do not wish to know the details may decide to omit these chapters. However, it is hoped that they will not make that choice, because an understanding of how genes work is crucial for an appreciation of the importance of genetics in relation to behavior – as well as to an understanding of the limits of genetics. Chapter 8 describes the methods used to find individual genes that may have effects on the behavior and summarizes what has been found with respect to the genes involved in susceptibility to develop certain key mental disorders.

Chapter 9 brings together genes and environment through a discussion of the role of gene–environment correlations and interactions.[6] In many respects, this constitutes the central issue for the book. That is because it shows that genes and environment cannot be viewed as totally separate and independent.

To an important extent, genes operate *through* the environment. That is, their effects come about first because the likelihood that a person encounters risky environments is influenced by that person's genetically influenced behavior in shaping and selecting their environments. The second way in which the environment is implicated is that genes influence a person's susceptibility to risk environments. People vary in their environmental vulnerability and genes are implicated in their individual differences.

Chapter 10, in effect, turns the tables by focusing on what environments do to genes. In the past, it has usually been assumed that genes do not change as a result of experiences. That is true insofar as gene sequences[7] are involved, but it is not true in the case of the expression of genes[8] in body tissues. That is to say, although the DNA is what a person inherits, the effects of that DNA are dependent on a chain reaction that ends up with the expression of the products of the DNA in the structure and function of individual cells (as described in Chapter 7). That is how environments can and do alter genes. The study of gene expression takes us into the realms of quite complicated basic science, but Chapter 10 concentrates on the fruits of that research (which is crucially important and readily understandable), rather than the biochemistry involved in the experiments.

Finally, Chapter 11 seeks to draw the threads together and to look ahead in relation to the likely implications for policy and practice.

Notes

See Reference list for full details.
1   Folstein & Rutter, 1977 a & b; Rutter, 1994, 2004
2   Rutter, 1972, 2002 a
3   Rutter, 1994; Rutter, 2004; Rutter & McGuffin, 2004
4   Rutter, 2002 b; Rutter & McGuffin, 2004; Rutter et al., 2001 a
5   Royal College of Psychiatrists, 2001; Rutter, 1999 a
6   Gene–environment correlations refer to genetic influences on the likelihood that individuals will encounter particular risk or protective environments. The genetic influence operates through effects on those behaviors that serve to shape people's choice of situations or experiences. Gene–environment interactions refer to genetic influences on people's sensitivity or vulnerability to particular risk or protective environments.
7   Gene sequences provide the genetic information and they comprise the particular order of the chemical bases (adenine, guanine, cytosine and thymine – A, G, C, and T for short) in the DNA (deoxyribonucleic acid) and then into translated protein (see Chapter 7).
8   Gene expression concerns the process by which the DNA exerts its effects through transcription into messenger RNA (ribonucleic acid) and then into translated protein (see Chapter 7).

Acknowledgments

For most of what I have learned about genetics, I am deeply indebted to colleagues at the Social, Genetic and Developmental Psychiatry Research Centre at the Institute of Psychiatry in London; to colleagues at the Virginia Institute for Psychiatric and Behavioral Genetics in Richmond, Virginia; to colleagues at the Wellcome Trust Centre for Human Genetics at the University of Oxford; and at earlier points in my career to working with Susan Folstein, Irving Gottesman, and Jerry Shields. I am particularly grateful to my wife Marjorie (with whom I collaborated on a book on development in the early 1990s), and to Avshalom Caspi, Kenneth Kendler, Terrie Moffitt, Tony Monaco, Barbara Maughan, Stephen Scott, and Anita Thapar, who read an earlier draft of the manuscript and who provided many helpful suggestions and comments. Needless to say, any misinterpretations that remain are entirely my responsibility. Deborah Ballinger-Mills and Jenny Wickham were enormously helpful in sorting out figures and references, in noting infelicities or ambiguities in wording, and in bringing the manuscript as a whole into its final state. To all of these people, many thanks.

Michael Rutter

Chapter 1

Why is the topic of genes and behavior controversial?

In this book, I set out to explain why the topic of genetics is so important for all of us, and specifically how it can be very informative with respect to questions about the causes and course of both mental disorders (such as depression or schizophrenia) and normal psychological characteristics (such as variations in scholastic achievement or **personality** characteristics). In the course of outlining the real value of genetics, I will, however, need to point out the "hype" and exaggeration associated with some genetic claims, as well as the widespread misunderstanding of genetics by some critics who have opposed its influence.

Before turning to a consideration of why the topic of genes and behavior has proved to be so surprisingly controversial, thereby setting the scene for the book, I need to say something of the achievements and claims of genetics. These involve both basic laboratory science and more applied studies.

Accomplishments of genetics

The history of genetics goes back to the mid-nineteenth century when, using studies of pea plants, Mendel (the Austrian monk, also trained as a scientist) concluded that genes were particulate factors that were passed on from generation to generation, each **gene** existing in alternate forms, now called **alleles** (see Lewin, 2004). Curiously, the importance of his discovery was not recognized at the time; indeed, it was not appreciated until well after his death. Also, it was not until the mid-twentieth century that it became clear that deoxyribonucleic acid (**DNA**) constituted the relevant genetic material. However, even then, there was no understanding of how it might work.

At the time I was a medical student in the early 1950s it was not even known how many chromosomes humans had (that was discovered in 1956) and there was discussion of how Down syndrome might be a result of stress!

(Its origin in an extra chromosome 21 was discovered only in 1959[1].) With respect to the basic biological mechanisms, the key breakthrough came in 1953, with the discovery by Watson and Crick that DNA had a paired helix (corkscrew) structure. In wonderful understatement, they concluded their paper by stating: "It has not escaped our notice that the specific pairing we have postulated immediately suggests a possible copying mechanism for the genetic material."[2] Another key step was Fred Sanger's description in 1977 of how to determine the precise sequence of **nucleotides** in any strand of DNA. Both these discoveries rightly led to Nobel prizes. Over the second half of the twentieth century, there was an awesome and spectacular series of scientific discoveries in molecular biology (some of which gave rise to further Nobel prizes), leading to a rich understanding of the detailed biology of how genes operated, a few key details of which are outlined in Chapter 7.[3]

Quite apart from the basic science elucidation of the biological mechanisms underlying gene action, technological (and conceptual) advances paved the way for the identification of genes associated with the liability to specific diseases. Perhaps the first crucial step was the discovery that enzymes could be used to cut the DNA at a particular sequence. A further step was the discovery of polymorphic markers (meaning that they took several forms that varied from individual to individual) that extended across the whole genome. The first type was called a restriction fragment length polymorphism (RFLD) but these have been largely superseded by microsatellite simple sequence repeats (SSRs) and more recently by single nucleotide polymorphisms (SNPs) – the advantage of the more recent developments being the far greater number of markers available. Two other advances had also revolutionized molecular genetic possibilities. First, the discovery of the polymerase chain reaction in the mid-1980s made it possible to have selective amplification of specific target **DNA sequence**s and permitted the cloning (i.e., reproduction) of genes, so facilitating their study. Second, high speed robotic methods were developed that enabled rapid screening of the whole genome for the markers being used. In addition, there have been important advances in the statistical methods needed in gene identification. Lastly, it is necessary to emphasize the importance of the discovery of the major extent of the overlap in genes across animal species, thereby making it possible to learn lessons from research on other organisms (including yeast and the fruit fly) and to test hypotheses on gene function through **animal models**.

The consequence of these revolutionary developments has been the identification of the individual genes responsible for a huge number of single-gene medical conditions (meaning those due to genes without the need for specific environmental factors – see Chapter 6). Progress has been slower with respect to the genes involved in susceptibility to multifactorial disorders in which there is a complex interplay among multiple genetic and environmental **risk factors** but, as discussed in Chapter 8, progress is now being made.

It might be thought that, although all of this is undoubtedly tremendously exciting from a scientific perspective, it may not have provided much understanding of the genetic issues involved in specific medical conditions. However, there have been important clinical advances, as exemplified by some of the unusual genetic mechanisms discussed in Chapter 6.

Because scientists recognized the huge medical, as well as scientific, potential of an adequate understanding of how individual genes worked and how they brought about their effects, the internationally collaborative Human Genome Project (HGP) was launched in 1990 to sequence the entire human genome. Draft reports were published in 2001 by both the HGP and a rival commercial concern, Celeron Genomics.[4] A further report was published in 2004. One key finding is that the number of protein-coding genes (20–25,000) is quite a lot less than used to be thought. This has implications for an understanding of gene action – discussed in Chapter 7.

In parallel with early developments in genetic mechanisms in the first half of the twentieth century, and the rapidly burgeoning field of molecular biology in the second half of that century, there was the somewhat separate development of population quantitative genetics. In a real sense, Francis Galton's study in the mid-nineteenth century of how talent ran in families provided the forerunner for this field, but it was the statisticians Karl Pearson and Ronald Fisher, together with the geneticist J.B.S. Haldane, who provided the foundation for this branch of genetics. Twin and adoptee studies were used to great effect to determine the relative importance of genetic and environmental influences on psychological **traits** and on mental disorders. With respect to the latter, Eliot Slater was a key figure, both through his setting up of the Maudsley Hospital Twin Register in 1948 and through the research in his own Medical Research Council Psychiatric Genetics Unit. During the second half of the twentieth century there were crucially important developments in both sampling and statistics and, as a result, an impressive corpus of knowledge was built up on the heritability of a wide range of psychological traits and mental disorders.[5] It was important, too, that there was a much more critical approach to twin and adoptee studies than there had been in the earlier days.[6] In particular, researchers appreciated the necessity of combining different research strategies. The outcome was the demonstration that genetic factors played a significant role in individual differences in the liability to show almost all human psychological traits and to suffer almost all mental disorders. In a few instances (such as **autism** and **schizophrenia**), genetic influences predominate, but in a larger number they are contributory to a lesser degree (accounting for some 20 to 60 percent of the variance in the general population).

Three key findings were particularly important. First, for the great majority of traits or disorder, *both* genetic and environmental factors were influential – meaning that any neat subdivision into those due to nature and those due to nurture was bound to be misleading. Second, except in rare circumstances, genes were not determinative of either psychological characteristics or mental disorders, and their influence involved a complex mix of direct and indirect effects operating on different parts of the causal chains. Third, the pervasive impact of genetic influences extended to social behaviors and attitudes, and even to the likelihood of experiencing particular types of risk environments.

It might be thought that these spectacular developments in genetics over the past half-century might be universally welcomed for the benefits that might be expected to follow. However, the reactions of professionals and the lay public alike have been quite mixed and I need to turn now to what is entailed in the various controversies.

Supposed lack of medical utility

Le Fanu,[7] whilst appreciative of the science, described "The New Genetics" as one of the major failures of modern medicine. He drew attention to the fact that the promise that genetic research would elucidate the causes of disease and thereby lead to effective new methods of treatment and of prevention had simply not been fulfilled because it had had such extremely limited success in producing successful genetic engineering, genetic screening, and gene therapy. He went on to argue that this was because, on the whole, genes do not play an important role in disease and, when they do (as in single-gene conditions such as cystic fibrosis), the genetic effects are so complex and elusive that not much can be done about them. He was undoubtedly correct in his assessment that gene therapy had been oversold,[8] and that genetics had not led to dramatic gains in drug discovery. Nevertheless, his conclusion was both premature and unduly pessimistic. The mistake was to equate genetic influences with single-gene disorders (it is correct that these account for a tiny proportion of medical conditions) and to assume (following, it has to be said, some genetic evangelists) that gene identification itself will elucidate the causes of disease (it will not). As discussed in Chapter 4, the findings from twin and adoptee studies are compelling in showing that genetic influences are highly important (albeit not determinative) in all medical conditions, including mental disorders. But the genes, in almost all cases, operate together with environmental influences as part of multifactorial causation (see Chapter 2 for a discussion of what this means).

The premature nature of the dismissal of "The New Genetics" arises from two different considerations. First, and most crucially, it ignores the need for biological research that uses pointers from genetics but which goes beyond it in order to elucidate *how* the causal influences operate. Gene discovery on its own will not do that. As discussed in Chapter 7, DNA itself does not cause any kind of disease process and, hence, identifying an individual gene that predisposes to some disease outcome is not directly informative. As Bryson[9] puts it, in his very readable popular gallop across the field of science, the cracking of the human genome constitutes only the beginning because it does not indicate *how* effects come about. Proteins are the workhorses that provide the action and, so far, we know remarkably little about their activity in relation to disease (and even less in relation to behavior). The term "**proteomics**" was introduced a few years ago to cover the new research field of the operation of protein interactions. If we are to understand how genes are involved in the causation of disease we will need major advances in proteomics and that will take time to happen.

However, understanding the chemistry, crucial though that is, will not be enough on its own. There is the further need to elucidate the complex pathways through which the chemical effects play a role in leading to a particular disease or a particular trait or characteristic. That will require an integrative physiology that moves from cell chemistry to whole body physiology, and that develops and tests hypotheses or ideas on how the processes may lead to the outcome being considered. In addition, there will be a need for the rather different field of molecular epidemiology in order to understand the interplay between genes and the environment as a crucial part of the causal processes. All of this is potentially doable but it will take time (many decades and not just months or a few years) and we are only just learning how to pursue the long path from gene discovery to determination of the causal processes.[10] The dismissal of "The New Genetics" was also premature because it failed to appreciate the time span required to identify the genes implicated in multifactorial disorders and traits. Again, the scientists have been responsible for arousing expectations that cannot be met. Thus Plomin and Crabbe[11] some five years ago claimed that we will soon "be awash with susceptibility genes." As Chapter 8 indicates, important progress has been made but it continues to prove quite difficult to identify genes for multifactorial traits (somatic or psychological) because most genes have such small effects and because their effects are often contingent on environmental circumstances (see Chapter 9 for a discussion of **gene–environment interactions**). As I hope this book will demonstrate, there is every reason to suppose that "The New Genetics" will deliver the goods but it will do so only if it combines effectively with other branches of science.

The supposed poor quality of the evidence from twin and adoptee studies

Quantitative behavioral genetics (as distinct from medical genetics) has been subject to particularly scathing and sweeping attacks on the supposed poor quality of twin and adoptee studies, as well as on the basic concept of heritability as applied to individual variations in psychological characteristics.[12] As discussed in Chapters 3 and 4, it has to be accepted that some of the methodological criticisms, particularly of the earlier research, has some validity. Not enough attention has been paid to questioning the assumptions of the twin design[13] and there has often been a failure to appreciate the consequences of the restriction in environmental range in adoptive families,[14] as well as concerns over sampling issues[15] and the effects of biased participation in studies.[16] These criticisms have some validity but the critics who have been keen to dismiss the whole of behavior genetics[17] have been equally guilty of selective attention to research findings. Any dispassionate critic would have to conclude that the evidence in favor of an important genetic influence on individual differences is undeniable, even though there are reasonable uncertainties over the degree of population variance accounted for.[18]

Three main points are relevant. First, particular attention needs to be paid to the studies that have addressed the methodological challenges most successfully (see Chapter 4). Second, attention needs to be paid to the extent to which different studies (with contrasting patterns of strengths and limitations) give rise to the same conclusions. Third, it is necessary to ask how likely it is that environmental influences could account for the overall pattern of findings. It is obvious that they could not. Opinions may reasonably differ on the strength of genetic influences but there can be no reasonable doubt that they are important.

Fraud and bias in behavioral genetics

A further concern stems from the evidence that behavioral genetic research has occasionally involved outright fraud, as exemplified by Cyril Burt's twin data.[19] Burt was a very distinguished British academic psychologist who undertook an important pioneering epidemiological study of mental retardation, who did much to establish applied psychology as a profession, and who played a key role in the development of factor analysis (a statistical method for studying how traits group together). However, he was also a strong proponent of the strength of genetic influences on intelligence and his published twin findings (for a variety of good reasons) came to be suspected of fraudulent manipulation. Some of the protagonists of behavioral genetics (especially those focusing on IQ) have strenuously sought to deny or downplay the evidence of fraud.[20] However, most dispassionate reviewers have concluded that the evidence of manipulation of data is sufficiently strong for it to be necessary to exclude Burt's data on the grounds of their untrustworthiness. In addition to rank fraud, there has also been concern over the ways in which some behavioral geneticists have been quite biased in their approach to research evidence.[21] These are serious scientific concerns, but it is important that the conclusions on genetic influences are much the same whether or not the disputed data are included or excluded. Nevertheless, the slipperiness has definitely not helped the behavioral geneticists' cause. It has been most unfortunate that, because some behavioral geneticists have been reluctant to accept the reality of fraud and bias, the far greater volume of high quality twin research has been unfairly castigated.

Acceptance of funding from organizations with an axe to grind

A somewhat related concern is that some behavioral geneticists have appeared to support the racist use of genetics and have definitely been willing to accept financial support for their research from highly suspect organizations. Thus, Eysenck and Jensen have seen no problem in their accepting funding from the Pioneer Fund, which has been widely regarded as having racist aims. Hans Eysenck, like Burt, was a very distinguished academic psychologist in London. He undertook some very important quantitative studies of personality dimensions as they related to mental disorder, and through his disciples he pioneered the use of behavioral methods of psychological treatment. He was a brilliant teacher and communicator and was a most effective popularizer of psychology, through a series of very readable paperbacks. However, he was also an enthusiastic controversialist in relation to race and IQ, smoking and cancer, and astrology. Throughout his career, he was suspected of being a bit dodgy in his use of evidence,[22] although he was never formally investigated for fraud. Nevertheless, his employing institution required him to hand back a research grant he had obtained from the Pioneer Fund for a study that he had "overlooked" submitting to the Ethics Committee.

Arthur Jensen, an American academic psychologist, is a world expert on the concepts and findings with respect to the notion of "g" as the central biological core of general intelligence.[23] He has undertaken some very important high quality research on this topic but, with respect to concerns over genetics, he is particularly associated with a scholarly paper that argued that the on-average lower IQ of African Americans as compared with Whites was likely to be due to their genetic endowment and also that attempts to raise IQ through educational interventions were doomed to fail.[24] Although he has been unwilling publicly to admit it, his arguments are known to be flawed (because it is not justifiable to infer the cause of a between-group difference on the basis of within-group findings[25] and because scarcely any of the twin data was on African Americans). He has argued that there has never been any attempt by the funding organization to censure his reporting of evidence[26] but there is good evidence that the source of funding does influence the ways in which findings are reported – as evident in the source of funding of drug studies.[27] Eysenck[28] similarly always argued that his critical discussion of the links between smoking and lung cancer were uninfluenced by his extensive support from tobacco companies. However, there is good evidence that British American Tobacco did suppress scientific findings[29] and, frankly, it is naïve to suppose that it is irrelevant who funds a particular scientist's research. Quite rightly, recommendations on ethical guidelines now stipulate that funding sources must be taken into account.[30]

In addition, there have been concerns over the misuse of genetic findings in support of discriminatory **eugenics** practices. Thus, for example, on the basis of eugenic principles, in the mid-1930s some 20,000 Americans were sterilized against their will.[31] Nazi Germany carried things even further, with some 322,000 suffering the same fate between 1934 and 1939. Of course, it is true that these abhorrent policies were based on a misunderstanding of the genetic findings but it is the case that they were supported by some very distinguished geneticists. Most people would consider that, although this historic past is both deplorable and extremely regrettable, it is not relevant to the situation today. But is that so? Müller-Hill[32] suggested that when susceptibility genes for IQ are discovered, there may well be a reemergence of concepts of genetic superiority and inferiority (because of views about IQ – see below) with consequent eugenic temptations. Also, there are reasonable concerns over the views of some distinguished (but ethically naïve) geneticists that "designer babies" (chosen on the basis of their genes) are an appropriate way forward.[33]

The holy grail of identifying the genes for intelligence

It is obvious that behavioral genetics has no particular focus on IQ or general intelligence; rather, it is concerned with genetic and environmental influences on all psychological characteristics and mental disorders. Nevertheless, it is the case that controversies have particularly concentrated on claims regarding the **heritability** of IQ. Kamin's book[34] on *"The Science and Politics of IQ"* includes the claim that: "there exist no data which should lead a prudent man to accept the hypothesis that IQ scores are in any way heritable." In fact, there is abundant evidence to indicate the importance of genetic influences on individual differences in IQ – most estimates put the heritability at about 50 percent. However, the basic critique is less about the precise level of heritability than it is about the tendency of some genetically minded psychologists to argue that a few traits are of such overwhelming importance that it is desirable that everyone should possess the same outstanding qualities. Thus, a regrettably large number of writers have sought to elevate IQ to a superordinate position in which it is seen as *the* human quality that is more important than all others, so that social or ethnic groups that are supposedly lacking in IQ should be treated differently and that the search for the genes that influence IQ should constitute the holy grail of behavioral genetics.[35] Of course, there is no denying that high IQ is quite a strong predictor of worldly success – both educational and occupational. Moreover, this appears to be the case in societies that differ widely in their political and social circumstances.[36]

On the other hand, follow-up studies of very high IQ individuals have shown that they are by no means all universally successful in adult life. Many human qualities other than IQ are vitally important in successful human adaptation. We are social animals, as well as thinking, talking animals, and success in a broad sense is much influenced by skills in social relationships, as well as by general intelligence. It would be foolish indeed to focus exclusively on IQ to the neglect of a much broader range of important adaptive human qualities. Also, however, it would be equally foolish to assume that it is desirable that everyone should be of high IQ and that genetic manipulation should be used to "design" high IQ children. To begin with, that could well mean inadvertent disadvantageous effects on other desirable human qualities. But, also, it is extremely questionable whether it would be either biologically or socially beneficial if everyone were similar with respect to high intelligence. Individual variation is an intrinsic part of biology and it would be ridiculous, as well as completely hopeless, to attempt to remove such individual differences and to seek to make everyone the same.

The supposed inequalities associated with individual differences

From a biological perspective, it is positively desirable to have individuals (both human and other animals) that vary in their skills, qualities, and limitations. There is no one "model" that would be ideal for all conditions, and there never could be. Traits that make for adaptability and success in one environment may not work so well in others. It is biologically advantageous for there to be individual variation so that there can be successful adaptation to new environmental conditions as and when they arise. That is, of course, one of the key features of how evolution takes place, and it is a central concept in genetics.

Nevertheless, over the years, social reformers and social scientists have often been concerned that individual differences create social inequalities, which are inherently undesirable. There is, indeed, much evidence of the adverse health consequences stemming from wide social inequalities, with the ill-effects evident in those at the bottom of the social hierarchy.[37] The precise causal mechanisms of these effects of social inequity remain ill-understood,[38] although part of the disadvantage stems from limitations in the availability and access to medical and other services[39] and part from lifestyle effects on features such as smoking, diet, and exercise. It is a matter of legitimate concern that social inequities have increased in countries such as the USA (especially) and the UK, with the gap between the rich and poor increasing.

However, this is not at all equivalent to a desire to remove individual differences. Tawney expressed the issue this way: "While . . . natural endowments differ profoundly, it is the mark of a civilized society to aim at eliminating such inequalities as have their own source, not in individual differences, but in its own organization . . . Individual differences that are the source of social energy are more likely to ripen and find expression if social inequalities are, as far as practical, diminished."[40] In other words, the problem lies in the ways in which societies put in place artificial disadvantaging "blocks" that impede people's performance and which prevent them reaching their potential and exercising their skills to their best advantage. It is clear that such "blocks" are brought about by discriminatory housing policies, lack of educational opportunities, and the various forms of racial and religious discrimination that are endemic in most societies. It is crucially important that a focus on the importance of genetic influences does not lead to a neglect of these vitally important societal influences. We need to understand better how they operate and we need to take the appropriate societal actions to deal with the damaging and disadvantaging inequities. But that should not get muddled up with a futile, and damaging, quest to get rid of bio-logically influenced individual differences.

Nevertheless, some psychologists have been worried that a focus on genetics may divert interest and attention from the important social influences on behavior.[41] It has to be admitted that this worry has both historical and contemporary roots in the writings of genetic enthusiasts. Thus Eliot Slater, who did so much to establish psychiatric genetics in Britain (see above), was notoriously hostile to social psychiatry and to those working in that field.[42]

Also, his championing of biology was associated with an uncritical advocacy of brain surgery as a treatment for mental disorders – so much so that he saw this likely to develop as a distinct specialty.[43] Similarly, Steven Pinker – a most distinguished language expert – set up the ridiculous "straw man" that non-geneticists believed that the mind is "a blank slate" (meaning that nurture can change everything) and thereby condemned the entire field of social research.[44]

The worry that a focus on genetics may lead to a neglect of social influences has some validity in addition because the dominance of genetic, and broader biological, concepts focuses on individual differences rather than on levels of either disorder or psychological functioning as known to vary either over time or between populations.[45] Thus, environmental factors have to be implicated in the major increase over the past half-century or so in levels of crime, substance use and misuse, and suicide in young people. Equally, they are involved in the rise in the average level of intelligence.[46] That does not mean that there are not continuing major genetic influences on individual differences in all these traits but it does mean that there have to be non-genetic factors that are responsible for the changes in level. Changes in the gene pool take place too slowly to account for such major time trends. Equally, it is obviously implausible that genetic factors are responsible for the fact that homicide is at least a dozen times as common in the United States as it is in Europe. In all probability, there are genetic factors involved in propensities to engage in such violent behavior but the national differences are not likely to be attributable to genetic factors; rather, the evidence indicates that they are a function of access to firearms.[47] Behavioral genetics has rightly been criticized for ignoring this evidence. Of course, that does not mean that genetic factors are not involved through interplay with the environment but it does mean that a straightforwardly deterministic view of genetic factors is unwarranted.

Overstatement of genetic claims

A related concern is that not only are the genetic claims overstated, but some geneticists resolutely ignore the evidence that runs counter to their evangelism. Thus, both Baumrind[41] and Jackson[41] drew attention to the limitations in some behavioral geneticists' considerations of the evidence, but also took exception to the claims that only extreme environments matter and that variations in rearing in families is of no real consequence.[48] As discussed in Chapter 5, these sweeping assertions on the irrelevance of the family environment are not supported by the research evidence. It is quite striking that behavioral genetics reviews usually totally ignore the findings on environmental influences. It is almost as if research by non-geneticists is irrelevant. The underlying problem is that many behavioral geneticists have been reluctant to pay attention to evidence that does not derive directly from the use of genetic designs. The end product has been a rather one-sided approach to research findings.

There is no doubt that some of the proponents of behavioral genetics have been guilty of evangelistic overstatement and misleading claims, but that does not mean that they are wholly wrong in the arguments that they are putting forth. The purpose of this volume is to try to take a dispassionate view of the research evidence and, thereby, to come up with conclusions on the probable role of genes in influencing individual differences in behavior. Inevitably, that will mean a cool hard look at the evidence on what genes actually do, as well as an equally rigorous look at how genetic mechanisms might play a role in shaping individual differences in behavior.

How could there be genes for social behavior?

Critics of behavioral genetics have cast scorn on the apparent absurdity of the idea that there could be genetic influences on behaviors that are manifestly social, such as crime, divorce, and homosexuality. However, this attack rather misses the point. Of course, it is the case that there is not, and could not be, a gene for any of these behaviors, but individuals do vary in their propensity to show those behaviors and, insofar as that is the case, there is every reason to suppose that genetic factors will be implicated (see Chapters 4 and 8). It makes no sense to try to subdivide behaviors into those that are social and those that are not. To a degree, all behavior is influenced by social context and social forces, but that does not mean that it is not also influenced by genetic factors. It would be truly absurd to suppose that, although there are genetic influences on everything else, susceptibility to the environment is unique in not being influenced by genetic factors. Evolutionary concepts make clear that genes are very much involved in adaptation to different environments, and the empirical evidence (see Chapter 9) provides demonstrations of such gene–environment **correlation**s and interactions.

The supposed inappropriateness of neurogenetic determinism

Finally, and perhaps most importantly, there have been critiques of what seems to be neurogenetic determinism.[49] Some of these arguments are better based than others. For example, Rose[50] argued that the behavioral genetics claims imply a directness of genetic effects (as exemplified by references to genes "for" **schizophrenia** or "for" **autism** or "for" **bipolar disorder**) that are out of keeping with the evidence that genetic pathways are much more indirect than that. The DNA influences the **RNA**, which influences the production of polypeptides and thereby proteins, which influence the metabolic pathways that cause disorder (see Chapter 7), but it is much more complex than implied by statements that genes lead to any kind of disorder. Such statements also ignore the influence of gene–environment correlations and gene–environment interactions and, especially, ignore the effects of environmental influences on gene expression (see Chapters 9 and 10). In all of these respects, the arguments of the critics of behavioral genetics are on target. Genetic influences are indeed all-pervasive, and extremely important, but they are frequently indirect.

But that is exactly what some leading psychiatric geneticists have themselves been arguing. Kendler[51] firmly states that "the strong, clear and direct causal relationship implied by the concept of 'a gene for' does not exist for psychiatric disorders. Although we may wish it to be true, we do not have and are not likely ever to discover 'genes for' psychiatric illnesses." That accepted (as clearly it must be), it is nevertheless important to be clear what neurogenetic determinism does, and does not, mean. A reductionist approach in science implies that, ultimately, everything is derivable from first principles, that everything at one level is explicable in terms of some lower level, and that what appears to be complex will prove to be accountable for in terms of a limited set of concepts and simpler, more basic, constituents.[52] Rose[50] has objected on the grounds that it transfers the burden of explanation from the social to the individual and, within the individual, from the biological system to the molecular. However, that is to take an unduly narrow view of biology. Dennett[53] has argued convincingly that evolution has meant that humans are thinking, feeling beings with the capacity to imagine what might be, to conceptualize the consequences of different actions, and hence the capacity to evaluate the ends and not just the means. In other words, through our thought processes (and their effects on our behavior) we can influence what happens to us. Determinism definitely does not imply inevitability (because avoidance and prevention may be possible); indeterminism would actually provide less room for maneuver (because it is determinism that allows us to decide how to change things), and real options (and not just apparent ones) exist in a deterministic world. Determinism means that there is a logical structure to how genes operate but it does not mean that genes provide direct causal links with any behavior. Manifestly, they do not.

Rose's[50] other objection is that neurogenetic determinism seems to place all mechanisms within the organism, thereby ignoring both environmental influences and social contextual effects. As discussed throughout the book, that kind of reduction is out of keeping with the evidence.[54] The good side of reductionism lies in the attempt to derive simplifying principles and to identify both organizational constructs and causal pathways. However, the bad side of some forms of reductionism is to seek to do this entirely at the molecular level, ignoring the different levels that have to be considered in terms of what is known about the biology.

Lewontin,[55] whilst noting that holistic explanations cannot provide the answer (because everything is not connected to everything else), emphasizes three main features. First, developmentally there are random effects and not just the specific effects of genes and environment. Second, evolution involves construction, and not just adaptation; in other words, to an important extent organisms shape their environments, just as their environments shape organismic development. Third, there are important feedback loops; a perturbation in one point of a connected system may be the cause of a change in another part, which then leaves a cause for a change in the first part.

Morange[56] put the same point in a slightly different way. He noted that biology is almost always based on a strictly regimented, structured, and dynamic order. Once the processes are properly understood, it is clear that they follow a regular pattern. To that extent, a deterministic view is correct. Genes *do* provide the basis for the process of development and for the functioning of the mature organism.

On the other hand, because the effects of genes are indirect, it is not possible to reduce everything to the molecular level. Organisms are made up of a hierarchy of organizational levels. There is a precise causal chain linking the product of a gene to the actions of that gene within the organism, but this causal chain passes through several different levels of organization. At each level, the chain is transformed and obeys different rules. The complexity starts with the fact that any given gene can have several rather different effects (see Chapter 7). Thus, a given DNA fragment may be involved in making several different messenger RNAs and thus several different proteins, each of which can have different functions. Also, it is misleading to think of a gene as a single thing. The process leading to the production of proteins involves various other genes that do not themselves have a direct effect on proteins but which, nevertheless, exert important effects through their action on genes that do. The route from the protein products to a particular functional feature, such as a behavior, involves yet more indirect links. The finding that a gene is implicated in some way in the pathway leading to a particular behavior does not mean that it causes such a behavior. The protein products of genes do not act in isolation but participate in the formation of complex networks and structures which are then integrated into an overall hierarchical organization. Moreover, with multifactorial traits (and these account for the great majority of behaviors of interest) there is an interplay with the environment that may involve gene–environment correlations, genetic influences on sensitivity to the environment (see Chapter 9), and the effects of the environment on gene expression (see Chapter 10).

The situation may be summarized by saying that basic science genetic studies have been hugely helpful in identifying some of the key organizing principles of how effects come about, but equally they have emphasized that the causal pathways are often probabilistic and indirect.[56]

Also, the genetic effects operate on causal pathways that will often not be specific to particular diagnostic endpoints. We need to be concerned with what these pathways might be (see Chapter 7) but it would be absurd to restrict attention to particular psychiatric diagnoses. There is every reason to suppose that genetic effects apply across all varieties of individual differences in human functioning and there is absolutely no reason to suppose that genetic effects will operate directly on psychiatric diagnoses.

In addition, many concerns have been expressed over the extravagant claims of protagonists of genetics such as Sandra Scarr[57] or David Rowe[58] or Steven Pinker[44] or Judith Rich Harris.[59]

Again, some psychiatric geneticists have expressed much the same views. Kendler[54] has argued that there is a need for a coherent conceptual and philosophical framework for psychiatry that rejects mind–body dualism; that psychiatry is irrevocably grounded in mental, first-person experiences; that a multilevel systems approach is essential; and that it is necessary to embrace complexity and to support empirically rigorous and pluralistic explanatory models. As he explains, using examples, this is *not* to argue for a compromise "bits of everything" concept, but rather it is an acceptance that, as a U.S. National Research Council entitled their report,[60] the science must extend *"From Neurons to Neighborhoods."*

Conclusions

In summary, behavioral genetics has proved controversial because of much of the "hype" associated with it. It has to be said that this is as much a fault of its protagonists as it is of the media account of genetic findings. In this book, I seek to consider the extent to which, beneath the hype, there is real substance in genetic influences on behavior and that there are important implications of genetic findings for our understanding of causal mechanisms with respect to individual differences in both normal behavior and the occurrence of mental disorders. Before turning to the empirical findings on genetics, however, it is necessary to discuss concepts of risk and protective factors in relation to the variations in behavior for which genetic influences might be relevant (Chapter 2).

Notes

See Reference list for full details.

1   See Valentine, 1986; also McKusick, 2002
2   Watson & Crick, 1953
3   See Lewin, 2004 and Strachan & Read, 2004 for clearly expressed authoritative descriptions of the technical details, and Weatherall, 1995 for a very readable account of some of the scientific highlights and their meaning for medicine.
4   International Human Genome Sequencing Consortium, 2001, 2004; Venter et al., 2001; see Sulston & Ferry, 2002 for a more personal account of what was involved in this pioneering international collaboration.
5   Plomin et al., 2001
6   Rutter et al., 1990 & 1999
7   Le Fanu, 1999
8   See Kimmelman, 2005; Marshall, 1995 a & b; Relph et al., 2004
9   Bryson, 2003
10   See Rutter, 2000 a, for a very brief note on this need in relation to autism and Rutter & Plomin, 1997 and McGuffin & Rutter, 2002 for a broader discussion of the role of genetics in providing an understanding of the neural underpinning of mental disorders.
11   Plomin & Crabbe, 2000
12   See Joseph, 2003; Kamin, 1974; Kamin & Goldberger, 2002
13   Rutter et al., 2001 a
14   Stoolmiller, 1999
15   Devlin et al., 1997
16   Taylor, 2004
17   e.g., Joseph, 2003; Kamin, 1974
18   Kendler, 2005 a
19   See Mackintosh, 1995 for a very clear and fair account of the issues.
20   See Miele, 2002 re Jensen's views
21   See Rutter & Tienda, 2005 with respect to Jensen's dealing with the Minnesota Transracial Adoption Study.
22   See Storms & Sigal, 1958 and Pelosi & Appleby, 1992
23   Jensen, 1998
24   Jensen, 1969
25   See Tizard, 1975
26   See Miele, 2003
27   Antonuccio et al., 2003; Bekelman et al., 2003; Blumenthal, 2003
28   Eysenck, 1965, 1971 & 1980
29   Glantz et al., 1995; Hilts, 1996; Ong & Glantz 2000
30   Royal College of Psychiatrists, 2001
31   Devlin et al., 1997; Black, 2003
32   Müller-Hill, 1993
33   See Rutter, 1999 a; Nuffield Council on Bioethics, 2002
34   Kamin, 1974

35   Herrnstein & Murray, 1994; Jensen, 1998
36   Firkowska-Mankiewicz, 2002
37   Marmot & Wilkinson, 1999
38   Rutter, 1999 b
39   Starfield, 1998
40   Tawney, 1952, p. 49
41   Baumrind, 1993; Jackson, 1993
42   Rutter & McGuffin, 2004
43   Sargant & Slater, 1954
44   Pinker, 2002
45   Rutter & Smith, 1995; Rutter & Tienda, 2005
46   Flynn, 1987; Dickens & Flynn, 2001
47   Rutter & Smith, 1995
48   See the extravagant claims of the protagonists of genetics such as Sandra Scarr
     (1992) or David Rowe (1994) or Steven Pinker (2002) or Judith Rich Harris (1998)
49   Rose, 1995, 1998; Rose et al., 1984
50   Rose, 1998 – see pp. 272–301
51   Kendler, 2005 c
52   Bock & Goode, 1998
53   Dennett, 2003
54   See Kendler, 2005 b
55   Lewontin, 2000
56   Morange 2001
57   Scarr, 1992
58   Rowe, 1994
59   Harris, 1998
60   Shonkoff & Phillips, 2000

Further reading

Morange, M. (2001). *The misunderstood gene*. Cambridge, MA & London: Harvard University Press.
Nuffield Council on Bioethics. (2002). *Genetics and human behaviour: The ethical context*. London: Nuffield Council on Bioethics.
Rutter, M. (2002 b). Nature, nurture, and development: From evangelism through science toward policy and practice. *Child Development*, *73*, 1–21.

Chapter 2

Causes and risks

Necessary and sufficient causes

Before discussing the role of genetic influences on behavior and on mental disorders, it is necessary to consider what is meant by "causation." The media often refer to the "cause" of some disease as having been discovered by a new piece of research. The implication is that there is a single factor that fully accounts for the fact that someone develops the disease in question. Rothman and Greenland[1] used the analogy of how the flick of a light switch appears to be the singular cause that makes the light go on. There is a one-to-one correspondence between flicking the switch and the lights turning on. You do not need to do anything else to make this happen and, at first sight, that seems to provide the complete cause. However, as they point out, even in this simple case, other factors are crucially involved in the causal process. For the light to go on there must be a live bulb in the light socket, the wiring from the switch to the bulb must be intact, and there must be sufficient voltage to produce a current when the circuit is closed. In a real sense, all of these constitute essential components in the causal process. The flick of the light switch provides the immediate act that makes the light turn on, but this will not happen if the other components are not functioning as they should. Causation necessarily consists of a set of components acting in concert. That is so even with the most direct types of causation. It is even more so in the much more complicated situation of behaviors and mental disorders.

The next consideration is whether a causal factor is "necessary," meaning that, quite apart from the operation of other factors, the outcome will not happen unless that one necessary causal factor is present. This would apply, for example, in the case of both infectious diseases and disorders wholly due to a single gene (see Chapters 7 and 8). Thus, no one will get a streptococcal sore throat unless they are exposed to the streptococcus. The bacillus is a necessary component in the causal process. The same applies to the viral causation of the common cold. In much the same way it applies to genetic diseases such as **tuberous sclerosis**, which may cause mental retardation and sometimes autism (see Chapters 6 and 8). However, what is notable, even with many necessary causes, is that they are not in themselves "sufficient" to cause the disease. We are all familiar with the fact that, even when exposed to disease-causing bacilli or viruses, not everyone develops the infectious disease. Research has shown that whether or not the disease occurs is dependent on the person's immune system and this may be compromised by stress and emotional disturbance,[2] or by the presence of some other disease (such as HIV or tuberculosis). Also, a person's susceptibility to particular infectious agents has been shown to be influenced by particular genes.[3] The infectious agent is a necessary cause but it is not entirely sufficient; other influences constitute components in the causal process.

The concept of risk and protective effects

In biology and medicine, the situation is much more complicated in the vast majority of cases because the various components act in a probabilistic, rather than deterministic, fashion. That is to say, the factors involved in the causal process increase the likelihood of some particular outcome but they do not determine it (or guarantee that it will happen), and the outcome may still come about even in their absence. When that is the case, which it is with most factors involved in causation, we refer to the feature as a "risk factor," meaning that it increases the risk of some specified outcome, but does not determine it. This would apply, for example, to smoking with respect to lung cancer. Most of us know heavy smokers who live to a ripe old age without developing lung cancer. Equally, many people develop lung cancer without having ever smoked. On the other hand, the evidence is unequivocal that smoking greatly increases the chance of getting lung cancer.[4]

This concept of probabilistic risk is fundamental for the understanding of genetics because most genes operate in that way. They make it more likely that the person will show some trait or have some disorder, but they do not determine that outcome. Whether or not the trait or disorder happens will depend on other genes as well as a range of environmental influences. Nevertheless, for a gene or an environmental factor to be considered as a risk factor, it must be involved in the risk process in some way. Another medical example may serve to illustrate the point. High cholesterol levels are known to constitute an important risk factor for coronary artery disease, and cholesterol constitutes one of several key elements in the deposition of atheroma, which is what clogs up the arteries serving the heart. However, high cholesterol does not, on its own, cause the disease. It increases the risk to a major extent (and a reduction in cholesterol levels brought about by taking statins reduces the risk proportionately). But high blood pressure, obesity, an abnormal clotting tendency, a lack of exercise, smoking, and chest infections also have risk effects for coronary artery disease and, therefore, for heart attacks. It is noteworthy that the risk effect associated with cholesterol applies even at the bottom of the normal range. It is not just a consequence of abnormal levels. The same applies to genes. Most genes that carry risk are normal genes, rather than pathological mutations; it is just that particular variations of those genes involve an increased likelihood that some trait or disorder will develop. But, as in the case of the cholesterol example, these genetic variations do not cause the outcome on their own. They just contribute to the overall risk – sometimes in a minor way, and sometimes in a major way.

The same considerations apply to protective factors. These may be viewed in two rather different ways. First, they constitute no more than the positive end of the same continuum as the equivalent risk factor. Thus, a low cholesterol level may be labeled as a protective factor for coronary artery disease, whereas a high cholesterol level is a risk factor. Similarly, parental negativity is a risk factor for **antisocial behavior** just as a positive parent–child relationship is a protective factor. Viewed in this way, the distinction between risk and protective factors is meaningless because they merely constitute the opposite ends of the same continuum. However, the second concept is quite different in that a protective factor is defined in terms of an effect that operates only (or mainly) as a resistance effect against a risk factor. Thus, the acquisition of immunity against a particular infectious pathogen, as a result of either natural exposure or immunization, provides a protective effect against that pathogen. It provides no positive benefit in itself; its benefits arise only when there is later exposure to the infectious agent. Similarly, vigorous exercise and the regular eating of green vegetables provide a degree of protection against coronary artery disease in the presence of other risk factors. Adoption constitutes a protective factor for various adverse psychological outcomes for children exposed to abuse or neglect by their biological parents, but it makes no sense to view a lack of adoption as a risk factor, because it provides no protection or positive effect for children who do not come from high-risk families.

The relevance of this distinction for genetics is that some genes operate through their impact on protective functions. This is most strikingly evident in relation to the development of cancer. Because cellular proliferation is a normal biological phenomenon, there is a potential for it to get out of hand in the form of cancer. Two sorts of genes are implicated – oncogenes that promote cell proliferation, and tumor suppressor genes that either help keep cell proliferation under control or steer deviant cells into apoptosis (the term used for the normal phenomenon of cell death). The interplay between these two opposing genetic influences and their interplay with environmental influences that can interfere with the "expression" of the protective genes (the process by which genes act – see Chapter 7) lead to the multiphase process that gives rise to cancer. Mental disorders may have more parallels with cancer, with respect to risk and protective forces, than usually supposed. Thus, it is normal to respond to stress or adversity with feelings of anxiety or depression, together with their physiological con-comitants. A complete lack of response would not be adaptive but, equally, an excessively strong and prolonged response would be damaging and lead to disorder. We are only just beginning to understand these processes, but what is clear is that we need to consider both risk and protective processes in relation to genetic, as well as environmental, effects.

Testing causation

In studying risk factors, there are five main considerations. First, it is necessary to undertake research that can find out whether the factor is truly involved in the causal process. The alternatives are that the association is coincidental or that it arises only because the supposed risk factor happens to be associated with some other "third" variable that is the one really involved in the causal process. Even very strong associations need not mean causation. Rothman and Greenland[1] used Bertrand Russell's example of two clocks to illustrate the point. Both clocks are highly accurate and both always chime on the hour. However, because they were originally set slightly differently, one always chimes a couple of minutes before the other one. The association is perfect but the chiming of the first clock does not cause the second clock to chime. Similarly, there are very strong associations between where someone lives and how they vote in an election, but that does not mean that living in a particular area "causes" you to vote for one party rather than another one. In the medical arena, an example would be the association between where you live, or the job you hold, and the likelihood of developing disease or dying young.[5] The associations are both strong and remarkably consistent over time, but neither geography nor occupation, as such, causes disease or death. Rather, they stand for, or index, a range of other risk factors that *are* involved in the causal process. In this instance, we use the term **risk "indicator"** rather than risk factor or risk mechanism to signify that direct causation is not involved. There are many issues to be considered in testing hypotheses about causation; some of those concerned in genetic effects are discussed in Chapter 3 and those for environmental effects in Chapter 5.[6]

Strength of specific risk in the individual

Once it is established that a factor truly causes risk, the second question concerns the strength of the risk effect. This is usually measured by what is called "**relative risk**," meaning the degree to which a person's risk for the outcome being considered is increased by virtue of having that risk factor. Thus, a relative risk of 2 would mean that the factor doubled the likelihood that someone would have the outcome, as compared with the likelihood for someone without the risk factor. Sometimes this is expressed as an "odds ratio" – roughly speaking, meaning the odds of having that outcome in the presence of the risk factor as compared with its absence.

Although there are a few risk factors carrying a strong relative risk, they constitute the exception rather than the rule. As discussed in Chapter 8, most individual genes carry a relative risk of much less than 2. Similarly, the relative risk associated with single environmental risks is of the same order (see Chapter 5). This is so despite the fact that the cumulative risk provided by multiple genes is much greater than that, as is the cumulative risk stemming from multiple environmental risk factors.

Overall level of a risk in the population as a whole

The third issue concerns the degree to which a particular risk factor accounts for the whole of the causation of some outcome in the population as a whole. That is usually known as "attributable risk." Of course, that will be influenced by the strength of effect as indicated by the relative risk but it will also be crucially influenced by the frequency of occurrence of the risk factor. The example that I used some years ago was provided by **Down syndrome**.[7] It has a hugely strong effect on IQ; overall, individuals with Down syndrome have an IQ that is some 60 points below that of the general population. This is equivalent to an enormous relative risk. Despite this, Down syndrome has a very low attributable risk with respect to variations in IQ within the normal range. That is because Down syndrome affects such a small proportion of the population. What this means in practice is that if Down syndrome ceased to exist, it would make virtually no difference to the overall IQ level in the general population.

Down syndrome provides another illustration of the same point. As most people are aware, the chances that a pregnancy will result in the birth of a child with Down syndrome is very strongly affected by the age of the mother.[8] The relative risk for Down syndrome if the mother is aged 40 is 1 in 100 births. The temptation is to assume that most children with Down syndrome are born to mothers in their 40s, but, in fact, that is not so. The great majority are born to younger mothers. The relative risk is low for young mothers (1 in 1,600 births at age 25) but because younger mothers are so much more numerous than mothers in their 40s, older maternal age carries with it only a modest attributable risk.

Another relevant statistic concerns what may be called the "absolute risk." This means the actual probability of some outcome if a person has the relevant risk factor. Thus, to continue the Down syndrome example, the relative risk of Down syndrome for a mother in her 40s is very high but the "absolute risk" is nevertheless very low. That is, the likelihood that the baby will have Down syndrome is tiny, even though the risk is raised in comparison with younger mothers. The relative risk for the birth of a Down syndrome child for a mother aged 30 is approximately 16 times that for a mother aged 15, but the absolute risk is only 1 percent.

Induction periods

The fourth issue concerns what is called the "induction period" – meaning the time between the onset of the causal factor and the initiation of some particular outcome. This is frequently quite long when the risk is provided by some genetic factor. Thus, there are strong genetic influences on diseases such as **Alzheimer's disease** or **Huntington's disease** (see Chapters 4 and 8) that do not usually begin until middle age or later. The same applies to many environmental risk factors with respect to disease outcomes. For example, exposure of female fetuses to a high dose of a particular sex hormone causes an increased risk for a certain form of cancer of the vagina, but the cancer does not usually develop until 15–30 years later.[9] Similarly, various environmental risk factors operating while the baby is in the womb increase the risk for schizophrenia, which does not usually develop until late adolescence or early adult life.

The frequently long induction period for causal processes brings up a related consideration – namely, that causation may involve several different phases, each of which is dependent on the one before it. This is known to apply to the development of some cancers, and, when this is the case, the causes cannot be considered to operate independently of one another, as Pickles pointed out.[10] Thus, many cancers have a precancerous phase (certain forms of polyps in colon cancer, and the changes in the cervix that precede cancer of the womb, are examples). They are not themselves cancerous but they increase the risk of cancer developing later if further risk factors (often of an unknown type) occur. That is, if the cause operating in the second or third phase is dependent on that phase having been reached as a result of different causal factors operating in an earlier phase, there is a necessary interaction involved. It makes no sense to treat the risks in the later phase as parallel to those in the earlier phases because the later phase risks only come into operation if different risk factors have meant that causal process has progressed to the relevant phase. That may mean that the causes of a disorder beginning at an early age will differ from what seems to be the same disorder beginning much later. For example, that appears to be the case with both **depressive disorder**s and antisocial behavior.[11]

Interactions among risk factors

The fifth consideration concerns the importance of interactions among risk factors. It might be thought that the attributable risks associated with specific risk factors should always add up to 100 percent, but that would not apply when there are interactions among risk factors.[1] What is meant by an interaction is that there is a synergistic interplay such that the risk associated with one risk factor is increased (or decreased) by the presence of some other risk factor. This applies among genes (discussed in Chapters 4 and 8), and between genes and environments (as discussed in Chapter 9), and it also applies among different environmental risk factors. The implication is that outcomes often depend not just on multiple risk factors (which is almost always the case), but also on the specific pattern of co-acting risk factors. In other words, for a specified outcome, a particular two (or more) risk factors must *both* be present. The topic is more fully discussed in Chapter 9, in relation to gene–environment interactions, but an example here may serve to illustrate how it can work.

Flamingos everywhere are famous for their spectacularly beautiful pink color. It is known that this is entirely dependent on a particular diet of shrimp and plankton. If flamingos do not have access to their usual diet for any reason, they are white, not pink. Their color is entirely dependent on the environmental influence of diet. On the other hand, the flamingos' ability to turn pink with diet is entirely dependent on their genes. You could feed seagulls for ever on the same diet and they would never turn pink. It would make no sense to say that the flamingos' color was 50 percent due to genes and 50 percent due to diet. It is 100 percent due to genes (which *have* to be present) and 100 percent due to the environmental diet (which *has* to be present). Neither, on their own, will bring about the pink color. The color is essentially due to the *joint* action of the genes and the environment.

The dimensional operation of genes

With traits that are dependent on multiple genes and multiple specific environmental factors, it will be usual for the genes to operate on dimensional features and not diagnostic categories. Sometimes this has been shown directly in relation to measures and dimensions (as is the case with reading and hyperactivity) and sometimes it is assumed in the mathematical model used to quantify genetic effects. Thus, for example, **schizophrenia** is clearly an abnormal condition involving qualitatively peculiar features such as thought disorder, hallucinations, and delusions. At first sight, it would seem that this must be quite distinct from variations within the normal range. It does not seem reasonable to consider the general population as all showing a degree of schizophrenia, with some having the trait only to a very slight degree, others more so, and those with the greatest degree of the trait having the overt mental disorder. Yet that is what the model, as applied to twin and adoptee studies, assumes. Accordingly, before turning to the genetics we need to consider whether this dimensional approach makes sense in terms of what we know about both somatic diseases (such as heart attacks and strokes) and mental disorders (such as schizophrenia or autism). The issue is crucially important with respect to the question of whether the genetic research is dealing with "real" entities, and whether it is reasonable to consider genetic influences on behaviors that are both widespread in the normal population and clearly subject to social and psychological influences of various kinds.

Much heat, and not much light, has been generated over discussions with respect to the continuities and discontinuities between overt disorder or malfunction or disease and normal variations in either risk factors or symptomatology. Throughout its history psychiatric classification has been bedeviled by supposed clashes between dimensional and categorical approaches. The dominant classifications such as the *American Diagnostic and Statistical Manual for Mental Disorders* (DSM-IV)[12] and the *World Health Organization International Classification of Diseases* (ICD-10)[13] are exclusively categorical in organization. This is partly for the good practical reason that many clinical decisions have to be categorical.[14] Thus, clinicians have to decide whether a patient is, or is not, to be treated with antidepressant medication. It would make no sense to give a lower dose of the drug if the dimensional score was only moderate but a higher dose if the dimensional score was much greater. That is because there is no indication whatsoever that mild depressive disorders respond to lower doses of medication than those required for more serious mental disorders. The drugs do not relieve depression if given in very low dosage. Nevertheless, it has long been recognized that there are advantages to combining dimensions and categories[15] and a recent volume on a research agenda for DSM-V[16] accepts this as an important possibility.

Dimensions assume continuity between normality and psychopathology, involve linear quantification, and use internal empirical data to quantify and separate dimensions.[17] By contrast, categories function as if there were discontinuity between normality and psychopathology and they use quantification (either on symptoms or impairment or both) to decide diagnostic cut-offs and presuppose the need to validate by criteria that are external to the defining symptoms.[18] It has been recognized that such external validation could be provided by biological findings, drug response, genetic findings, epidemiology, and course of disorder, to mention only some of the many possibilities. When the comparison is expressed in this way, it is tempting to suppose that empirical research should be able to decide which is correct or valid. However, this is based on the misconception that there can be one universally "right" answer, whereas it is obvious that that is not so.[19] Thus, for example, IQ works best as a dimension if the interest is in predicting someone's scholastic attainment or even social functioning in adult life. On the other hand, it works much better as a category if the interest is in biological causes because the causes of severe mental retardation are so different from those that concern individual differences within the normal range.[20]

It is sometimes argued that dimensions are more open to psychosocial explanations, whereas categories lend themselves better to neurobiological ones,[21] but this is actually not the case. For example, within the field of internal medicine as a whole, blood pressure, degree of atheroma, and height are important dimensional within-individual features but they all involve a major biological component. Both the risk factors for coronary artery disease (such as cholesterol levels, neonatal nutrition, smoking, and clotting tendencies) and the pathological processes involved in coronary artery disease are dimensional, despite the fact that the final outcomes (such as death from coronary occlusion – heart attack) have to be categorical. In the field of psychopathology, epidemiological findings have been consistent in showing that most forms of common mental disorder show continuous distributions, with no clearly discernible point of demarcation between normality and psychopathology. Indeed it has been further argued, on the basis of empirical analyses, that the underlying distributions of people's liability to experience mental disorder show very little evidence of non-normality.[22] The suggestion is that the apparently skewed nature of many measures of deviant behavior may be largely measurement artifacts. In other words, there is no indication that a qualitatively distinct process generates disorder.

Most people readily accept this argument for features such as depression or antisocial behavior. That is because it is obvious that everyone is liable to feel depressed when faced with severe social stresses, and that most individuals engage in at least minor antisocial behavior at some time. Accordingly, it seems reasonable to consider that major depressive disorders, leading to serious malfunction, could be a consequence of a more severe variety of the same thing. On the other hand, until relatively recently, handicapping disorders such as autism and schizophrenia have been thought of as entirely separate from variations within the normal range. However, genetic evidence has forced some rethinking on this issue. Thus, schizophrenia and schizotypal personality disorder appear to show the same genetic liability.[23] Similarly, autism is associated with a much broader range of social communicative abnormalities.[24] Broadly similar findings apply to both specific developmental language disorders[25] and dyslexia[26]. In both cases, the genetically influenced liability extends well beyond the traditional diagnostic boundaries. In other words, in all of these cases, both the twin data and the family data show that the risk not only includes the diagnostic category but also includes a wider range of impairments, some of which involve rather more general cognitive and behavioral deficits than implied by the diagnostic category.

The findings would seem to suggest that the genetic liability is less specific than used to be supposed, and that it involves a dimension or continuum that extends into the general population. However, some caution must be exercised before concluding that there are no discontinuities between normality and psychopathology. First, it is necessary to appreciate that the findings derive from studies in which the starting point is an individual with a traditionally diagnosed handicapping disorder. The evidence shows that, given this starting point, close relatives in the same family have a much increased rate of the same handicapping disorder but also a spectrum of impairments that are both less severe and more varied in their manifestations. The key question is whether, if the starting point was someone in the general population without a handicapping disorder, this mixture of mild and marked disabilities found in relatives would reflect the same genetic liability as seen in the families of people with a handicapping disorder as ordinarily diagnosed. It could turn out to be the case that this is so but it is by no means self-evident that this will be so.

For example, although in the general population the evidence indicates that there is a huge overlap in the genetic influences operating on general intelligence and those that apply to specific skills in reading, mathematics, and the like,[27] that does not necessarily mean that there will be no specific genetic effects on the more extreme handicapping conditions of **language impairment**, **dyslexia**, **autism**, and **ADHD**. What the genetic evidence on these conditions shows is that the genetic liability extends beyond the traditional diagnostic boundaries, but that does not necessarily mean that these extensions are synonymous with variations within the normal range in the general population. Thus, for example, Knopik et al.[28] found that genetic influences were stronger for reading difficulties in children of higher IQ than in those of lower IQ and that this applied to the genetic locus for dyslexia previously identified on chromosome 6.

The distinction is most easily illustrated by taking the example of mild mental retardation (general learning difficulties). Some of the individuals with mild retardation have a medical condition such as **Down syndrome** or **Angelman syndrome** (see Chapter 6). With each of these conditions the range of IQ extends downward to severe retardation and upward into the normal range. Because the range includes a normal level of intelligence, one might be tempted to infer that variations in IQ in the general population are, therefore, due to variations in the same factors causing the medical condition. In other words, Down syndrome occurs because the individuals have less of the positive influences (genetic or environmental) that lead to high IQ in other people. Of course, we know that is not true. We know that because these medical conditions have specific genetic causes that play little or no part in influencing individual differences in IQ in the general population. High IQ is not due to having less of the chromosomal abnormality that causes Down syndrome. By contrast, the majority of individuals (the precise proportion is not known) do not have any such medical condition. In these people, it is likely that their lower IQ *is* due to the same factors (genetic and environmental) that influence variations in IQ within the normal range. They have less of the positive influences and/or more of the negative ones, but there is no qualitative difference. The question, therefore, is whether dyslexia and specific language impairment fall into the former category, with specific causes to a substantial extent separate from those affecting general intelligence in the population as a whole, or into the latter category with their specific deficits merely part of the normal variation in patterns of intellectual skills. Most people view the causation as likely to involve considerable specificity (that would also be my view), but whether or not that is so remains uncertain, and awaits answers from further research.

The evidence is far too slender for any firm conclusions but research needs to consider both the possibility that dimensions extend right across the general population with a high degree of non-specificity, together with the contrasting hypothesis that although there are important dimensions within specific genetic liabilities, they are distinct from one another and do not encompass the range of variation seen in the general population.

The further point is that the evidence on these broader manifestations indicates that, in some respects, they do seem to be rather different from the traditional diagnostic condition. For example, with respect to **autism**, the broader phenotype, unlike traditional autism, does not seem to be associated with either mental retardation or epilepsy. The reasons for this difference remain unknown but there is the possibility that there may be some kind of two-hit mechanism whereby there is one set of causal influences that leads to the broader phenotype and another, possibly overlapping, set of causal factors that are responsible for the translation of the broader phenotype into the more seriously handicapping disorder.

Multiple causal pathways

Much of the writing on risk factors for mental disorders has tended to make the implicit assumption that there is likely to be just one causal pathway for each mental disorder. The implication is that the research challenge should be to search for just what that pathway might comprise and, also, what might be the basic fundamental cause that sets the causal pathway in operation. For several different reasons, that is a profoundly wrong-headed assumption, not just in the field of mental disorders and psychological functions but also in relation to the whole of medicine and biology. To begin with, in the great majority of cases, both psychological traits and mental disorders are multifactorial in origin – meaning that they involve some kind of combination, and interplay, among several genetic factors providing contributions to susceptibility or liability and several environmental factors that similarly play a part in the causal pathway. Given that situation, it makes little sense to use a concept of any single cause that is more basic or more fundamental than others.

However, there is also another, rather different, reason why the assumption is wrong-headed and that is that it is often the case that there are several rather different routes by which causal factors tend to exert their effect. For example, in the field of respiratory disease there is a seriously handicapping disorder of obstructive airway disease that usually brings about premature death. However, it can begin in several different ways.[29] For example, heavy smoking, or repeated asthma attacks, or lung infections can each set in motion a set of changes that ultimately lead to the same endpoint of gross disease. The initial proximal effects of smoking, of asthma, and of infections are all very different. On the other hand, they do have various features in common that mean that they predispose to changes in the respiratory pathways that end up at the same life-threatening disease endpoint. Each causal pathway involves multiple causal factors sometimes acting additively but quite often synergistically. Any adequate understanding of the disease process involves not just an appreciation of the multiple factors that play a part in causation, and not even of how they come together, or even the pathophysiological changes that ultimately lead to the obstructive airway disease, but also that, at least in the initial stages, the causal process may look rather different.

Exactly the same considerations apply with respect to mental disorders. For example, Kendler et al.[30] brought together findings from their twin study in adult women. The detailed findings are quite complex and were presented in full in the published paper but Figure 2.1 provides a much simplified portrayal of the several pathways that seem to be involved (focusing only

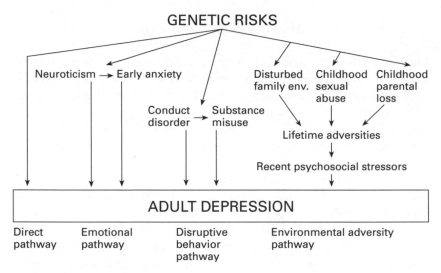

Figure 2.1 Simplified causal pathways from genes to adult depression.
Source: from Kendler et al., 2002.

on those that follow from genes). It is not suggested that these are utterly distinct from one another but what is emphasized is that there are several contrasting pathways all leading to depression and involving somewhat different mixes of risk factors operating in different ways. The figure also brings out that these risk factors operate to some extent at different points in the life span. Thus, for example, there are early adversities in life that are important, because, amongst other things, they set in motion chains of events that make it more likely that the individuals will experience severely negative, more acute negative life events in adult life. These later life events serve as important provoking factors for the onset of depression but the propensity of the individual to experience such factors to an unusual degree has been influenced both by their genetic susceptibilities and by their earlier life experiences. It might seem that all this looks very complex but the point is that each of these steps in the multiple causal chains is analyzable, and alternative mediating mechanisms involved in each step can be contrasted and tested against one another. However, what does come through loud and clear is that it would make little sense to try to say that any one of these factors is more or less important overall than some other one. To attempt such over-simplified quantification would ignore the multiplicity of causal pathways and would ignore the fact that most of the pathways involve multiple steps. It will be apparent from the figure that the fingerprint of genetics is evident throughout and, hence, the importance of understanding the role of genetic mechanisms. Equally, however, it is clear that the genetic factors operate in conjunction with non-genetic influences and that any understanding of the causal process must incorporate an adequate appreciation of the mechanisms involved in their interplay.

Multifaceted nature of causal concepts

In this discussion of multiple causal pathways, there has tended to be the implicit assumption that, even if the causal pathways are multiple, they are basically all dealing with the same thing. But, that is not the case.

Figure 2.2 provides a simple illustration of the point with respect to antisocial behavior. Thus, individuals differ in their propensity to engage in antisocial behavior. That constitutes the arrow beginning on the extreme left and, in a real sense, it has to constitute the starting point. However, by no means all individuals with a high propensity to engage in antisocial behavior actually do commit delinquent acts, and quite a few individuals with a relatively low propensity to engage in such behavior do commit delinquent acts in particular circumstances. The individual liability is multifactorial – that is to say it involves multiple genes and multiple environmental factors. However, it is necessary to go on to ask whether there are different sets of influences that are involved in the translation of that propensity (however caused) into actual delinquent acts. Situational stresses might include social circumstances such as being in a crowd of people engaging in violence at a football match or it might involve personal factors such as being intoxicated with alcohol or under the influence of drugs. Then there are other factors involved with emotional provocation. These might include someone picking a fight or making taunting derogatory racial insults, or someone behaving aggressively in a way that puts their own driving at risk (road rage).

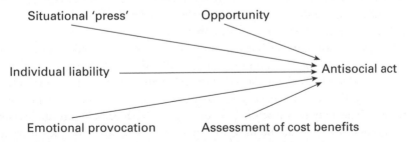

Figure 2.2 Causal scheme for processes leading to crime.
Source: Rutter, Giller, & Hagell 1998. Copyright © 1998 by Cambridge University Press. Reprinted by permission of the publisher.

Further, even with those three sets of factors providing risk, whether or not a person engages in an actual criminal act would depend on opportunity. If they are out on their own walking in the mountains, however antisocial they feel, there is not a lot of scope for engaging in crime. On the other hand, in a crowded urban situation, there are many more opportunities. However, even in those situations, the level of opportunity varies. Has someone left their car door unlocked? Is there an unprotected handbag that has been left on the floor in a restaurant? Finally, there is the need to consider cost benefits. Is there anyone about who is likely to observe the crime and take action to apprehend the offender? Is there a camera monitoring the area? How likely is it that the crime will be quickly noticed and detected so that there is no time to make a getaway? It will be readily appreciated that these various considerations would differ in importance in different individuals in different circumstances but they are all potentially important in the causal pathways.

Of course, one may think that, although this applies to a behavior such as a delinquent act over which a person has choice, it is not applicable in the same way to clinically significant mental disorders. But that distinction is not as clear-cut as it might seem at first sight. For example, it really does not need spelling out that a precisely parallel set of considerations applies to suicidal acts. Thus, for example, there will be individual liability based perhaps on a combination of depression and a risk-taking propensity but, in addition, there may be situational factors such as being intoxicated, in many cases there is an acute provoking incident (such as a quarrel or a humiliating failure), there will be the matter of opportunity in terms of access to the means to kill oneself, and some kind of assessment of cost benefits. Very similar issues apply to substance misuse, for which a multiple-step causal pathway is likely to be involved. That is to say, there must be access to drugs, there must be factors involved in first using the drug in an experimental way, there will be the progression to regular heavy use, and there will be the factors involved in becoming psychologically and/or pharmacologically dependent on the drug. It is clear that the causal influences that operate at each of these stages may not be exactly the same.

In perhaps not quite such an obvious way, the same considerations apply to mental disorders that are not a matter of individual choice (in the way that a suicidal act or delinquent activities are). Thus, there will be an individual propensity that is influenced by a mixture of genetic and environmental factors; there may be situational circumstances such as being in unpleasant living conditions, or attending a low-morale school that provides little in the way of rewards, or of having a job that involves few rewards and little sense of autonomy. In addition, however, many major mental disorders are provoked or precipitated by acutely negative life events that carry long-term threat – such as rejection by a loved one or a humiliating experience. Again, none of these can be seen as independent if only because the likelihood of experiencing, say, acute life events is influenced by prior circumstances and earlier behavior.[31]

One final point about causation is that the endpoint can be conceptualized in a number of rather different ways. Most of the literature on causes, whether it is based on genetics or psychosocial studies, has tended to focus on the question of individual differences. In other words, the question is why this person has a depressive disorder and that one does not, or why this individual has schizophrenia and someone else does not. The answers provided may be quantified in terms of probabilistic risks but they are, in essence, concerned just with individual differences in the likelihood of someone experiencing a disorder (or showing a particular psychological trait). That is a very important way of thinking about causation but it is far from the only way. For example, a high proportion of the population will suffer from a major depressive disorder at some point in their life. The figures put forward vary but they are of the order of a fifth to a third of the population for women. Many of these people will have just a single episode of depression and it might be quite short-lived. At the other extreme, there are people who are plagued by frequent episodes of prolonged depression that may be profoundly handicapping and disruptive of their lives.[32] From a public health point of view, or a service planning perspective, the main interest may be less focused on why someone develops depression at some point in their life than on the different question of whether they are likely to have just one transient episode or be recurrently impaired over the years ahead. The causal factors involved with recurrence or course of disorder are likely to overlap with those involved with whether someone gets depressed at all but they may not be quite the same. For example, numerous studies have shown that physical or sexual abuse in childhood is associated with a substantially increased risk of developing a depressive disorder later. However, the follow-up into middle age of young people first seen in childhood and adolescence on the Isle of Wight has shown that this risk mainly applies to recurrent depression (rather than single episodes) and possibly it tends to have most impact on depression beginning in adolescence rather than adult life.[33] Other research has also shown that once a person has had a handicapping disorder of depression, the very experience of suffering the disorder does something to the organism that makes it more likely that depression will recur – the so-called kindling effect.[34]

A third way of thinking about causes is to focus on levels of disorder in the population as a whole or on population-wide traits. The question in this case is not who has the trait or shows the disorder but rather, what proportion of the population is affected. Thus, the evidence shows that over the past

50 years or so,[35] there has been a quite substantial rise in the rate of crime among young people, in the use and misuse of drugs, and in the rate of suicide (especially in young males). Interestingly, these population-wide trends do not necessarily apply to all age groups. Thus, for example, during the same period of time that the rate of suicide in young males was rising, it was actually falling in older age groups. In many cases, the causes of individual differences and the causes of changes in rate over time may be the same or at least overlapping to a considerable extent. On the other hand, they may be rather different. For example, it is very striking that the homicide rate in young people living in the United States is at least a dozen times as high as the comparable figure for homicide in young people living in most European countries.[36] The evidence shows that the main factor responsible for this extraordinary difference in rate is the availability of firearms. On the other hand, within the United States, relative ease of access to firearms is not particularly associated with homicide rate. That is likely to be because the variations in access are relatively small within the USA whereas the differences in access between the USA and Europe are quite large.

In even more striking fashion, it is well known that over the past century or so there has been, in almost all industrialized countries, a massive reduction in infantile mortality and almost a doubling in the life expectancy at birth. Thus, in the UK at the beginning of the twentieth century the life expectancy at birth for males was about 42 years whereas it is now something like 76 years.[37] Over the same period of time there has been a major increase in the average height of the population.[38] Almost certainly the main explanation for these extremely dramatic, and crucially important trends over time are to be found in the public health arena rather than in either the medical causes of illnesses or the medical treatment of illnesses.[39] Thus, better nutrition and improved sanitation are probably the two most important factors. But, note that these huge changes over time apply to features that involve a strong genetic component. Thus, for example, height has a heritability of about 80 percent. For reasons discussed in Chapter 3, even such a high heritability does not mean that environmental factors of a new kind cannot make a huge difference and clearly they did. Does that mean that genetic factors play no role in these tremendously large changes over time or dramatic differences in rate across countries or across other populations? Not necessarily. It is not in the least bit likely that genes account for the changes in rate or level, because gene pools do not ordinarily change so rapidly. On the other hand, it may be that they do have an indirect effect in some circumstances. For example, Flynn[40] showed convincingly that over the past 50 years or so there has been a substantial rise in the average level of intelligence. It may well be that some of this rise is a function of people becoming more familiar with, and more used to dealing with, intelligence tests but a critical look at the evidence gives a convincing impression that, in addition to such factors, there has been a real rise. What has seemed a paradox, however, is that the rise has appeared to be greater than it would be sensible to suppose has occurred in the environmental factors that seem to be important in cognitive development. Dickens and Flynn[41] have put forward the interesting hypothesis that that is because there must be a multiplier variable of some kind and they have suggested that this may be genetic in origin. In other words, because some people are better able to profit from educational opportunities (at home and at school) this creates the sort of multiplier that seems to be operating. It is a highly plausible hypothesis but it has yet to be put to the test in rigorous fashion. However, there is evidence that if interventions (with respect to a variety of outcomes) are applied to the whole population, this may increase inequalities simply because (other things being equal) those who are advantaged are better able than the disadvantaged to make effective use of what is provided.[42] The point is that it is necessary to think of genes playing roles, sometimes of a very important kind, in indirect effects of one kind or another that are being driven primarily by environmental factors. The old dichotomy implied in the question as to whether something is mainly due to nature or due to nurture is simply not the right way of thinking about things.

Specificity/non-specificity of risks

One of the objections sometimes put forward by critics of behavioral genetics is that genetic influences have been considered in relation to a wide range of poorly defined and poorly conceptualized concepts of behavior – such as antisocial behavior. The implication has been that it may be entirely appropriate to look for genetic factors in relation to "proper" diseases such as diabetes or coronary artery disease and, just conceivably, this might also apply to severe handicapping psychiatric disorders such as schizophrenia or autism or bipolar disorder, but it cannot possibly make sense to seek to assess the heritability of characteristics that have no independent standing outside of the social context. The same objection has been put forward with respect to the genetics of intelligence on the grounds that people cannot really agree on what intelligence is and that they tend to fall back on the feeble rationale that intelligence is what intelligence tests measure. On the face of it, these critiques sound reasonable but actually they are mistaken.[43] That is because there is no reason to suppose that genes map on to human traits or human disorders as they are traditionally characterized or diagnosed.

Genes do not code for behaviors. Genes are causally implicated (albeit by a more dynamic pathway than usually realized – see Chapter 7) in the biochemical pathways that play a role in individual differences in susceptibility to behaviors of all kinds, normal and abnormal. To stick with the example of antisocial behavior, the genes that play a role in the individual differences in liability to engage in antisocial behavior may have nothing directly to do with criminality as such. Rather, they may be concerned with risk taking or sensation seeking or susceptibility to peer group influences, or educational attainments, or drug taking. However, that does not in any way negate the value of undertaking genetic research that is planned in order to determine which of these various alternative routes is the one through which genetic influences operate. Genetic research, too, may be helpful in providing a way of sorting out different varieties of antisocial behavior according to the different genetically influenced causal pathways that are found. Exactly the same applies to the kind of objections that have been put forward in relation to the genetic study of intelligence or attention deficit disorder with hyperactivity (**ADHD**). Intelligence may or may not turn out to boil down to some unitary factor such as "g," and ADHD may or may not turn out to be a qualitatively distinct psychiatric condition. The point is that genetic research may be helpful in sorting out these alternatives and it is completely neutral with respect to which it may turn out to be. The empirical findings will push conclusions in one direction or another; genetic theory will not.

An alternative objection is that medical research into, say, intelligence or ADHD may distract attention away from the important non-genetic influences on both and, also, may convey a misleading impression of both the importance of these features and the extent to which they are inbuilt into the individual. It has to be admitted that the ways in which enthusiasts write about intelligence from a genetic perspective do sometimes leave themselves open to this criticism[44] and, somewhat similarly, the enthusiasts for the disease concept of ADHD tend to overplay the certainty that it is a qualitatively distinct condition.[45] Nevertheless, there is no denying that, however it is conceptualized, measures of intelligence have a powerful predictive value. They certainly do not account for all aspects of academic achievement, and even less so do they account for all aspects of social success. Nevertheless, it would be to put one's head in the sand to suppose that intelligence is of little consequence. The same applies to ADHD. Research findings are in good agreement in showing that it is a phenomenon that is associated with considerable social malfunction both in the short term and in the long[46] If genetic research can help provide an understanding of the meaning of the causal factors involved in traits of this kind, it will perform a valuable service and there is every reason to suppose that that is the case.

There is another aspect to specificity and that is whether the individual risk factors (be they individual genes or individual environmental risks) have specific or non-specific effects. At one time, genetic studies did tend to be predicated on the basis that it would be possible to find genes that were specific for specific psychiatric conditions. That may still be possible for some mental disorders but there is a growing body of evidence that, in many cases, the genetic effects do not coincide at all exactly with either the traditional psychiatric diagnoses or, indeed, the ways in which psychological traits tend to be conceptualized and subdivided. That is scarcely surprising because the risk pathways leading from either the genes to disorder or the environments to disorder are indirect. If the effects of the genes are on biochemical pathways of one kind or another (as is the case), it would not be surprising if the same pathway might lead to different end results according to the presence or absence of other risk factors either genetic or environmental. These possibilities are considered further in Chapters 7, 8, and 9.

Somewhat comparable considerations apply to environmental risk factors. Thus, if the environmentally mediated risks influence physiological pathways, or **neuroendocrine** function, or patterns of thinking, or styles of interpersonal interaction, it is obvious that each of these may have effects that go beyond a single psychological outcome. In addition, however, it is necessary to appreciate that many environmental risk factors that sound as if they are unitary actually involve a quite diverse range of risk mechanisms. For example, there is good evidence that smoking is a risk factor for lung cancer, for coronary artery disease, for respiratory disease, and for wrinkling of the skin, to mention but a few adverse outcomes. However, this certainly does not mean that the same risk mechanisms apply to each of these. We know, for example, that it is the carcinogenic tars that predispose to cancer of the lung and that the other effects involve quite different mediating factors such as the effects of carbon monoxide or the nicotinic effects on blood vessels. In the same way, obesity predisposes to osteoarthritis, diabetes, and hypertension but, once again, it does so through quite different mechanisms. The effects of osteoarthritis come about through the wear and tear on joints, as a result of carrying such a lot of weight around all the time. Diabetes arises through the strain put on pancreatic function, and hypertension through yet other mechanisms. In much the same sort of way, psychosocial risk factors in psychiatry are likely to involve a substantial degree of non-specificity of both kinds. That is to say, some of the effects will be on aspects of function that carry risk for several different sorts of outcomes and, equally, some of the supposedly single risk factors will actually involve risk mechanisms of quite disparate kinds.

On the other hand, these considerations definitely do not mean that we should abandon concepts on the distinctiveness of different psychiatric syndromes, or throw away our concepts on the distinctions among different psychological traits or features. Equally, it does not mean that we should move to a concept of global risk. It would be a counsel of despair to move to a causal model that is, in effect, a conceptual soup in which causation derives from an unanalyzable mix of multiple diverse risk factors. Instead, we need to take seriously the challenge to delineate specific causal pathways, without the presupposition that there has to be just one, without the expectation that cause will involve one basic causal factor or one fundamental single causal step, and without any assumption that the risks will be either specific or non-specific. The strong likelihood is that it will be a mixture of the two. The chapters that follow consider some of the ways in which this may come about.

Conclusions

The concept of some simple "basic" cause appears attractive because of its simplicity. Nevertheless, the concept is misleading because it implies a deterministic mechanism that rarely applies, rather than the probabilistic processes that are much more usual; because it ignores the interplay among risk and protective factors; and because a single causal pathway is implied, rather than the multiple pathways that have been found to operate in many circumstances. The notion of probabilistic risk is basic to most of medicine and it applies in similar fashion to the operation of genetic influences on mental disorders and psychological traits.

Notes

See Reference list for full details.
  1   Rothman & Greenland, 1998
  2   Cohen et al., 1991; Petitto & Evans, 1999; Stone et al., 1992; Wüst et al., 2004
  3   Hill, 1998 a & b; Kotb et al., 2002
  4   Doll & Crofton, 1999; Doll et al., 2004
  5   Townsend et al., 1988
  6   See Kraemer, 2003 for a discussion of some of the key statistical issues that need to be considered,
  7   Rutter, 1987
  8   Aitken et al., 2002
  9   Rothman, 1981
 10   Pickles, 1993
 11   Rutter, in press a
 12   APA, 2000
 13   WHO, 1993
 14   Rutter, 2003 a
 15   Kendell, 1975
 16   Kupfer et al., 2002
 17   Achenbach, 1985, 1988

18 Rutter, 1965, 1978; Taylor & Rutter, 2002
19 Taylor & Rutter, 2002; Pickles & Angold, 2003
20 Volkmar & Dykens, 2002
21 Sonuga-Barke, 1998
22 van den Oord et al., 2003
23 Kendler et al., 1995; Siever et al., 1993
24 Bailey et al., 1998; Rutter, 2000 a
25 Bishop et al., 1995 & Bishop, 2002 a
26 Snowling et al., 2003
27 Plomin & Kovas, 2005
28 Knopik et al., 2002; Wadsworth et al., 2000
29 Rutter, 1997
30 Kendler et al., 2000 a
31 Champion et al., 1995; Robins, 1966
32 Lee & Murray, 1988; Angst, 2000
33 Maughan et al., to be submitted
34 Kendler et al., 2000 b, 2001
35 Collishaw et al., 2004; Rutter & Smith, 1995
36 Rutter et al., 1998
37 Office for National Statistics, 2002
38 Weir, 1952; Tizard, 1975; van Wieringen, 1986
39 McKeown, 1976
40 Flynn, 1987 & 2000
41 Dickens & Flynn, 2001
42 Ceci & Papierno, 2005
43 Rutter, 2002 b
44 Jensen, 1998
45 Barkley et al., 2004
46 Schachar & Tannock, 2002

Further reading

Rutter, M. (1997). Comorbidity: Concepts, claims and choices. *Criminal Behaviour and Mental Health*, 7, 265–286.

Rutter, M. (2003 a). Categories, dimensions, and the mental health of children and adolescents. In J.A. King, C.F. Ferris, & I.I. Lederhendler (Eds.), *Roots of mental illness in children*. New York: The New York Academy of Sciences. pp. 11–21.

Rutter, M., Giller, H., & Hagell, A. (1998). *Antisocial behavior by young people*. New York: Cambridge University Press.

Chapter 3

How much is nature and how much nurture?

Quantitative genetics is concerned with estimating the relative strength of effects of genes and of environmental influences on the variation within populations with respect to some trait (feature). It does not deal with genetic effects on traits that occur universally. For example, the fact that all human beings have the power to develop language (unless there is some disease or damage), the ability to walk upright, and to have hands that allow a prehensile grip is obviously attributable to genes that have come to operate in all human beings as the result of evolution. Quantitative genetics does not deal with genes that are possessed similarly by everyone; rather it is solely concerned with traits that vary among people. Thus, this applies to features such as height, intelligence, and the liability to develop disorders of particular kinds.

The findings give rise to population statistics that concern the differences among individuals. Thus, a statement that the heritability (meaning overall genetic influence) of a trait is, say, 60 percent does not mean that 60 percent of that trait in a particular person is genetically determined. Rather, it means that genetic factors account for 60 percent of the variation among individuals within a particular population with respect to that trait. It follows from this consideration that the findings are necessarily population specific. Suppose, for example, that the population studied consisted of people all of whom had HIV, with the research question being what accounted for the variations in the transition to the full syndrome of AIDS. The findings would show that much of the variation was attributable to genetic factors despite the fact that the basic cause was an infection. Similarly, suppose that the population consisted of children all of whom had **phenylketonuria**, but with some treated early with a low phenalanine diet, some with such a diet beginning later, and some on an ordinary diet. The research question might be the importance of genetic and environmental influences on the likelihood of children developing mental retardation. In this case, although phenylketonuria is an entirely genetic condition, the findings would show that the liability to develop mental retardation was entirely environmentally determined. Obviously, these two examples are extreme cases but the point applies much more broadly. In interpreting the findings from quantitative genetics, careful attention needs to be paid to the populations being studied. Two studies, for example, have shown that the genetic influence on variations in intelligence is much stronger in children from well-educated or socially advantaged families than in those coming from families that are disadvantaged socially and educationally.[1] The matter has been too little examined up to now to be at all sure whether or not this is a general finding, but the point remains that great caution must be taken in generalizing the findings from one sort of population to other, different populations.

The whole basis of quantitative genetics lies in the use of natural experiments of one kind or another that separate the genetic and environmental influences that in ordinary circumstances go together. The two most used approaches are provided by the range of twin and adoptee designs.

Twin designs

Twin designs use the contrast between **monozygotic** (identical) and **dizygotic** (fraternal or non-identical) twin pairs for this purpose. The rationale is quite straightforward in its reliance on the fact that monozygotic (MZ) twin pairs share all their segregating genes inherited from their parents (i.e., identical by descent), whereas, on average, dizygotic (DZ) pairs share only 50 percent of such genes. If MZ pairs are much more alike in the traits being studied than are DZ pairs, it may be inferred that this comes about through genetic influences. However, in order to make that inference, it is necessary to rely on what has been called the "**equal environments assumption**" (EEA). In other words, one has to assume that the contrast between MZ and DZ pairs can be wholly attributable to genes because the environmental variation within MZ pairs should be much the same as within DZ pairs.[2]

Equal environments assumption

At first sight, that seems a most implausible assumption. It is obvious, for example, that MZ twins are more likely to be dressed alike than are DZ twins. Also, (for genetic reasons) MZ twins (within any pair) are more likely than DZ twins to be similar in their behavior, attitudes, and interests. It may safely be assumed that this is almost bound to lead to their choosing more similar experiences and also eliciting more similar patterns of interaction with other people. However, the EEA will not be violated if that is all that is occurring. That is because if the environments are being entirely driven by genes, it is reasonable to attribute the effects to genes provided, and only provided, that the environments that differ between MZ and DZ pairs do not have an effect on the trait being studied. Thus, for example, no one would suppose that whether or not a pair was dressed alike would make any difference to their intelligence or their liability to develop schizophrenia.

Behavioral geneticists have almost always focused on the possibility that a greater environmental similarity between monozygotic twins than between dizygotic twins (in both cases within the same pairs) has led to an **environmentally mediated** greater similarity for some trait or disorder within MZ pairs.[3] This is because this possibility has been a particular focus in criticisms of the twin strategy. There are various ways in which the possibility can be tested but one key quantitative approach has been to introduce the postulated biasing influence into a multivariate statistical model. The result has almost always been demonstration of no biasing effect (that is, the estimate of the genetic effect has been the same whether or not the biasing influence was taken into account). The finding has led to the conclusion that the EEA is fully justified. However, the problem is that the biasing influences that could operate in this way are very limited and none constitute plausible environmentally mediated influences on either psychological traits or mental disorders. Thus, physical similarity or frequency of contact is most unlikely to have any significant psychological effect, and that is just what has been found.

A second possible threat to the EEA is provided by circumstances in which the experiences of MZ twins within the same pair tend to be *less* alike than those of DZ twins. When this is the case the violation of the EEA will lead to a misleading *under*estimate of genetic effects if the environmental influences have effects on the trait or disorder being studied. The main circumstance in which this could be the case concerns obstetric factors.

For example, MZ twins tend to differ more in their birth weight than do DZ twins. This usually comes about because **monochorionic** MZ twins can share their circulation of blood (that arises because there is no division between the portions of the placenta that provide their blood supply). The net effect is what has been called the "transfusion syndrome" in which one twin, relatively speaking, gets overstuffed with blood and the other twin gets relatively exsanguinated. It might be thought that the greatest risks would apply to the twin who has lost blood, but, in fact, on the whole the greater risks are for the twin who receives too much blood. In severe degree the transfusion syndrome, as reflected in a large difference in birth weight, can carry important risks, although it does not always do so. For most traits, the effect is quite minor and it does not threaten the logic of the twin strategy to any appreciable extent.[4]

Neither of these threats to the EEA is likely to be operative other than rarely. However, there is a third scenario of much greater importance that has received only systematic attention in recent times. This is the circumstance in which there is a strong genetic effect on some environmental variable that, in turn, has effects on the psychological feature or mental disorder being investigated. That applies, for example, to the risk environments that are relevant for either antisocial behavior or depression.[5] In both cases, it has been found that there are genetic effects on exposure to environments such as negative life events, parent–child conflict, and parental negativity. Each of these environments has, moreover, been shown to be significantly associated with individual differences in the traits of antisocial behavior and depression. That is to say, within an MZ pair who share all their genes, the twin who receives the most parental negativity tends to be the twin who also shows the most antisocial behavior. The same applies to negative life events and depression. In other words, with respect to these traits, some of the difference in similarity between MZ and DZ pairs will be due to environmental influences. This means that, to a degree, EEA is violated. It is important to emphasize that this is not an artifact of twin studies; rather, it is an expected consequence of the ways in which genes work with respect to environmental exposure. However, it will mean that the standard way of measuring heritability will tend to overestimate the genetic effect. It is difficult to quantify the extent of this inflation of the genetic effect but it is not likely to make a major difference to conclusions. Thus, for example, if the estimated heritability was 50 percent, but the true heritability was actually 40 percent, the conclusion would still be that there was an important meaningful genetic influence. Accordingly, although it is important to recognize that there is likely to be some violation of the EEA with respect to some traits, the effect is unlikely to be of sufficient magnitude to jeopardize the overall twin strategy. Also, whether or not the EEA is, or is not, violated will vary by traits. There cannot be any general conclusions on the EEA.

Most behavioral geneticists have ignored this biasing effect because they assume that the environmental influence within MZ pairs will tend to lead to an underestimate, rather than overestimate, of genetic effects. That is inappropriate on two grounds. First, there has to be a concern over possible bias in both directions. Second, the net effect is likely to be an artifactual inflation of genetic effects. That is because heritability is not determined by the MZ correlation on its own, but rather by the *difference* between the MZ and DZ correlations. The key point is that because the environmental similarity (for example, on parental negativity) will be so much greater in MZ pairs than in DZ pairs (as a result of the **gene–environment correlation**), the parental negativity will tend to make the MZ pairs more similar than

DZ pairs on the psychological feature (e.g., depression or antisocial behavior) as a result of environmental influences, as well as genetics.

There have been various attempts to look for possible violations of the EEA with respect to twin studies of schizophrenia and other major mental disorders,[6] with the conclusion that the EEA is not violated. However, it must be said that, so far, the EEA has not been systematically examined with respect to the environmental factors for which there is evidence that they play a likely role in the causal process for schizophrenia – namely obstetric complications, serious life events, urban living, and heavy early use of cannabis.[7] Nevertheless, because the effect of these environmental factors is quite small, it is unlikely that there would be a serious violation of the EEA.

Differences between twins and singletons

A further assumption of the twin strategy is that it can be assumed that twins and singletons are roughly the same with respect to the likelihood that they will show particular traits such as intelligence, emotionality, depression, or antisocial behavior. The question has been closely examined on many occasions with many different samples and the general conclusion is clear-cut – namely that twins and singletons are basically very similar with respect to the distribution of most psychological traits. However, there are a few exceptions that need to be noted. The two most important concern language development and the frequency of obstetric complications. It has been well demonstrated that as a group, twins tend to be a bit slower in their language development than do singletons.[8] The difference amounts, on average, to about 3 months at 3 years of age. The evidence suggests that the difference concerns variations within the normal range rather than an excess of severe language delay in twins. Also, the explanation seems to lie in the differences between twins and singletons in the pattern of mother–child interaction and communication that they experience. That is, having to deal simultaneously with two children of the same age and with roughly the same developmental needs is a somewhat different situation for the family than having one child at a time to deal with.[9] Once more, the effect, although of considerable interest, is not sufficiently great to bias the use of the twin design to examine genetic effects. It does indicate that there must be some caution when studying environmental influences on the development of language and language-related features but the researchers who have made such studies have been well aware of the issue and the research findings appear solid.[10]

The other well-known and well-documented feature is the substantially higher rate of obstetric complications, particularly low birth weight and premature gestation in twins as compared with singletons.[11] The evidence indicates that considerable caution needs to be applied when dealing with twins who are born after a very short period of gestation (say, 32 weeks or below) and/or are of extremely low birth weight. This group has a markedly increased mortality and morbidity.[12] However, this accounts for a tiny proportion of twins and the high rate of obstetric complications in the remainder seems of little consequence, and the twin–singleton differences in no way threaten the twin research strategy unless dealing with traits for which obstetric factors constitute a major risk.

Zygosity

For obvious reasons, the whole twin research strategy is predicated on the basis of accurate identification of which pairs are MZ and which pairs are DZ. Some of the early twin studies relied on parents' judgment. However, although parents are correct in their judgment much more often than they are wrong, they do sometimes draw wrong conclusions.[13] The bias can arise because judgments may be influenced by the extent to which twins behave in similar ways. This is most likely to occur when dealing with extreme behaviors of one kind or another. Thus, for example, in a study of twins with autism,[14] there were a few examples in which parents wrongly concluded that a pair was dizygotic because their behavior (including their facial expression) made it so easy to tell them apart. Interestingly, however, the twins were much more readily confused when dealing with photographs because there were not all those other cues that enabled other people to tell which twin was which. This sort of confusion is much less common in more ordinary circumstances. In any case, reliance on global parental judgment about **zygosity** was soon replaced by carefully constructed questionnaires. Comparisons with biological measures of zygosity have shown that such questionnaires have an overall accuracy of about 95 percent, which is adequate for most purposes. However, even more accurate decisions on zygosity became available through the use of fingerprints, then blood groups, and in recent years DNA. Sometimes, DNA methods are applied to full samples and sometimes only to subgroups for whom zygosity is in doubt. Either way, the slight uncertainties about zygosity that apply to earlier twin studies raise no serious concerns with most modern twin research.

Possible sampling biases

Sampling biases constitute rather more of a possible problem. For many years, the majority of twin studies that were concerned with traits in the general population (rather than serious mental disorders) were based on volunteer samples of one sort or another. Findings showed that, in general, MZ twins and concordant pairs were more likely to participate in such studies. This tendency would not necessarily affect the differences between MZ and DZ pairs, but it could do so.

By contrast, most twin studies of serious mental disorders have relied on clinic or hospital samples of one kind or another. With mental disorders that almost always result in referral (as would be the case, for example, with schizophrenia) it is not likely to be a serious problem. On the other hand, with disorders, such as depression, where that is not the case, it does constitute a potential source of bias. It is not just that the individuals who were referred may be different but also that the referral may be influenced by the characteristics of the co-twin. That is, when there is more than one reason for referral, referral is much more likely to take place.[15] It is also a potential problem when referral may lead to a rather diverse range of clinical facilities or to special schools rather than hospitals. That would be the case, for example, with autism. Accordingly, in the first twin study of autism, a nationwide search (spanning not only child psychiatric facilities but mental retardation facilities and special schools) was undertaken in order to ensure as near as possible total population coverage.[16] A further study more than 10 years later showed that the multifaceted, multifacility screening had resulted in very few cases being missed.[14]

With more common conditions, general population epidemiological samples are almost always to be preferred. However, they too have their problems. If the sampling is based on school registers, rather than birth registers, there is the uncertainty as to whether cases may be more likely to be missed if the two twins go to different schools (as might well be the case if either they are placed with different parents following parental separation and divorce, or special needs mean that one of the twins is placed in a school offering special facilities of one kind or another). However, whether or not this actually results in appreciable bias can be checked and, when this has been done, the results are generally reassuring.[17]

Birth registers manage to avoid this particular problem but, even with the best epidemiological studies, it is usual to have non-participation rates of 30 percent or so, and, with longitudinal studies, attrition may further increase the loss. The available evidence suggests that it is highly likely that the non-participating families will not be fully representative of the original population.[18] Those missing from the sample are likely to include a disproportionate percentage with psychopathology in either the parents or children. This crucial epidemiological consideration has received too little attention in twin studies in the past. Attrition biases, similarly, will distort the pattern of associations among variables[19] and hence these too are likely to give rise to misleading inferences about nature–nurture interplay. The problem of attrition leading to serious bias is well illustrated by a general population study of language.[20] Twins born to very young mothers and those from socially disadvantaged backgrounds were substantially under-represented. An opportunity to examine this matter in a quantified fashion was presented by the Moffitt and Caspi Environmental Risk Study (E-Risk), which constituted a subset of the original sample. In the E-Risk subsample, strenuous efforts were made to obtain information on the children and families who had dropped out of the overall study. This exercise was strikingly successful and it meant that it was possible to compare the results of analyses based on the full E-Risk sample and analyses using the overall sample that had been subject to attrition and, therefore, non-response bias.[21] The findings were salutary in indicating that the attrition had indeed brought about significant bias in the genetic inferences. The primary effect of the bias was a failure to detect shared environmental effects, an inflation of **additive genetic effects** and **nonshared environmental effect**s, and sometimes the spurious identification of rating contrast effects or **non-additive** (i.e., synergistic) **genetic effects**.

Sibling interaction effects

Most studies of psychological traits or of psychopathology inevitably involve judgments on whether an individual shows an unusually high or low rate of a particular feature (such as depression or antisocial behavior). At least two somewhat different issues arise in this connection. First, parents rating one twin may be influenced in their ratings by the characteristics of the other twin. In other words, if one twin is very overactive the parent may underestimate the level of overactivity in the other twin because, although greater than in most other children of the same age, it is so much less than that in the first twin. Where this tendency is marked, it will lead to an artifactually misleading exaggeration of the differences with the twin pair. This has often, although not always, been the case with respect to the ratings of hyperactivity. One way round the problem is to determine what happens with the ratings made by teachers, when a different teacher rates each twin. When such analyses were undertaken it was indeed found that there was a parental rating bias that led to an underestimate of the degree of similarity within dizygotic pairs.[22] Similarly, there may also be a sibling interaction effect that is independent of rating biases. Interaction could lead in either of two directions.[23] Thus, it could result in a contrast effect if the behavior of one twin led the other twin to strive to behave differently. This does some-times happen. Alternatively, if twins tend to share leisure activities it may lead to an increase in similarity because of this sharing of activities. For example, this tends to happen with antisocial or delinquent activities.[24]

Imprecision in measurement

It has been clear for a long time that there is inevitably a substantial amount of error whenever there is reliance on just one measure from one data source. This is not just because there may be bias deriving from particular perceptions of that one informant (although that may well be the case), but also from the fact that all measures involve a substantial amount of random error. Accordingly, it has become standard for there to be reliance on multiple measures from multiple informants.[25] Multivariate statistical techniques, involving various sorts of modeling (see below), have been invaluable in combining multiple measures in order to derive estimates of the latent trait that each of these specific measures aims to tap. Broadly similar issues apply to the reliance on measures that concern manifestations of a trait at just one single point in time. The point is that the overall balance or pattern of influences on a trait shown at just one time may be rather different from the influences that operate with respect to the persistence of a trait over time.

The evidence indicates that, on the whole, genetic influences on a liability to a disorder as shown over time, or for a persistent trait, tend to be substantially stronger than those that apply to a single episode or a measurement point.[26] That is scarcely surprising because all sorts of transient environmental influences may play a considerable role in emotions or behavior shown at a particular time when stress or opportunities are maximal. The picture is likely to be rather different if the focus is on emotions and behaviors that persist over time and over a varied range of circumstances. Nevertheless, care must be exercised when putting together information from several data sources that show rather low levels of agreement. When this is the case, it can occasionally turn out that the estimates of genetic effects are unrealistically high.[27] That is because, although they may accurately reflect the situation that applies to the agreement across data sources, it is important also to bear in mind that, because the agreement is so low, this accounts for only a tiny proportion of the overall population variance. There is no entirely satisfactory answer to the problem when little is known on the sources of disagreement among measures and among informants (which is often the case), and it is always necessary to combine statistical skills with common sense and good judgment. Having said that, the conclusion remains that genetic influences on recurrent disorder or persistent traits tend to be substantially stronger than on time-specific measures, particularly when they are derived from just one informant.

Statistical model fitting

One of the most important advances in quantitative genetics has been the development of sophisticated statistical modeling techniques. They have been crucially important, not only for the purpose of combining data sources (as noted above) but in going beyond simple quantitative estimates of the proportion of population variance accounted for by genetic effects to the testing of much more interesting and important specific hypotheses on questions such as whether different forms of psychopathology share the same genetic liability,[28] or hypotheses about possible mechanisms involved in sex differences in rates or patterns of psychopathology,[29] or hypotheses about the number of genes that are likely to be playing a part in genetic liability.[30] The use of modeling methods has been immensely helpful both in deciding between alternative hypotheses and in clarifying the nature of the phenomena to be explained. Their use undoubtedly carried the field forward in a major way.

On the other hand, they have involved two important considerations that involve the potential of introducing bias. First, the basic strategy works on the principle of parsimony. That is, the ideal model should both fit the data and be simple. The usual approach involves the systematic comparison of different models so that the consequences of dropping particular effects can be examined. When the elimination of an effect does not result in a significant worsening of the fit of the model, it has become standard practice for it to be dropped from the model in order to produce a simpler one. On the face of it, that sounds a reasonable strategy but it is essential to appreciate that a lack of a significant effect is not synonymous with a demonstrated lack of effect. The main reason why this is such an important issue is that, even with very large samples, it is usual to find that the confidence interval for particular effects are very wide and, therefore, the decision to drop a parameter is based on the lower end of the 95 percent confidence limits without reference to its upper end. The point was thoughtfully discussed by Slutske et al.[31] and their data well illustrate the matter. Their sample involved 2,682 twin pairs from the Australian twin register, a substantial sample by any reckoning. Nevertheless, the confidence interval for a shared environmental effect on antisocial behavior extended from 0 to 32 percent. Because the lower limit included 0, the overall effect was not statistically significant and, hence, shared effects were not included in the best-fitting model for conduct disorder symptoms. However, it follows that a variable that might, in truth, have quite a large effect was being eliminated as if it were known that it was of no consequence. In practice, this approach has often led to a dropping of shared environmental effects with a resulting exaggeration of genetic and nonshared environmental effects (see Chapter 4 for the meaning of the distinction between shared and nonshared environmental effects).

It is clear that this parsimony rule sometimes results in the dropping of a variable that absolutely must have had an effect. For example, Maes et al.[32] examined alcohol use in 8- to 16-year-old twins in the Virginia Twin Study. The best-fitting model for lifetime alcohol use included no genetic effect. By sharp contrast, the model for lifetime alcohol use without permission had genetic effects accounting for 72 percent of the population variance! Clearly, that result was impossible, as the investigators themselves appreciated. The difference is all the more striking because not only was the group who used alcohol without permission a subset of individuals in the overall population of alcohol users, but it made up over half of them. It has become increasingly recognized by behavioral geneticists that the mechanical operation of model-fitting rules can lead to ridiculous conclusions and it is necessary to consider the meaning of the findings, together with the confidence interval of the various estimates.[33]

The second point about statistical modeling is that the models are often based on quite implausible assumptions. Thus, at least until recently, it has been usual for them to assume that there is no assortative mating, no synergistic interactions among genes, no gene–environment correlations, and no gene–environment interactions. Although these assumptions may be justified for some characteristics, they quite definitely are not so for others (as discussed more fully below). Some of the assumptions will lead to an exaggeration of genetic effects and some to an underestimate of their importance, but there is one assumption that matters rather more than the others.

That is, in the traditional way of partitioning genetic and environmental effects, the effects of gene–environment correlations and gene–environment interactions will be largely included in the genetic influence estimate if the environmental effect is shared and in the nonshared environmental effect if the gene–environmental interplay operates in a twin-specific fashion. The rationale is that because the origins of an environmental risk factor derive from genetics (as will be the case with a gene–environment correlation), it is reasonable to attribute the whole of the environmental effect to the genes that provided the basis for the risk environment. The falsity of this argument is well illustrated by the example of cigarette smoking.[34] In this instance, the reasons why people smoke cigarettes have got virtually nothing to do with the causal mechanisms involved in the damaging consequences of smoking. Thus, people smoke through a mixture of influences deriving from genetically influenced propensities, pharmacological effects on dependency, cultural influences, personality features, and availability. However, none of those account for the carcinogenic effects of the tars in the cigarette smoke or the effects on coronary artery disease, chronic bronchitis, osteoporosis, and skin wrinkling (to mention but a few of the wide range of sequelae) which are attributable to the nicotinic effects on blood vessels and the effects of carbon monoxide. Of course, in other circumstances with other outcomes, there may be more of a connection between the causes of the risk factor and the mode of mediation of the risk influence, but the crucial point is that there is no necessary connection between the two and it is seriously misleading to incorporate all of that into the genetic estimate. The same applies to gene–environment interactions. However, it makes no sense to attribute these either to genetics alone or to the environment alone in that the effects, in actuality, result from the co-action of the two operating together. Of course, these effects can be disaggregated,[35] but they rarely are.

Assumptions on general population base rate

The calculation of degree of genetic influence (often summarized under the overall heading of heritability) is very dependent on the assumptions made about the rate of the trait in the general population. That is, with mental disorders ordinarily dealt with in terms of a categorical diagnosis, there is an assumption that the genetic liability is actually distributed dimensionally, with the disorder becoming evident only above some particular threshold. The calculations on heritability, particularly with rare disorders, necessarily have to take into account the rate in the general population. Thus, for example, the rate in **siblings** of a child showing the syndrome of autism is only about 3–6 percent (depending a bit on how it is measured). That does not sound very high and, on the face of it, would seem to imply a rather low genetic influence. However, the point is that this is very many times higher than the rate in the general population. This is ordinarily expressed by the **lambda** statistic, which quantifies the relative frequency in siblings (or in any other specified relative) in comparison with the general population. When the general population base rate of autism was assumed to be about 4–10 per 10,000, the lambda value was 50–100, implying an extremely strong familial tendency. Given the general acceptance of the broadening of the concept of autism spectrum disorder (see below) and the appreciation that the true general population rate is more likely to be in the region of 30–60 per 10,000,[36] this necessarily means that the lambda must be much less than originally thought. It cannot be calculated very precisely because, in order to do so, it will be necessary that the definition of autism spectrum disorder in the twin studies should be identical to that in the general population epidemiological studies. However, it would be reasonable to conclude that the lambda is more likely to be in the region of 20 rather than of the original estimate of 100. That would still lead to the conclusion of a strong familial tendency and, in the light of the twin findings, to a very high heritability but not quite as high as first assumed.

Assumptions on the definition of diagnostic phenotypes

The early psychiatric genetic studies tended to assume that it was safe to rely on the use of traditional psychiatric diagnostic categories. That is, it was assumed that genetic influences would operate through risks for specific disorders. What rapidly became clear is that the genetic liability frequently did not coincide with the accepted psychiatric classifications. For example, the genetic liability for schizophrenia extended to include schizotypal disorders and paranoid disorders as well as schizophrenia "proper."[37] Similarly, the genetic liability for autism extends well beyond the traditional seriously handicapping disorder that usually involves a degree of mental retardation, to a much broader range of qualitatively similar, but much milder, abnormalities in communicative and social reciprocity and in repetitive stereotyped behavior.[36] Similarly, it seems that the genetic liability to depression includes generalized anxiety disorders and the temperamental trait of neuroticism.[38] Also, the genetic liability for Tourette's syndrome probably includes chronic tics and even some forms of obsessive–compulsive disorder.[39] Critics have had a field day in arguing that if researchers cannot even define the psychiatric categories properly, how can they possibly investigate genetic influences? However, that is to totally miss the point. Although the old assumption used to be that the genetic effects operate directly on traditional psychiatric disorders, no one believes that today. The traditional psychiatric diagnostic classifications do have important purposes but there is no reason to suppose that these categories coincide with either pathophysiological causal pathways or the routes of genetic influence. The argument that genetic research should wait for proper validation of psychiatric categories ignores the vital point that genetic findings will be very helpful in that validation.

Separated twins and offspring of twins designs

An appreciation by behavioral geneticists that twin designs, as usually undertaken, are not free of problems has led to the development of two potentially important variations on the twin strategy. First, there have been several studies focusing on twins who have been reared apart in different families.[40] The basic idea is a good one; namely, that if the two twins in MZ pairs are separated at birth and brought up in entirely different families, any resemblance between them (beyond that expected by chance alone) must be attributable to genetic influences. The findings from separated twins studies have certainly produced some quite remarkable examples of striking similarities that apply to details, as well as generalities, of behavior. At first sight, the inference that these similarities reflect genetic influences seems incontrovertible. However, the design has rather more problems than are usually acknowledged. To begin with, it is very unusual to separate twins at birth and there must be questions as to what was special about the circumstances that led to such a separation. Second, although the findings tend to be written up as if the separation was at birth, it is clear from the descriptions that the actual separation sometimes took place at a rather later age, leaving open the possibility of shared rearing influences. Third, there are inevitable question marks over the influences that led separated twins to volunteer to participate in the research. It seems likely that, at least in some instances, their making contact with each other and being struck by resemblances played a part in their volunteering for the research and this could well exaggerate the similarities. Fourth, although some of the separated twins were brought up in rather different family circumstances, in many instances the homes in which they were placed were somewhat similar. Finally, there are queries over some of the measurement approaches adopted as well as with the rather limited reporting so far of quantitative findings presented in scientific papers that have been subject to peer review. Without question, the separated twins findings serve to support the conclusion that genetic influences on behavior are substantial but there are too many queries for it to be reasonable to place great reliance on the findings.

Although the offspring of twins design was identified some years ago,[41] it is only very recently that it has been used in a systematic way to determine the effect of specific measured environmental influences on behavior. The basic rationale is quite straightforward.[42] The key consideration is that adult identical twins share all their genes. This means that their children are, genetically speaking, **half-siblings** (i.e., they share the same genes from one parent but not from the other parent) rather than cousins, as they would be in other circumstances. Accordingly, the comparison of the offspring of twins allows estimates of both genetic effects and the environmental effects of being brought up in different families. The quantification is, of course, strengthened by the inclusion of both MZ and DZ twin pairs in the design. It is an ingenious and neat approach that does, indeed, get over some of the disadvantages of the traditional twin design. However, there are several limitations. Because the offspring of the identical twins are half-siblings rather than **full siblings**, this much reduces the statistical power of the comparison with cousins. Second, both genetic and environmental influences on the now-adult twins as they were growing up will make it possible that there will be some similarities in the spouses they choose and in the environments that they provide for their children. Nevertheless, the design is unquestionably a useful one and its employment should add in an important way to the overall pattern of evidence on genetic and environmental influences.

Adoptee designs

Adoptee designs deal with the separation of genetic and environmental effects in a quite different way from that involved in the twin research strategy. The key separation here is between the biological parents who (provided that the children were placed for adoption at birth or in early infancy) played no part in the rearing of the children, and the adopting parents who were entirely responsible for the rearing but who do not have any genetic relationship to the children that they have adopted.

Comparability of biological and adopting parents

There are several different varieties of adoptee study[43] but, in one way or another, they make use of the biological parent–social parent contrast. As with any research strategy, it is essential to consider critically the various assumptions that have to be made in the relevant analyses. First, if like is to be compared with like, the two sets of parents should be broadly comparable.[44] Although behavioral geneticists frequently claim that that is the case, it is obvious that they are not. Numerous general population studies have shown that adoptees are much more likely than other children to be born to unmarried teenage mothers and much more likely to have received sub-optimal obstetric care.[45] In the Colorado adoption study, despite efforts to ensure that the two sets of parents were comparable, antisocial behavior in the biological parents was four times as common as in the adopting parents. Scandinavian studies, too, have shown that traits of criminality and alcohol abuse are two to three times higher in parents giving their babies up for adoption than in the general population.[45] Conversely, adopting parents tend to differ systematically from other parents in being better educated, more socially advantaged, and in having low rates of psychopathology (at least as manifest up to the time of adoption).

These differences are, of course, not surprising. Women with mental disorders may well be more likely than other women to give up their babies for adoption (although the characteristics of parents giving up their children for adoption vary both over time and across countries), and prospective adopting parents are specifically screened to ensure that, as far as possible, they do not have significant mental disorders that are likely to interfere with their ability to provide good quality parenting. As a consequence, the findings of adoptee studies are certainly likely to be distorted by the fact that the biological parents include a disproportionately high percentage of individuals with genetic risk characteristics, and that the adopting parents under-represent the proportion of high-risk environments found in the general population. However, it is not just that the rate of high-risk environments tends to be unusually low in adoptive families but also that the range of environments is quite restricted as compared with the general population.[46] The net effect is that there will be a tendency for adoptee studies to underestimate environmental effects.

A further consideration is that, on the whole, rates of psychopathology tend to be somewhat higher in adoptees than in the general population, although the extent to which this is so varies across the age span and across different sorts of psychopathology. The reasons why this is so are not adequately understood and the implications for conclusions on genetic and environmental influences will be crucially dependent on the explanation. Thus, for example, the higher rate of psychopathology in adoptees could be a consequence of the biological parents including an unusually high proportion transmitting genetic risks. Alternatively, the higher rate could reflect the stresses that are involved in being an adoptee. Although, for children from high-risk backgrounds, the overall effect of adoption may well be (and probably is) protective, being an adoptee is unusual and may carry with it some stresses as well as challenges. The fact that the rate of psychopathology in adoptees tends to rise, relative to singletons, in the teenage years (as compared with earlier childhood) suggests that this environmental risk effect may be operative to some extent. Because it will operate more generally across all adoptees, it may serve to underestimate the effects of environmental differences among the adopting families.

Selective placement

Critics of adoptee findings tend to place particular emphasis on the possibility of selective placement of children such that there is a built-in confound between genetic risk and environmental risk. In this connection, the selectivity concerns the possibility that more favorable adoptive homes will be chosen for children with a more favorable genetic background. This may be a problem with respect to some traits but it is not likely to be a concern with respect to major psychopathology (because adopting parents are generally chosen to be relatively free of serious psychopathology). In any case, because it has been obvious from the outset that the adoptee design depends so crucially on knowledge of possible selective placement, it has been a matter of routine for genetic studies to seek to determine the presence of any selective placement, and to undertake the necessary statistical controls when it has been found. Accordingly, although concerns about selective placement have often been raised by critics of adoptee studies, the distortions created are likely to be far less important than those inherent in the nonrepresentativeness of adoptees for the general population of non-adopted children, and the major differences between the biological and adoptive parents.

Gene–environment interaction

One of the great strengths of the adoptee design is that it provides a means of separating genetic risk from environmental risk. The basic feature of the design is that it removes the passive gene–environment correlation (meaning that the parents who transmit genetic risks also tend to provide risky environments) that ordinarily applies in non-adoptive samples. This is a major advantage in separating the effects of nature and nurture, but it carries with it the potential disadvantage that the proportion of the population where there are both genetic and environmental risks will be misleadingly small. Insofar as genetic effects operate through gene–environment interactions (see Chapter 9), genetic effects on population variance will be underestimated by adoptee designs.

Assortative mating

Yet another complication is provided by **assortative mating**, and especially by a tendency for a particular sort of psychopathology in one parent to be associated with a different sort of psychopathology in the other parent. This is particularly problematic if different forms of psychopathology are involved because the findings will make it seem that the two traits have a similar genetic liability when in reality they have a different one. The intermarriage between antisocial individuals and people with schizophrenia illustrates the problem.[47] If the psychopathology in the two biological parents is of a similar type, there will be a tendency to overestimate the genetic effects through the adoptee design because, in effect, there is a double genetic dose rather than a single one.

Blended families design

The blended families design[48] was developed as a way of overcoming some of the limitations of the twin and adoptee designs. Basically, it comprises a study of families in which divorce / separation has been followed by remarriage with children who vary in their **genetic relatedness** according to who were their parents. Thus, there may be children from the first marriages of each parent and children born to the two parents coming together for their second marriage. The design has two main attractions. First, in most modern-day industrialized societies, the rates of marriage breakdown and subsequent remarriage or cohabitation are high. Accordingly, large samples of blended families are likely to be much easier to come by than are twin and adoptee samples. Moreover, the complexity of patterns of marriage and remarriage, and the different backgrounds from which the remarrying couples come, mean that it should be readily possible to find families that include full siblings, half-siblings, and unrelated siblings. The second attraction is that the expectation from the degree of genetic relatedness is straightforward. That is, if a behavior is genetically influenced, it should show a genetic cascade in which within-pair correlations are highest for monozygotic pairs, lower for dizygotic pairs and for full siblings, but similar in the two, lower still for half-siblings, and lowest of all for unrelated siblings.[49] This means that it provides the opportunity to test whether the genetic expectations are borne out.

Unfortunately, some of the findings, and their implications, have proved difficult to interpret because the expected genetic cascade has not always been apparent. Thus in the O'Connor et al. study,[50] the expectation was nearly met with antisocial behavior. However, the intercorrelation within DZ pairs (.68) was substantially greater than that for full siblings either reared apart or reared together (.46 and .49). The departure from expectations was even more marked for depression. With the exception of a high correlation within MZ pairs there was very little difference in the correlations for the other different types of sibling pair, and although the differences were very small, the intercorrelation was actually highest for half-siblings and lowest for DZ pairs.

This almost certainly comes about because of one very serious disadvantage of the design. That is, the differences in genetic relatedness are accompanied by differences in environmental risk, making it extremely difficult to sort out the effects of the one from the effects of the other. Thus, children of the previous marriages of the two adults getting remarried will vary in the length of their time in the previous home, and will vary in their length of time (as well as their age at the time of joining the family) in the blended family home. In short, there is an essential confound between genetic risk and environmental risk. Although the blended family design was an interesting innovation, this confound makes for major problems in quantifying and comparing genetic and environmental influences.

Family genetic studies

Family studies differ from twin and adoptee designs in the key respect that they do not permit a clear separation of genetic and non-genetic influences (except in the context of molecular genetic designs – see Chapter 6 – or extended twin-family designs – see Chapter 5). Nevertheless, they are contributory in several different ways. To begin with, the observation that disorders or psychological traits tend to "run" in families has often been the first indicator that the **familial loading** *might* reflect a genetic liability. The inference is more plausible if the strength of the loading varies systematically with the degree of biological genetic relatedness – i.e., being greatest in first-degree relatives, lower in second-degree relatives, and lower still in third-degree relatives.[51] It may also be informative in connection with the pattern of features that run in families. For example, the broader (milder) phenotype seen in the co-twins of individuals with autism was closely mirrored by a similar pattern in the siblings and parents of such individuals.[52] Also, the finding that the familial loading with Tourette's syndrome extended to chronic multiple tics and some varieties of obsessive–compulsive disorder pointed to the likelihood that the genetic liability extended more broadly than had been supposed previously.[53]

Family studies may also be instructive with respect to the patterns found when two supposedly different disorders often co-occur. For example, does the familial loading differ according to whether attention deficit disorder with hyperactivity (ADHD) is, or is not, associated with conduct disorder/oppositional defiant behavior? The finding that it does not reinforces the conclusion from twin studies that, to an important extent, when the two co-occur they reflect the same genetic liability.[54]

But perhaps the most important contribution of family studies is to test the mode of transmission of **Mendelian** (single gene, wholly genetic) disorders. Thus, for example, the finding that autism not infrequently occurs in fathers and sons meant that (at least in those cases) it could not be due to a gene on the X chromosome because boys always get their X chromosome from their mother and their Y chromosome from their father.

Family findings may also be crucially important in identifying the risk characteristics that are present *before* the mental disorders develop. Thus, a prospective study of young people in families at high risk for schizophrenia showed that they were identifiable in terms of neuropsychological impairment and brain imaging findings.[55] The same strategy has been informative with respect to the early indicators of later reading difficulties.[56] These findings do not directly show that the precursor characteristics are genetically influenced but, in conjunction with twin and adoptee data, they point to the features that are likely to identify genetic risk at the individual level.

Finally, family data may be valuable in suggesting how many **susceptibility genes** are likely to be operative. The key point is that because MZ twins (within a pair) share all their genes whereas DZ twins (within a pair) share only half their segregating genes, the genetic risk can be portrayed as 1 for MZ pairs and 1/2 for DZ pairs. However, although DZ pairs have a 50:50 chance of sharing any one gene, they will share only 1/4 of two-gene combinations, 1/8 of three-gene combinations, and so forth. It follows that if the risk to the co-twin is much less than 1 in 2, it is likely that inheritance involves synergism between particular patterns of genes. Tackling the matter mathematically, Pickles et al.[30] were able to show on this basis that autism could not ordinarily be due to just 1 gene; an interplay among 3 or 4 genes was quite likely but as many as 10 to 12 genes could be involved. However, a very large number of genes acting independently on one another was unlikely. It will be appreciated that a precise figure for the number of genes cannot be calculated because the number will depend on the relative strength of effect of each individual gene. Nevertheless, it was useful to know that a relatively small number of genes acting in combination was likely.

Overall conclusions from quantitative genetics

Given the many concerns and criticisms of twin and adoptee strategies, it might be concluded that no firm inferences are possible on the strength of genetic influences.[57] That would be seriously mistaken. Of course, there are limitations, particularly in some of the earlier behavioral genetic studies. However, behavioral geneticists have, for the most part, taken on board criticisms and concerns and have taken the necessary steps in their research to meet these concerns. What is impressive is that the best conducted studies give rise to conclusions that are broadly in line with the earlier studies, albeit expressed somewhat more modestly and somewhat more cautiously. There has been a real problem with the overstatements and exaggerations of genetic evangelists[58] but, putting these aside, the findings are impressively robust.

In considering how much confidence can be placed in the findings of quantitative behavioral genetic research, five key issues need to be borne in mind. First, throughout the whole of science, all research has limitations and difficulties; that is not at all a feature that applies only to psychiatric or behavioral genetics. It is all too easy to criticize and point to problems. The standard way of dealing with this issue throughout science is to check whether the highest quality studies provide the same message as the more problematic ones; to determine whether research strategies that differ in their pattern of strengths and limitations give rise to similar conclusions; to consider carefully the degree to which findings can be generalized across populations and samples; and to check the relative plausibility of competing explanations and conclusions. When that is done with psychiatric and behavioral genetic findings, it is obvious that the overall pattern demands acceptance of the importance of genetic influences. That is, the findings are incompatible with a zero genetic effect. Equally, the findings are incompatible with any suggestion that genes control all behavioral variation in a deterministic fashion. That conclusion derives from the genetic findings but it also derives from studies using a range of strategies to test hypotheses on environmentally mediated risk effects.[59] It should be noted that the evidence is equally incompatible with any suggestions that environmental influences account for all individual variation. Any dispassionate, but critical, review of the research leads to the clear conclusion that there are substantial genetic *and* environmental effects on almost all types of behavior and all forms of psychopathology or mental disorder.

The second issue is that there is not, and cannot be, any absolute value for the strength of genetic influences on a trait, no matter how accurately the trait is measured or how carefully the genetic effect is assessed. As behavioral geneticists have long recognized, and emphasized, heritability figures are necessarily specific to populations and to time periods. That is not just a matter of scientific caution. Rather, it reflects an appreciation that heritability figures represent effects on the variations within populations. They do not apply to individuals, nor do they have a fixed relationship with any specific traits. What that means is that if environmental circumstances change (such as with the introduction of a new risk, or the removal of an old risk, or the operation of novel protective factors), the heritability figure will be affected. Having accepted that fact, the findings nevertheless show that across a range of circumstances, and across broad time periods, there are important differences among traits in the extent to which they are genetically influenced (see below). Alongside that conclusion must be placed an appreciation that there is very limited evidence on the extent to which genetic influences operate similarly across ethnic groups,[60] or within seriously disadvantaged segments of the population.

The third issue is that the quantitative genetic findings concern effects on individual differences within a population at some point in time. These are very important, but equal attention needs to be paid to changes over time in the *level* of a trait and the **incidence** of disorders. For example, over the past

100 years or so, the average life expectancy at birth has almost doubled in most industrialized countries – from a little above 42 years to 76 years in males.[61] Similarly, there has been a huge reduction in infantile mortality, and a marked increase in average height.[62] Almost certainly, these beneficial changes are due to improved sanitation (reducing infectious disease) and improved nutrition. Genetic factors throughout these 100+ years have probably remained at about the same high level of effect on individual differences, but it is environmental change that has brought about the changes in level. In short, causal effects cannot be reduced to one question; rather they apply to a range of questions. Of course, the answers must prove to be compatible with one another but they will not necessarily tell quite the same story. In the following chapter, the heritability findings for different traits and disorders are considered in greater detail.

Notes

See Reference list for full details.
1   Rowe et al., 1999; Turkheimer et al., 2003
2   See Rutter et al., 1999 a; Rutter et al., 2001
3   Hettema et al., 1995
4   See, for example, Rutter et al., 2003
5   Rutter et al., 1999 a; Rutter et al., 2001
6   Kendler et al., 1994
7   Arseneault et al., 2004; Boydell et al., 2004; Cannon et al., 2004
8   Rutter & Redshaw, 1991; Rutter et al., 2003
9   Thorpe et al., 2003
10 Bishop, 2003
11 Rutter et al., 2003
12 Marlow, 2004; Marlow et al., 2005
13 Goodman & Stevenson, 1989
14 Bailey et al., 1995
15 Berkson, 1946
16 Folstein & Rutter, 1977 b
17 Nadder et al., 2002
18 Cox et al., 1977
19 Berk, 1983
20 Dale et al., 1998
21 Taylor, 2004
22 Simonoff et al., 1998 a
23 Segal, 1999
24 Rutter et al., 1998
25 Bank et al., 1990
26 Kendler et al., 1993 a; Cherny et al., 1997
27 Simonoff et al., 1998 b

28   Kendler, 1996; Nadder et al., 2002
29   Waldman & Rhee, 2002
30   Pickles et al., 1995
31   Slutske et al., 1997
32   Maes et al., 2000
33   Sullivan & Eaves, 2002
34   Rutter et al., 1993
35   See, for example, Eaves et al., 2003 and Silberg et al., 2001 b
36   Rutter, 2005 a & 2005 d
37   Kendler et al., 1995
38   Kendler, 1996
39   Leckman & Cohen, 2002
40   e.g., Shields, 1962; Bouchard, 1997
41   Nance & Corey, 1976
42   D'Onofrio et al., 2003; Silberg & Eaves, 2004
43   Rutter et al., 1990 a
44   This does not necessarily mean a comparison of the biological and adoptive parents because many adoptee designs use comparisons based on contrasting characteristics of either the biological parents or the offspring. Nevertheless, generalization to non-adoptive samples will be constrained by the range of characteristics of both biological and adopting parents.
45   DeFries et al., 1994; Maughan & Pickles, 1990; Maughan et al., 1998; Seglow et al., 1972
46   Stoolmiller, 1999
47   Mednick, 1978
48   Hetherington et al., 1994
49   O'Connor et al., 2000
50   O'Connor et al., 1998
51   Loehlin, 1989
52   Bolton et al., 1994; Bailey et al., 1998
53   Leckman & Cohen, 2002; Rapoport & Swedo, 2002
54   Nadder et al., 2002; Levy & Hay, 2001
55   Johnstone et al., 2002; Whalley et al., 2004; Johnstone et al., 2005
56   Lyytinen et al., 2004; Snowling et al., 2003
57   See Joseph, 2003
58   See Rutter, 2002 b
59   Rutter, 2000 a & in press b; Rutter et al., 2001
60   Rutter & Tienda, 2005
61   Office for National Statistics, 2002
62   Tizard, 1975

Further reading

Kendler, K.S. (2005). Psychiatric genetics: A methodological critique. *American Journal of Psychiatry*, 162, 3–11.

Plomin, R., DeFries, J., McClearn, G.E., & McGuffin, P. (Eds.) (2001). *Behavioral Genetics, Fourth Edition*. New York: Worth Publishers.

Rutter, M., Bolton, P., Harrington, R., Le Couteur, A., Macdonald, H., & Simonoff, A. (1990 a). Genetic factors in child psychiatric disorders: I. A review of research strategies. *Journal of Child Psychology and Psychiatry, 31*, 3–37.

Rutter, M., Silberg, J., O'Connor, T., & Simonoff, E. (1999 a). Genetics and child psychiatry: I. Advances in quantitative and molecular genetics. *Journal of Child Psychology and Psychiatry, 40*, 3–18.

Chapter 4

The heritability of different mental disorders and traits

Before summarizing the findings on the heritability of a selective sample of different mental disorders and traits, it is necessary to consider how best to decide on the confidence that can be placed in the estimates derived from research findings. Basically, four main approaches may be followed. First, attention needs to be paid to the results of putting together all the findings from the twin studies of acceptable quality. Sometimes, this has been done through a statistical technique called meta-analysis that provides a quantitative estimate based on the findings of all the studies but taking into account the relative size of the samples in the individual investigations. However, it is also sometimes done by considering both the average figure and the confidence interval around that figure – meaning the range covered by 95 percent of the findings. The second approach is to focus on the best quality studies in terms of sampling and measurement, in order to see whether they provide findings that are substantially different from the overall average. The third approach is to determine the extent to which the findings from the twin studies are in line with other evidence – meaning, for the most part, family studies and adoption studies. Finally, attention needs to be paid to whether or not cautions or reservations need to be added because of conceptual or methodological concerns raised by critics. These four approaches are illustrated with respect to some uncommon severely handi-capping disorders, some more common disorders and traits for which there are rather more in the way of queries over diagnosis and definition, and, thirdly, findings on life experiences.

Uncommon disorders for which genetic influences predominate

Schizophrenia

Schizophrenia is a serious mental disorder (occurring in males and females at roughly the same rate) that most often begins in early adult life and which is characterized by a combination of both positive and negative phenomena.[1] Positive symptoms (meaning those involving qualitative abnormalities) include thought disorder, auditory hallucinations, and delusions. Negative symptoms (meaning those that involve impairment in normal functions) include social withdrawal and a loss of motivation. Although about a fifth of people with schizophrenia do recover or markedly improve, in the majority of instances, the disorder runs a chronic or a current course. There is a much increased risk of suicide and also an increased rate of death from a variety of causes. There is major social impairment and considerable personal suffering. About one in a hundred people develop schizophrenia. Although the onset is characteristically in early adult life, in many cases there have been manifest precursors in childhood that involve neurodevelopmental impairment, social deficits, and solitary antisocial behavior.

Cardno and Gottesman[2] have brought together the findings from the five systematically ascertained twin studies reported in the late 1990s. The proband-wise **concordance** rate for schizophrenia in monozygotic (MZ) twin pairs was 41–65 percent, as compared with 0–28 percent for dizygotic (DZ) twin pairs, giving rise to a heritability estimate of approximately 80 to 85 percent. Considering the five studies separately, the heritability estimates range from 82 percent (with a confidence interval of 71–90) to 84 percent (with a confidence interval of 19–92). These figures are closely similar to the findings from the much earlier, methodologically less satisfactory, studies summarized by Gottesman.[3]

In many respects the best twin studies are the Scandinavian investigations – such as the Finnish Twin Study – because they are based on systematic coverage of the whole population as well as systematic diagnosis.[4] However, the Maudsley Twin Register has the special merit of a systematic recording of all twins attending the hospital since 1948 (albeit not on a population sample), and it has the advantages of a substantial sample size, zygosity determination undertaken on all available information and blind to diagnosis, and the use of systematic standardized diagnostic methods.[5] Both these studies produced heritability estimates closely in line with other twin studies.

Adoption studies, similarly, have indicated a strong genetic effect on the individual variations to the liability to schizophrenia. Thus, when data from the Danish adoption study were reanalyzed using modern diagnostic criteria, nearly 8 percent of the first-degree biological relatives of adoptees with schizophrenia had schizophrenia themselves, compared with just less than 1 percent of the first-degree relatives of control adoptees.[6] The comparable figures for schizophrenia spectrum disorders were 24 percent vs. 5 percent. Most of Joseph's[7] criticisms of this study were met by this more rigorous approach to both the data used and the diagnostic methods, as well as the separation of full and half siblings. The Finnish Adoption Study findings by Tienari et al.[8] provided broadly comparable figures for the offspring: an 8 percent rate of schizophrenia in the adopted-away offspring of mothers with schizophrenia, compared with 2 percent in the offspring of a comparison group of parents without schizophrenia.

Family studies, similarly, have shown consistently that the risk of schizophrenia in the relatives of individuals with schizophrenia is a function of the extent to which they share their genes. Thus, in the general population the rate of schizophrenia is approximately 1 percent, in second-degree relatives it is about 2–6 percent, whereas in first-degree relatives it is about 6–13 percent.[9]

Various objections have been raised in relation to the genetic findings on schizophrenia.[7] Some of the concerns refer to the reporting of the earlier adoptee study findings, some to the problems that derive from the uncertainties over diagnostic boundaries,[10] and some focus on the variations within groups of similar genetic relatedness (for example, the fact that the rate in non-identical co-twins is nearly twice as high as that in siblings, although they have the same genetic relatedness[3]). Also, the rate in parents (about 6 percent) is half that in children (about 13 percent), despite the fact that they are similar in their genetic relatedness. However, this last difference is almost certainly due to the fact that, as compared with the general population, individuals with schizophrenia are less likely to marry and have children.[11] Some of the detailed methodological criticisms are valid but the overall consistency of findings, and in particular the fact that the findings of the best studies are so consistent, makes the overall estimate of heritability sound. It can be inferred that, in the populations studied, the heritability is something of the order of 80 percent.

However, there are two further points that need emphasis. The early genetic studies all indicated that schizophrenia seemed to be genetically rather distinct from bipolar affective disorder. Recent evidence[12] has indicated that if the diagnostic criteria are somewhat broadened and if rather arbitrary traditional diagnostic hierarchies are set aside, the evidence indicates that, to some extent at least, genetic liability for schizophrenia and for bipolar disorder may overlap. A recent brain imaging study[13] showed that the genetic risks for schizophrenia and for bipolar disorder were associated with similar findings regarding the white matter of the brain, but with differences regarding the gray matter. As the author concluded, the evidence points to overlap between these two psychoses in some respects, but separateness in others. The other consideration is that the genetic risk for schizophrenia may interact with environmental risk factors.[14]

Bipolar affective disorder

Bipolar affective disorder (previously called manic-depressive disorder) is a serious recurrent condition involving one or more episodes of mania, usually (but not always) with episodes of depression at other times. The mania is characterized by euphoria, an exaggerated sense of self-esteem, racing thoughts and undue talkativeness, sleeplessness, distractibility, and reckless impulsive behavior. Typically each episode begins and ends rather suddenly, after a period of disability that lasts several months, but may be as brief as a week. It has an incidence of about 1 percent in the general population and occurs at much the same frequency in males and females.

The evidence on bipolar affective disorder is substantially less than that available for schizophrenia. Jones, Kent, and Craddock[15] pooled the findings from six twin studies using a modern concept of bipolar disorder. None was methodologically strong, and only three had a sample size that warranted statistical analysis. The monozygotic concordance rates ranged from 36 to 75 percent and those for dizygotic from 0 to 7 percent. This is consistent with high heritability but the data are too sparse for any quantitative estimate to be made with confidence. However, there are rather more data from family studies, there being eight with appropriate control findings. The risk of bipolar disorder in first-degree relatives is about 5–10 percent, which is much higher than the general population rate of about 0.5–1.5 percent. It has generally been concluded that the heritability is in excess of 70 percent, but inevitably this is a very approximate figure given the limitations of the evidence. The main area of uncertainty stems from the difficulty in knowing quite where to place the diagnostic boundary. Recently, long-term follow-up studies have suggested that the concept should be substantially broadened.[16] It is not at all clear how this would affect the estimates of the strength of genetic contribution to the population variance for this disorder.

Autism spectrum disorders

Autism spectrum disorders are serious conditions that involve deficits in social communication, deficits in social reciprocity, and the presence of stereotyped repetitive patterns of behavior, and which are much more common in males.[17] Although many findings indicate the likelihood that the basis of the disorder is first evident in brain development before birth and in the infancy period,[18] in most instances the manifestations of the disorder are not readily apparent until about the age of 18 months. It is now generally accepted that it is a neurodevelopmental disorder with characteristic cognitive deficits, of which the most prominent are a difficulty in telling from social situations what another person is likely to be thinking (a so-called "theory of mind" or mentalizing deficit) and a difficulty in appreciating the overall gestalt of pictures (in other words, a tendency to focus on details rather than the meaning of the whole[19]). There are also characteristic findings from functional brain imaging.[20]

There have been three epidemiologically based twin studies of autism.[21] The concordance rate in monozygotic pairs ranged from 36 to 91 percent; in dizygotic pairs the rate was just 0 percent (but probably 5 percent is a more realistic figure, this reflecting the rate in siblings as well as DZ twins on the grounds that the two are genetically comparable). The two combined British twin studies[22] had the considerable advantage of using well-tested standardized methods of diagnosis with DNA testing for zygosity in the great majority of cases, and checks that the findings were not an artifact of obstetric complications. The finding in the second study that very few new cases were found that would have been eligible for the first study (but were unused) means that the general population coverage was successfully thorough.

Family studies have provided further evidence of a strong genetic influence on the liability to autism. The rate of about 3 to 6 percent in the siblings of individuals with autism is many times higher than that in the general population. At the time the twin and family studies were undertaken, the evidence suggested a general population rate of approximately 1 per 1,000, meaning that the increase in rate among siblings was of the order of 30 to 60-fold. More recent epidemiological studies[23] have suggested that the true figure in the general population might be as high as 3 to 6 per 1,000. That would still mean an increase of 10-fold. However, for a proper comparison, the broad definition of autism used in the modern epidemiological studies would have to be applied to the twin and family studies, and this would mean that the increase in risk would be somewhat higher. Putting the findings together, the estimate of heritability is something of the order of about 90 percent. Because the twin and family studies provide the same conclusions, there can be considerable confidence that the heritability is very high, with genetic factors accounting for the majority of the population variance in liability to develop the disorder.

The main caution about the findings stems from the evidence that the genetic liability to autism extends much more broadly than the traditional diagnostic category of a seriously handicapping condition.[24]

Attention deficit disorder with hyperactivity (ADHD)

The fourth disorder for which the evidence suggests that genetic factors account for the majority of the population variance in liability is attention deficit disorder with hyperactivity (ADHD). It is a disorder that is more common in males and that is characterized by severe hyperactivity, impulsiveness, and inattention, that is pervasive across situations (although the intensity of its manifestations may vary according to circumstances), that is evident by the time the children start school, that shows substantial persistence into adult life, and which is associated with a range of other problems including antisocial behavior and poor scholastic achievement.[25] The majority of children with this disorder show a beneficial response to stimulant medication provided that it is part of a well thought out therapeutic plan tailored to the needs of the individual child.[26] Not surprisingly, because the diagnostic features overlap with "ordinary" forms of disruptive behavior seen in many normal children, there has been controversy over the validity of the diagnostic concept. Both the genetic evidence and the findings of longitudinal studies suggest that the liability is dimensionally distributed, without a clear watershed between variations within the normal range and a clinical condition requiring treatment.[27] On the other hand, there is much evidence showing important differences between ADHD and other forms of disruptive behavior, brain imaging findings show distinctive features, and the disorder is associated with substantial social impairment. Accordingly, although there is legitimate concern over the excessive use of stimulants in the United States for the treatment of very young children (an age group for which there is a lack of good evidence that stimulants are effective), there is every reason to regard ADHD as a clinically meaningful disorder that, when severe, warrants treatment by methods that include the use of stimulant medication.

There have been at least a dozen twin studies of ADHD symptoms[28] The heritability estimates range from 60 to 88 percent when based on information from parents and 39 to 72 percent when based on ratings by teachers. Consistency of the heritability estimates across studies using a diverse range of questionnaire and interview measures is certainly impressive; the inference of a strong heritability seems justified. Nevertheless, there are reasons for being somewhat cautious about the strength of genetic influences. The data from family studies are supportive in showing an increased risk in biological first-degree relatives, as compared with controls, but the estimated increase of 4 to 5-fold[29] would seem to suggest a moderate rather than a very high heritability. There have been a number of adoption studies but, because of their weak methodology, they are essentially non-contributory.

There are also concerns with respect to some uncertainties on the diagnostic boundaries of ADHD, the fact that the findings are based on symptom scores rather than clinical diagnoses (although the evidence suggests that the heritability findings are similar for the two), and that there is some evidence that there may be contrast effects. What this means is that parents, when rating hyperactivity or inattention in their twins, under-rate these behaviors in the one twin because the contrast with the more seriously affected twin is so great. There are ways of dealing with this problem and, when this has been done, the heritability rate is still well above 60 percent.[30] Despite these concerns, the consistency of the evidence is sufficient to conclude that genetic influences on ADHD are substantial. Moreover, there is evidence that the well-documented association between ADHD and cognitive impairment arises to a predominant extent from a shared genetic liability.[31]

Disorders and traits with queries over diagnosis or definition

Antisocial behavior

Antisocial behavior is a general term used to cover acts that involve breaking the law irrespective of whether the individual is caught or prosecuted.[32] However, children below the age of criminal responsibility (which varies widely among different countries) engage in similar behavior for which they cannot be prosecuted and these are similarly incorporated in the same overall term. The origins of antisocial behavior frequently lie in early-onset physical aggression, which tends to be accompanied by oppositional/defiant behavior. Accordingly, both of these may be included in a broader concept of antisocial behavior. Overall, it is more common in males, but the sex difference varies according to the type of antisocial behavior.

In many respects, claims on the strength of genetic influences on antisocial behavior have proved particularly controversial because of the fact that it involves socially defined behavior occurring in social contexts, rather than something that can be unambiguously measured in an objective fashion. However, that concern, although relevant for interpretation of the meaning of the findings, is not relevant with respect to the heritability findings. There have been a huge number of twin studies on large samples using sound measures of antisocial behavior. Rhee and Waldman[33] undertook a meta-analysis of the findings, which produced an overall heritability estimate of 41 percent. Moffitt[34] adopted a slightly different approach by examining the distribution of heritability estimates across studies, as shown in Figure 4.1. The findings show that the peak is around the 50 percent mark, with small tails to the bell-shaped distribution at both extremes. On the whole, the

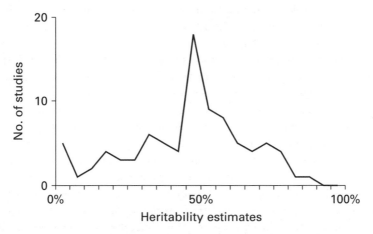

Figure 4.1 Percentage of genetic influence reported in behavioral genetic studies of antisocial behaviour.
Source: Moffitt, personal communication, derived from Moffitt, 2005.

findings at the extremes derive from somewhat unusual samples or measures. This variation across studies is precisely what one would expect in putting a heterogeneous group of studies together.

Because of the need to be concerned about possible rater biases, the greatest confidence can be placed on the studies that have used multiple informants and multiple measures. These have tended to give heritability estimates that are rather higher than most. There are a few adoptee studies but the evidence they provide is too limited to offer much help in conclusions. Family studies are consistent in showing a 3 to 4-fold increase in the rate of antisocial behavior in the first degree of biological relatives of individuals showing antisocial behavior themselves.[32]

Putting the evidence together,[34] it is clear that there is a moderately strong genetic influence on the liability to exhibit antisocial behavior but the effects of genetic factors are far from determinative. The heritability of 40–50 percent means that there are strong non-genetic influences, and more detailed findings indicate that these account for both similarities among siblings in the same family and also differences. That is to say, some of the environmental influences tend to impinge similarly on all children in the family whereas others are particularly focused on just one child.

It is necessary to come back, however, to just what this moderate, but not overwhelmingly strong, heritability means. To begin with, it certainly does not mean that it is at all likely that antisocial behavior as such is inherited. That is really rather unlikely. What is much more probable is that the genetic factors influence temperamental or personality features that play a contributory role in making it more or less likely that individuals will engage in antisocial behavior. In other words, the effects are indirect. Also, as discussed further in Chapter 9, the genetic factors may be important in rendering people more vulnerable to adverse environmental features. It also should not be assumed that the genetic influence operates equally across all varieties of antisocial behavior. For example, there is some preliminary evidence that genetic influences may be more important in relation to early-onset antisocial behavior associated with hyperactivity and which tends to persist into adult life. There is a strong tendency for hyperactivity/inattention to be associated with oppositional/defiant behavior and with conduct problems and the evidence indicates that genetic factors play the major role in the associations among these different forms of disruptive behavior. The public tends to assume that genetic factors are likely to be maximal with violent crime, rather than with petty theft, but, although the evidence is far from conclusive, it does suggest that the reverse may be the case.

In summary, antisocial behavior constitutes a good example of behavior that is certainly heterogeneous in type and which is much influenced by social factors of both a societal and personal kind, but which, nevertheless, involves moderate genetic influences on individual differences in the liability to behave in antisocial ways.

Unipolar depression

Common varieties of depressive disorder constitute another example of the same kind. The adjective unipolar means depression that is not associated with episodes of mania or hypomania (meaning a lesser degree of mania) in which there is an abnormal elevation in mood that is accompanied by widespread disturbances in behavior. These ordinary varieties of depression are very common and indeed it is part of the normal human condition to feel depressed in some circumstances. What is called depressive disorder differs from this normal variation in mood in that it is accompanied by marked suffering and impairments in social functioning. Thus, the depressed mood tends to be accompanied by a loss of energy and of interest in life, changes in sleep and appetite, psychomotor agitation or retardation, feelings of worthlessness or unwarranted guilt, diminished concentration, and recurrent thoughts of death or suicidal ideation. In short, it is not at all like ordinary sadness, although there is unhappiness. Over the course of a lifetime, probably about one in four females and one in ten males suffer from a major depressive disorder. For some people, there is just one such episode but for others there are many recurrences and it has been shown from many studies that not only is there a substantial increase in the rate of suicide but there is also a substantial increase in mortality from other disorders. Numerous twin studies, based on both general population and hospital clinic samples, have been undertaken. Sullivan et al.[35] undertook a meta-analysis from the five twin studies meeting the most stringent criteria, and produced a heritability estimate of 37 percent (with a confidence interval extending from 31 to 42 percent). However, the McGuffin et al.[36] study based on the Maudsley Hospital Twin Register found a heritability of between 48 and 75 percent, depending on what assumption was made about the rate in the general population. Kendler et al.[37] also showed that the heritability tended to be substantially greater when account was taken of both the reliability of measurement and multiple times of measurement.

Several concerns have been expressed with respect to the genetic findings on depression.[38] Thus, in relation to the general population studies, it has been objected that, because most of the sample will not have been depressed, the findings mainly show a genetic effect on not being depressed, rather than on having a depressive disorder. Of course, in a sense, that is correct because most of the variance will be within the normal range, but the objection does not really have validity because, as discussed in Chapter 2, the liability to depression is based on a continuously distributed dimension that extends throughout the population. The findings do not suggest that the disorder of depression is inherited as such; rather, the evidence suggests that the liability to have such an episode is influenced by genetic and environmental factors to an approximately equal degree. Surprise has also been expressed that relatively small differences between monozygotic and dizygotic pairs result in an estimated heritability as high as 40 percent. However, that, too, represents a misunderstanding of the situation. Heritability of 40 percent means that, overall in the population, environmental influences are having more effect than genes and, therefore, you would not expect a very big difference between monozygotic and dizygotic pairs. The situation is quite different from that seen with, say, schizophrenia or autism. Attention has also been drawn to the difficulties of defining the boundaries of depression, a problem that pervades the whole field of mental disorders. None of these concerns seriously challenges the conclusion that genetic factors are of moderate strength in relation to the ordinary varieties of depression, but that environmental influences are of roughly comparable importance. It is scarcely a very startling or surprising finding.

Temperament, personality and personality disorder

The notion that people differ in their temperamental qualities goes back at least to the time of Galen in the second century, who postulated a subdivision into four qualities – melancholic, sanguine, choleric and phlegmatic[39] With various modifications, the concept of biologically based differences in psychological style persisted until the twentieth century when, following the emergence of both psychoanalysis and behaviorism (led respectively by Freud and Pavlov), a belief in the overwhelming importance of the rearing environment took over. A key turning point was provided by the research and ideas of Alexander Thomas, Stella Chess, and Herbert Birch, working in New York. Based on an inductive analysis of detailed parental accounts of their children's behavior from infancy onwards, they emphasized the importance of distinctive styles of behavior, rather than motives, goals and competence.[40] Initially, they used the term "primary reaction patterns" in order to focus on both the constitutional origin and the role of the behavioral style in shaping children's responses to their environment. Later, they adopted the more straightforward term of "**temperament**."

During the years that followed, in keeping with the concepts of Buss and Plomin, it came to be accepted that temperamental features constituted a subclass of traits that showed marked individual variability and that were distinctive in emerging early in life, in exhibiting high stability over time and over situations, and in showing high heritability.[41] This view has not stood the test of time[42] because temperamental features are not noticeably more heritable than other behaviors, because there is low stability in early infancy (although much higher stability from age 3 years onwards[43]), and because traits that index reactivity to the environment will be most evident in high stress or challenge situations, rather than in ordinary everyday life.[44] Accordingly, although there is no clear consensus on how temperament should be conceptualized, many researchers follow Kagan's preference for low-level traits that are concerned with some aspect of reactivity and which show good conceptual and empirical links with biology (and hence are best measured through a combination of behavior and physiology). He has argued that such temperamental features create an envelope of potential outcomes, creating a behavioral tendency that is not easily limited by life events but yet does not determine a particular personality type.

A quite different approach has been adopted by researchers who have focused on the coherence of reported behavioral features as observed in adult life. The preference here is for higher-order abstractions as exemplified by the so-called Big Five traits of extraversion/positive emotionality, neuroticism/negative emotionality, conscientiousness/constraint, agreeableness, and openness to experience.[45] This approach differs from Kagan's notion of temperamental reactivity in its inclusion of coherences that stem from attitudinal features, patterns of thought, and from motivational considerations, as well as simple dispositional attributes.[42] Although derived initially from adult research, the approach works reasonably well in childhood[46] and the measures provide important predictors of later mental functioning. Nevertheless, longitudinal evidence indicates that personality is far from fixed in early childhood; changes continue well into adult life.[45]

Personality disorder involves yet another concept that needs to be differentiated from temperament and personality. Traditionally, they have been conceptualized as malfunctioning extremes of personality traits, but this concept has little empirical justification.[42] Probably, the personality disorder concept of the greatest contemporary interest is "psychopathy," a category first put forward by Cleckley to describe a lack of normal socio-emotional responsiveness characterized by lack of remorse for wrong-doing, an absence of close relationships, egocentricity, and a general poverty of affect.[47] Some researchers have sought to relate "psychopathy" to the Big Five dimensions of personality but, in my view, it is more fruitful to define it in terms of an abnormal lack of responsiveness to emotionally laden cues, as examined by both Blair and Patrick using experimental paradigms with adult criminals.[48] The interest lies in the possibility that the emotional detachment constitutes an unusual risk factor for antisocial behavior that is not particularly associated with social disadvantage or family adversity.

These three aspects of psychological individuality (temperament, personality, and personality disorder) have been discussed at some length because of their centrality in dimensional approaches to risk (see Chapter 2) and in considerations of gene–environment interplay (see Chapter 9). However, that being noted, it has to be added that twin and adoptee studies have not been particularly informative in casting light on causal mechanisms. There is consistency in the finding of a substantial genetic influence on personality dimensions with heritabilities of about 50 percent from twin studies and about 30 percent from adoptee studies,[49] but with not much variation across different dimensions. There is rather less evidence on temperament studies[50] but the findings are broadly comparable. There is some suggestion that genetic influences on psychopathy are possibly somewhat stronger than other dimensions studies.[51] It is reasonable to infer that temperament, personality, and personality disorder all show a moderate heritability (as is the case with most behaviors), but caution is needed in going any further than that in view of the fact that most research is based on single informant measures (parent reports in childhood and self-reports in adult life). The very limited evidence from the few multi-informant studies provides much the same picture, but the hope that behavioral genetics would show how temperament leads on to personality functioning and mental disorder has yet to be realized.

Substance use, and substance use disorder

A key feature of substance use and abuse is the very high frequency of occasional recreational use of illicit drugs (and of alcohol and tobacco products), but the relative infrequency of abuse and dependency.[52] The terminology applied to the various patterns of misuse and their consequences is both complex and varied. However, the patterns include "dependence" (meaning a state involving various admixtures of increasing tolerance, physical withdrawal effects, difficulties in controlling the use of the substance, and a strong desire to take the substance despite harmful consequences), and "harmful use" (meaning that it leads to psychological, social, or somatic complications). It is also typical that the use of illicit substances includes a range of chemically disparate drugs, and that it is usual for the substance misuse to be associated with a mixture of mental health problems. A particularly common pattern is for early conduct disturbance to lead on to drug use and misuse and for such misuse to increase the later development of depression.[52]

In undertaking twin and adoptee studies, it is obvious that a developmental approach is essential. Thus, it cannot be assumed that the genetic and environmental influences on occasional recreational use of substances will be identical to those predisposing to later regular heavy use or to those involved in dependence. Because of these complications, it is perhaps not surprising that the estimates of heritability vary considerably,[53] although overall most estimates are in the 25 to 50 percent range. The more interesting aspects of the findings concern the evidence that genetic influences tend to be much weaker for initial experimental use of drugs than for abuse or dependency, which has quite a strong heritability, and that there is substantial overlap in the genetic liability for the use and abuse of different drugs. On the other hand, there is some drug-specificity. Also, adoption study findings suggest that there are two genetic pathways leading to drug abuse/dependency.[54] The first involves a main effect on drug problems, and the second involves a more indirect causal route that operates through antisocial behavior. Moreover, the genetic effects on antisocial behavior include a gene–environment interaction whereby the genetic risk involves an effect on susceptibility to environmental hazards.

Dyslexia

Dyslexia, a specific reading disability, is characterized by a persistent failure to acquire skills in reading despite adequate intelligence, adequate opportunity, and satisfactory teaching.[55] Although there is evidence from twin studies of a substantial genetic influence, dyslexia is a multifactorial disorder that is influenced by environmental as well as genetic factors. Thus, for example, specific reading disability was found to be much more common in inner London children than in those living in a less disadvantaged area of small towns.[56] This geographical difference held up after taking account of the children's measured intelligence and also patterns of in- and out-migration from the area.[57] Also, there are differences among schools in rates of reading difficulties that cannot be accounted for by differences in intake to the schools.[58] As well, there is evidence that children's opportunities to read at home affect their reading.[59] It is also notable that there are important differences in the rate of difficulties according to the language of upbringing.[60] The genetic findings cannot be used to infer that the reading difficulties have been caused by changes in the brain but they can be used to infer important connections between the workings of the brain and the acquisition, or failure to acquire, reading skills, as well as the fact that reading difficulties have a strong tendency to persist from childhood into adult life.

Dyslexia has also been found to be about twice as common in males as females.[61] Because of the influence of environmental factors, and because of difficulties of providing a satisfactory unambiguous definition of the disorder, the concept has given rise to some controversy. However, there is now substantial evidence that the reading difficulties are associated with measurable changes in brain functioning as studied through functional imaging. Moreover, brain changes are associated with both learning to read[62] and persistence of reading difficulties.[63]

Much of the uncertainty over genetic influences on dyslexia (specific reading disability) stems from the difficulties in knowing how best to conceptualize and measure it. It is generally regarded as a specific disorder that is not accounted for by limitations in general intelligence. However, IQ and reading skills are associated and therefore there is a need to separate the two when examining dyslexia. Also, although conceptualized as a specific disorder, from a genetic perspective it may function as a dimensionally distributed liability.

It has been known for many years that specific reading disability tends to run in families and both the Colorado Twin Study[64] and the London Twin Study[55] have shown that there is a substantial genetic influence.[66] Interestingly, heritability may be higher for reading disability in children of above average IQ (72 percent) than for those of below average IQ (43 percent)[64]; this finding still needs confirmation.

The sampling and measurement in the Colorado Twin Study were good and provide sound evidence of a substantial genetic influence but, in the absence of sound data from multiple studies of equal quality, uncertainty remains on the aspects of reading disability that are most influenced by genetics.

Specific developmental disorders of language
(specific language impairment – SLI)

Specific developmental disorders of language, now more commonly termed **specific language impairment** – SLI – concern marked delays in language development in children whose psychological development is proceeding relatively normally otherwise and who do not have an obvious disorder that might be causal (such as hearing loss, an acquired neurological condition, or mental retardation).[67] Such delay may involve only expressive language (i.e., use of language), or may include receptive abnormalities (i.e., the understanding of language), or may largely concern pragmatics (i.e., the social communicative aspects of language). Although essentially normal children may be remarkably late in gaining spoken language, the research findings are clear-cut in showing that the deficits associated with SLI that includes receptive problems often persist into adult life, with accompanying social deficits[68] It is unlikely that this form of SLI constitutes just a variant of normal.

There are only a small number of twin studies but both those based on clinic samples and those based on general population epidemiological samples are in agreement in showing that SLI has substantial heritability.[69] In Viding et al.'s 2004 general population study, it was notable that the heritability was significantly greater for severe SLI than milder degrees of SLI.[70] It is notable that the genetic liability in high-risk groups, however, extends to include milder, as well as severe, SLI and that it does not fit at all neatly into the traditional diagnostic categories of SLI.

Alzheimer's disease

Alzheimer's disease is a progressive neurodegenerative disorder involving memory loss and then a more global decline in intellectual function, which typically comes on in old age. In the later stages, there is a loss of self-help skills (feeding, dressing, etc.), there may be wandering, and also episodes of delusions and hallucinations. It has a distinctive pattern of brain changes that can be seen microscopically after death. Thus, there is extensive loss of **neurone**s and the deposition of extracellular plaques (made up of beta amyloid protein) and intracellular neurofibrillary tangles (made up from a particular kind of tau). There are two varieties of Alzheimer's disease: a rare early-onset variety (beginning before the age of 65 years), that is inherited in autosomal dominant fashion; and a much commoner late-onset variety that occurs in some 40 percent of individuals (both male and female) over the age of 90 years.

It is generally considered that Alzheimer's disease is quite distinct from normal ageing and from the deterioration in short-term memory and new learning that is so common in extreme old age. Certainly Alzheimer's disease involves a serious and general dementia that extends far beyond decrements in memory and new learning. Nevertheless, it may be that the genetic liability spans both the disease and normal memory decline.

Although Alzheimer's disease is a common condition, there are three main problems in assessing heritability.[71] First, clinical diagnosis is not completely accurate because of possible confusion with dementia due to cerebrovascular disease; second, because of the late onset of the condition, many individuals with a genetic liability die before reaching the age of risk; and third, family members may be assessed as free of the disease but nevertheless develop it some years later. Nevertheless, it is apparent that some 6 to 14 percent of the first-degree relatives of people with Alzheimer's disease also have the disease – approximately a doubling or trebling of risk. The twin data are based on very small samples but suggest a heritability of 40 to 80 percent. The family data suggest that most of the genetically influenced familial increase in risk has already come into play by age 90, with a lesser effect on Alzheimer's disease with an onset in extreme old age.

Life experiences

There are now quite a number of studies that have examined genetic effects on a diverse range of experiences including threatening life events, differential parenting, parental negativity, and divorce.[72] Because the life experiences examined have been rather diverse and have involved a disparate range of measures, it is not possible to combine the studies in quite the same way that was done with the various mental disorders. Nevertheless, the findings are consistent in showing a significant genetic effect on people's likelihood of experiencing negative events or happenings of the kind that could be influenced by their own behavior. That is to say, the genetic influence is not on the events as such, but rather on the way people behave, and it is through their behavior that they shape and select their environments. The genetic effect is a far from overwhelming one, with most heritabilities in the region of 20 percent or so, although sometimes they have been higher than that. The evidence is certainly quite sufficient by now to conclude that there are genetic effects on the likelihood that people will have negative experiences that put them at risk of mental disorders, that the genetic effects are modest rather than strong, but they are pervasive.

How confident can we be on the heritabilities that have been found?

Despite the critics who cast scorn on quantitative behavioral genetics as a whole, there can be reasonable confidence in the findings. However, all heritability estimates have four key limitations.[73] First, the heritability figure includes the effects of gene–environment correlations and interactions and not just a pure genetic effect. Because of that, it is measuring both the effects of genes that are separate from environmental effects plus the effects of genes that require a co-action with the environment in order to bring about their effects.

Second, heritabilities are population statistics and not measures of either individuals or even traits as such. Thus, it is appropriate to note that, in all the populations studied so far, the heritability of schizophrenia and autism is substantially greater than that for the common varieties of depression or antisocial behavior, and stronger still than the effects on the liability to experience particular environmental hazards. Nevertheless, these are statistics of the heritability of these behaviors within particular populations. The level of heritability will change if either the gene pool or the mix of environments alters. Thus, for example, there are two studies[74] that found that the heritability for IQ was less for children reared in socially disadvantaged circumstances than for those brought up by well-educated parents.

Third, the heritability measures genetic effects on the population variance of traits, but it does not indicate *how* the relevant genes operate and it definitely does not mean that the genes operate on the trait as such, rather than through the effects on some intermediate variable. Thus, it has already been noted that it is most unlikely that genes affect antisocial behavior directly, but it is probable that they have indirect effects through influences on the metabolic pathways concerned with temperament or personality variations.

Fourth, heritability does not measure the strength of genetic effects in any absolute sense; it is solely concerned with effects on variance. It has already been noted that genes determine capacities possessed by all humans (such as the ability to develop spoken language, or to walk upright). Because these are universally part of what humans are like, there is no population variation to be measured by heritability. Also, however, there can be hugely important environmental influences on the *level* of a trait in the population, without it making much, if any, difference to heritability. The increase in height (a strongly genetically influenced trait) during the past century, almost certainly due to improve nutrition, provides a striking example.[75] Accordingly, it is necessary to appreciate what heritability estimates cannot tell us.

Conclusions on heritability of psychiatric disorders

Nevertheless, if properly interpreted, heritabilities can provide a reasonable rough-and-ready estimate of the degree to which genetic factors contribute to individual differences in the liability to experience psychiatric disorders, as well as to show individual differences on particular psychological traits. As discussed, the findings are reasonably consistent in showing that some mental disorders (especially schizophrenia and autism but probably also bipolar affective disorder and ADHD) are strongly influenced by genetic factors, with heritabilities in the 60 to 90 percent range. We do not have good genetic evidence on all psychiatric conditions but the available evidence indicates that virtually all psychiatric disorders show a significant genetic contribution to individual differences, with heritabilities at least in the 20 to 50 percent range.

Most crucially, it is clear that virtually *all* behaviors are genetically influenced to a significant extent. The effects are by no means restricted to psychiatric diseases. The implication is that most mental disorders are multifactorial, meaning that they arise from the effects of several (often many) genes, and the effects of several (often many) environmental factors. There is also the further implication that, in many instances, the effects are likely to operate on population-wide dimensional features. Furthermore, in most cases the susceptibility genes are likely to be common allelic variations that influence normal functioning, rather than rare pathological mutations that directly cause malfunction and which, therefore, almost inevitably lead to disease.

Conclusions regarding genetic influences on individual differences in environmental risk exposure

One important conclusion, from quantitative studies, is that the genetic effects extend beyond psychological traits and beyond mental disorders to include environmental features such as divorce, family discord, and life stresses. At first sight, that sounds an implausible finding because there cannot possibly be genes in environments. However, it is necessary to recall that the quantitative genetic findings concern population variance and not individual features as such. In other words, the findings apply to individual variations in the likelihood of having particular experiences. How could that come about? It arises because most (but not all) experiences are influenced to a greater or lesser degree by how people behave.[76] Thus, for example, the likelihood that someone will be rebuffed or rejected by friends will be influenced by the style of their interactions with those friends. Similarly, the likelihood that someone will experience divorce will be influenced, amongst other things, by whether or not they married as a teenager (which is a well-demonstrated risk factor for marriage break-up), by the quality of the relationship they form with their spouse, by their propensity to engage in extra-marital liaisons, and by their tendency to respond to marital difficulties by taking up the option of divorce or separation. In other words, of course, it is inconceivable that there is a gene for divorce; the very idea is ridiculous. However, what is not ridiculous is that there are genetic influences on behaviors that will play a part in the likelihood that someone will have a divorce.

What is the nature and quality of the evidence? The Kendler et al.[77] findings on life events are illustrative. First of all, the findings are based on a reasonably representative general population sample with a high level of participation in the study. The information on life events was obtained through the use of a standardized structured interview and the interviews with each twin were undertaken by different researchers. The findings are informative in showing a moderate heritability for major life stresses, but it is important to note that the heritability varies according to the type of life event. Thus, genetic influences did not play any major role in life events that were outside the person's control (such as deaths in the social group) and were greater for events such as divorce or separation where it is fairly obvious that a person's own behavior is likely to have played some part. The difference among types of life events is important because non-geneticists sometimes tend to assume (wrongly) that twin studies inevitably land up with showing a genetic effect. The findings here clearly indicate that that is not so. Moreover, the variations among life events and the extent to which there is a genetic component fit in with expectations based on the likelihood that the experiences have been selected or shaped to some degree by the behavior of the individuals.

What traits do genes affect?

A main conclusion from quantitative genetics studies is that genes have an effect, sometimes greater and sometimes lesser, on virtually all aspects of behavior. Many people are willing to accept that there may be abnormal genes that give rise to a susceptibility to overt diseases or clear-cut mental disorders, but they are much more skeptical about the possibility that genes influence behaviors, attitudes, and environmental experiences that are obviously embedded in, and influenced by, the social context. However, that skepticism is misplaced. The relevant genes are by no means confined to those that might be conceptualized as "abnormal" in the sense that they interfere with vital functions of one kind or another. Most genes are "normal" in the sense that everyone has a variant of these genes. The differences lie in the particular allelic variation (meaning the specific sub-variety of the gene) possessed by the individual. These genes are part of the normal biological constitution but the allelic differences are associated with variations in particular types of biological functioning.

Some of these biological variations have behavioral implications. In this way, genetic influences may lead people to be more or less emotional in their functioning, more or less impulsive in their style of reacting, more or less sociable and outgoing in their personality, more or less stable or labile in their mood, and more or less assertive or aggressive in their interpersonal interactions. All of these traits are quantitative, rather than of a presence or absence variety. In other words, the world does not divide up into individuals who are aggressive and those who are not; rather, people simply vary in the likelihood that they will feel or behave aggressively. Moreover, it would be a mistake to see these traits as simply features of the mind. All of them involve somatic accompaniments, many of which can be measured by the appropriate physiological tests. Nevertheless, that is not to say that the traits are caused by the somatic, or physiological, features. It is much more accurate to see these as two sides of the same coin. If we have experiences that make us feel dispirited or downcast, that will bring about changes in our bodily functions. Conversely, if there are physiological changes in our body (brought about by disease or drugs or genetic liability), this will have concomitant consequences for our feelings and behavior. A neat example of that is provided by studies of men that show that the winner of a competitive tennis match will show a rise in testosterone levels and his defeated opponent will show a fall.[78] It is not just a matter of the effects of exercise because the same thing is found with competitive chess matches.[79] Experiences affect physiology. Equally, however, experimentally induced or naturally occurring changes in the physiology will have emotional and behavioral consequences.[80]

Interplay among genes and among alleles

Most standard estimates of heritability assume that the effects of multiple individual susceptibility genes summate in a simple additive fashion. However, it is known that some genetic effects are dependent on the interplay among a specific combination of genes (termed **epistasis**) or among different alleles of the same genes (termed dominance). Originally, the concept of epistasis was introduced to describe a masking effect whereby a genetic variant (allele) at one locus prevents a variant at another locus from manifesting its effect. However, in recent times, there has been at least as much interest in synergistic (potentializing) interplay.[81] The concept is essentially biological but necessarily it has to be examined by statistical methods. In principle, these can be applied to twin data but the possibility of true biological interactions really requires molecular methods identifying specific genes. There are documented examples of epistasis with **Mendelian** disorders (for example, sickle cell anemia), but they are likely to be more frequent with multifactorial disorders, if only because more genes are involved. However, there are substantial statistical hurdles to be overcome because of the major influence of scaling on all interactions.[82] Changes in scaling readily produce artifactual interactions, but also may conceal true interactions. Understanding of biological interplay among genes remains very primitive at the moment but it is of considerable potential importance because of the implications of how genes work (see Chapter 7).

What do quantitative genetic findings tell us about environmental influences?

As is very clear from the heritability findings, quantitative evidence is clear-cut and consistent in indicating that the individual variation in virtually all traits is influenced by both genetic and non-genetic factors. The relative importance of the two varies substantially across traits, but, with a few rare exceptions, in all cases environmental factors are influential and, with many traits, their impact is as great as, or greater than, those of genetics. However, because most behavioral genetic studies have had little interest in environmental influences and have, therefore, included rather weak measures of possible environmental risk factors, behavioral genetics has, at least until recently, been much less helpful on the specific effects of specific measured environments (but see exceptions as discussed in Chapter 5).

Shared and nonshared environmental effects

However, there are a few general messages that warrant attention. Almost certainly, the one message that created the greatest stir initially was the Plomin and Daniels[83] claim that **shared environmental effects** were of only quite minor importance and that **nonshared environmental effects** were much more influential. Because this claim has been widely misunderstood, it is important to clarify just what it does, and does not, mean. Both some geneticists (who should know better) and many non-geneticists have concluded that the finding means that the sort of family that provides the rearing of children is of negligible importance.[84] However, what the terms "shared" and "nonshared" environmental effects mean is simply whether the effect of environments is to make children within the same family more alike (which would be a "shared" effect) or unalike (which would be a "nonshared" effect). It has nothing directly to do with measures of influences in or outside the family.

Four main points need to be made with respect to the differentiation between the two contrasting types of environmental effects. First, there are two important methodological reasons for treating the empirical findings with substantial caution. To begin with, by the way it is ordinarily calculated, any errors in measurement automatically go into the nonshared environment effect term. Accordingly, this necessarily means that (unless some form of modeling is undertaken that takes account of error) nonshared environmental effects will be inflated in a misleading fashion, whereas shared environmental effects will not. In other words, like is not being compared with like. The other methodological consideration is that the environments that impinge generally on all children in the same family tend to be much more persistent over time than are the variety of one-off experiences that impinge on just one child. Accordingly, there is likely to be a difference between effects as measured over repeated measurement and those that are restricted to just one point in time. It is the one-off assessments that are most likely to exaggerate nonshared environmental effects. The empirical findings confirm that the difference between shared and nonshared environmental effects is substantially diminished in most cases when these methodological factors are taken into account.[85]

The second consideration is that there are important differences among traits with respect to the relative importance of shared and nonshared environmental effects. Thus, if traits that involve roughly the same heritability are contrasted, there are some (such as antisocial behavior) that show a strong tendency to affect multiple children in the same family, whereas there are others (such as depression) where it is much more frequent that just one child in the family is affected. What this means is that, although it is true that, on the whole, many traits have environmental effects that are more nonshared than shared, that is not true for all.

The third consideration is that the conclusions apply strictly to individual differences and the picture may look quite different if attention is focused instead on effects on level of a trait or a disorder. For example, Duyme et al.[86] studied children in France who had been removed from their biological parents because of concerns over abuse or neglect and who were subsequently adopted after the age of 4 years. The findings showed that, in the group as a whole, the overall family environment had made a big difference to the level of IQ but it had made much less difference to the individual differences in IQ among the children.

Much the same was evident in our study of children from extremely depriving Romanian institutions who were adopted into generally well-functioning UK families.[87] The radical change from an appalling environment to a rearing environment that was at least average in quality was associated with a massive improvement in the children's psychological functioning all around. Again, therefore, the overall family environment had a hugely strong and beneficial effect. On the other hand, again, the individual differences among the children remained very large. The findings were also different, however, in that the overall rise in IQ was not associated with variations in the educational qualities of the adoptive families. In this instance, the main persisting effect derived from the pre-adoption depriving experiences in the institution.

It also follows that, because the shared or nonshared effects are inferred, the shared effects may actually derive from experiences that are not individually shared at all. For example, if a pair of twins went to different schools but were very similar in the type of friends they chose and in the qualities of the peer groups into which they entered, their peer group experiences might serve to make them more, rather than less, alike. The experiences would be outside the home and the particular friends and peer groups would be quite different. Nevertheless, the effect will be categorized as shared because it tended to make them alike. In other words, the findings on shared environmental effects have no implication for whether or not the formative experiences are within or outside the family and they definitely do *not* mean that family influences have little effect on children's psychological development or mental functioning.

A further point that is often misleadingly made is that because, on the whole, shared environmental effects tend to become weaker as children grow older, this means that environmentally mediated family influences become less important as children age. The finding means nothing of the kind. Rather, it simply reflects the obvious fact that, with increasing age, children become more able to select and shape their environments (both within and outside the family) and hence that siblings, and twins, become less likely to have the same experiences.

It is also necessary to note that the influences that bring about shared or nonshared environmental effects need not apply either to postnatal experiences or indeed to specific experiences of any kind. That is to say, the effects are strictly speaking non-genetic, rather than environmental. What might that mean? Three possibilities illustrate the range of influences that must be considered. First, there are experiences in the womb that may impinge differentially on the two trends. The example of the transfusion syndrome has already been mentioned but there are other possibilities. Second, there are differential epigenetic influences that could play a role. For example, in females, all of whom inherit two X chromosomes, it is standard for one of the X chromosomes to be inactivated. Which X chromosome is inactivated appears to be a largely random process. Thus, for example, if one of the X chromosomes involves a pathogenic mutation and the other one does not, it may happen that one of the twins mainly has X chromosomes carrying the pathogenic mutation and the other twin mainly has normal X chromosomes without the mutation. In this way, differences may come about within identical twin pairs. Third, somatic development is a probabilistic process in which minor errors quite commonly arise.[88] Thus, it is quite frequent for children to have one or more extra teeth, or to be missing a tooth (or some other body part), and these errors in development, which are not due to specific environments, could have functional consequences (although in most cases they do not). We need to bear in mind, therefore, that when considering nonshared environmental effects, these may not necessarily derive from specific environmental influences as they are ordinarily understood.

Despite these important methodological and conceptual considerations, the basic message remains valid and important. That is, it is usual for family-wide influences to impinge differentially on the children in the family. For example, when one parent is depressed and irritable, it will often be the case that just one of the children receives the main brunt of the parental irritability. Accordingly, what has become appreciated is that the key need is not to get involved in fruitless arguments about shared and nonshared environmental effects but, rather, to make sure that our measurement of possible environmental influences is undertaken in such a way that we can determine how these actually impinge on individual children.[89] It is no longer acceptable to measure risk or protective environments at a general level and assume they will affect everyone the same way. That is unlikely to be the case, although sometimes it may be.

Casting light on possible processes

In the absence of actual identified genes, quantitative genetic findings can provide only clues about causal processes. Nevertheless, the findings have proved useful. For example, epidemiological studies have amply documented the statistical associations among antisocial behavior, drug taking, and depression, but it has remained unclear which causal mechanisms underlie these associations. Twin study findings in adolescence suggest that, whereas there is a substantial shared genetic liability between antisocial behavior and drug taking, the connections between drug taking and depression seem rather different, probably reflecting some kind of non-genetic mechanism. Taken in conjunction with longitudinal study findings, the implication is that although there may be two-way interconnections, the more usual risk pathway is from drug taking to depression, rather than the other way around as was once thought to be the case.[90]

Genetic data have also shown that co-occurrence of ADHD and reading difficulties,[91] as well as that between ADHD and disruptive behavior,[92] to a large extent reflects a shared genetic liability.

Twin data in both adolescence and adult life have indicated that, to a considerable extent, generalized anxiety disorders and depressive disorders share the same genetic liability.[93] That does not necessarily mean, of course, that the traditional psychiatric distinction between these two groups of emotional disorders is meaningless. Thus, there is some evidence, at least in adults, that the life events that provoke the onset of anxiety are somewhat different in kind from those that provoke the onset of depression.[94] Also, the response to medication is somewhat different, although there is some overlap. The course over time between childhood and adult life is similarly somewhat different for anxiety disorders and depressive disorders. Geneticists have sometimes claimed that genetic data may be informative in forcing a revision of psychiatric diagnostic conventions. Certainly, diagnostic and classification issues in the future will need to take genetic findings into account. On the other hand, when dealing with multifactorial disorders across the whole of medicine, it is rarely useful to rely on just one type of cause to define diagnosis. Rather, diagnoses are usually based on pathophysiological causal pathways, each of which will usually have multiple origins.

Twin data may also be helpful in casting light on age differences in psychopathology. For example, although major depressive disorders can begin in childhood, and sometimes do, they become much more frequent in adolescence. The findings suggest that depressive disorders beginning after puberty, however, are often preceded by prepubertal anxiety, which shares the same genetic liability. Although not yet certain, it also appears that the rise in depression in girls during adolescence may, at least in part, be a consequence of an emerging genetic vulnerability to life stressors, which is stronger in girls.[95] There is also some (not entirely consistent) evidence that genetic influences on depression tend to be greater during adolescence than in earlier childhood.[96] Although genes are present from birth, their effects may not become manifest until very much later. This is usually discussed in terms of the concepts of genes being "switched on." Thus, for example, genetic influences on the timing of the menarche are quite strong but the menarche nevertheless only occurs in adolescence. A rather different age-related effect concerns old age. Longevity does tend to run in families and it had often been assumed that genetic factors played quite a large part in such longevity. It now seems apparent that the genetic influences largely operate through their effects on diseases that lead to early death. Once early death has been taken into account, it seems that there may be only quite a limited genetic influence on living into extreme old age.[97] As we shall see in Chapter 9, genetic findings have also been crucially important in indicating that many genetic influences operate only indirectly through effects on individual differences in exposure, and susceptibility, to environmental risk and protective factors.

Conclusions

In conclusion, it is evident that quantitative genetic findings have been most useful in causing people to think somewhat differently about the nature of mental disorders. In particular, the findings are clear-cut in indicating that genetic influences apply to some degree to all forms of behavior, both normal and abnormal. However, in both cases the relevant genes are likely often to involve common, normal allelic variations rather than rare pathological mutations with major effects. It is not that, on its own, it matters very much whether the heritability is 20 percent or 80 percent, but the more hypothesis-driven multivariate analyses using twin and adoptee data have been helpful both in elucidating some matters and in raising fundamental questions about others. None of the findings are in the least bit compatible with a genetically deterministic view. The evidence does indicate that genetic influences are all-pervasive but the same evidence also indicates that they operate through a variety of mechanisms both direct and indirect. These are considered more fully in Chapters 7 and 9.

Notes

See Reference list for full details.

1 Jablensky, 2000; Liddle, 2000
2 Cardno & Gottesman, 2000
3 See Gottesman, 1991. The **proband**-wise concordance rate is that based on probands, rather than pairs. In other words, a concordant pair is counted twice, once for each proband. This is appropriate provided that each proband has been independently ascertained; that is, the schizophrenia (or whatever disorder is being studied) has not been diagnosed only as a result of special assessment as a consequence of being a co-twin. For a variety of technical reasons, the proband-wise concordance rate is usually regarded as preferable to the pair-wise concordance rate.

4   Cannon et al., 1998
5   Cardno et al., 1999
6   Kendler et al., 1994
7   Joseph, 2003
8   Tienari et al., 2000
9   Gottesman, 1991; Jablensky, 2000
10 See, e.g., Kendler et al., 1995
11 McGuffin et al., 1994
12 Cardno et al., 2002
13 McDonald et al., 2004
14 Carter et al., 2002; van Os & Sham, 2003; Wahlberg et al., 1997
15 Jones, Kent, & Craddock, 2002
16 Angst et al., 2003
17 Lord & Bailey, 2002
18 Bock & Goode, 2003; Courchesne et al., 2003
19 Frith, U., 2003
20 Frith, C., 2003; Volkmar et al., 2004
21 Rutter, 2000 a and in press b; Steffenburg et al., 1989
22 Bailey et al., 1995
23 Rutter, 2005 a
24 Bailey et al., 1998; Pickles et al., 2000; Rutter, 2000 a, 2005 a
25 Schachar & Tannock, 2002
26 MTA, 1999 a & b, 2004 a & b
27 Levy & Hay, 2001
28 Levy & Hay, 2001; Thapar et al., 1995; Waldman & Rhee, 2002
29 Faraone et al., 1998
30 Eaves et al., 1997; Simonoff et al., 1998 a
31 Kuntsi et al., 2004
32 Moffitt et al., 2001; Rutter et al., 1998
33 Rhee & Waldman, 2002
34 Moffitt, 2005
35 Sullivan et al., 2000
36 McGuffin et al., 1996
37 Kendler et al., 1993 a
38 Brown, 1996
39 Kagan, 1994; Kagan & Snidman, 2004
40 Thomas et al., 1963; Thomas et al., 1968
41 Buss & Plomin 1984; Kohnstamm et al., 1989
42 Rutter, 1987
43 Caspi et al., 2005 a; Shiner & Caspi, 2003
44 Higley & Suomi, 1989; Kagan, 1994; Kagan & Snidman, 2004
45 Caspi et al., 2005 a
46 Shiner & Caspi, 2003
47 See Cleckley, 1941; Rutter, 2005 f
48 Blair et al., 1997 & 2002; Patrick et al., 1997

49 Bouchard & Loehlin, 2001
50 Nigg & Goldsmith, 1998
51 Viding et al., 2005
52 Rutter, 2002 c
53 Ball & Collier, 2002; Rutter, 2002 c
54 Cadoret et al., 1995 a & b
55 Démonet et al., 2004; Fisher & DeFries, 2002; Knopik et al., 2002
56 Berger et al., 1975; Rutter et al., 1975 a, b
57 Rutter & Quinton, 1977
58 Rutter et al., 1979
59 Hewison & Tizard, 1980
60 Wimmer & Goswami, 1994; Aro & Wimmer, 2003; Paulesu et al., 2001
61 Rutter et al., 2004
62 Turkeltaub et al., 2003
63 Shaywitz et al., 2003
64 Wadsworth et al., 2000
65 Stevenson et al., 1987
66 Williams, 2002
67 Bishop, 2002 b
68 Clegg et al., 2005
69 Bishop, 2001
70 Viding et al., 2004
71 Liddell et al., 2002
72 Plomin, 1994; Rutter, 2000 b; Rutter, Caspi, & Moffitt, in press
73 Rutter, 2004
74 Rowe et al., 1999; Turkheimer et al., 2003
75 Tizard, 1975
76 Scarr & McCartney, 1983; Rutter et al., 1997; Plomin et al., 2003
77 Kendler et al., 1993 b
78 Booth et al., 1989
79 Mazur et al., 1992
80 Rowe et al., 2004
81 Cordell, 2002; Grigorenko et al., 2002
82 Greenland & Rothman, 1998
83 Plomin & Daniels, 1987
84 Rowe, 1994; Harris, 1998
85 Rutter et al., 1999 a; Rutter et al., 2001
86 Duyme et al., 1999
87 Rutter, in press b
88 Molenaar et al., 1993
89 Rutter & McGuffin, 2004
90 Silberg et al., 2003
91 Stevenson, 2001
92 Nadder et al., 2001 & 2002; Waldman et al., 2001
93 Kendler, 1996; Eaves et al., 2003; Silberg et al., 2001 a

94 Brown et al., 1996; Eley & Stevenson, 2000; Finlay-Jones & Brown, 1981
95 Silberg et al., 1999; Silberg et al., 2001 a & b
96 Eley & Stevenson, 1999; Silberg et al., 1999; Thapar & McGuffin, 1994 & 1996
97 Pedersen et al., 2003

Further reading

McGuffin, P., Owen, M.J., & Gottesman, I.I. (Eds.) (2002). *Psychiatric genetics and genomics*. Oxford: Oxford University Press.
Plomin, R., DeFries, J.C., Craig, I.W., & McGuffin, P. (Eds.) (2003). *Behavioral genetics in the post-genomic era*. Washington, DC: American Psychological Association.

Chapter 5

Environmentally mediated risks

For most of this book, the main emphasis is on the role of genes and how they lead to particular psychological and psychopathological outcomes. However, because one of the main messages is that most psychological and psychopathological endpoints are the consequence of both genetic and environmental influences, it is necessary to ask first whether or not there is robust evidence that environments truly do have effects. As noted in the introduction, many behavioral geneticists, and many protagonists of behavioral genetic viewpoints, have scoffed at the notion that rearing environments make much of a difference other than when the environments are obviously extreme and manifestly damaging.[1] These critics were correct in pointing out that many of the claims by psychosocial enthusiasts were based on evidence that failed to take adequate account of the possibility of either genetic mediation or the effects of the child on the family and on other individuals in the environment that might have effects that shape development. However, there is a growing body of evidence that has put environmental mediation hypotheses under test in a rigorous fashion. What kind of research does that and what do the results show?

Research design requirements

It has been argued that there are six main requirements for research that can truly provide an adequate test of environmental mediation.[2] First, the research design that is used must be able to "pull apart" variables that are ordinarily together. For example, a range of different twin and adoptee designs do that

This chapter is largely based on Rutter, M. (2005). Environmentally mediated risks for psychopathology: Research strategies and findings. *Journal of the American Academy of Child and Adolescent Psychiatry*, 44, 3–18.

by various techniques to separate genetic and environmental effects. Twin studies do so by contrasting monozygotic twin pairs (who share all of their genes) and dizygotic twin pairs (who share, on average, half of their segregating genes). Adoptee studies provide a separation of nature and nurture through ways of comparing the effects of biological parents who have not reared their children and adoptive parents who have no genetic link with their children but who have provided their upbringing. In addition, research leverage may be provided by "natural experiments," by which extraneous circumstances that are outside the control of both the parents and the children give rise to markedly contrasting environments that can be compared with respect to their effects. Examples are given below. Experimental interventions can achieve the same objective by determining both the effects of the therapeutic or preventive intervention, and relating such effects to changes in the postulated environmental mediating mechanism.

This first requirement serves the essential function of being able to separate environmental mediation deriving from the postulated environmental risk or protective factor from alternative influences (such as genetics). However, that in itself is not enough. It is also necessary to have longitudinal data in order to study within-individual change by which each subject serves as their own control. In other words, the idea is to determine whether the behavior of someone before some particular experience changes following the experience that is hypothesized to have the predicted effect. The demonstration that changes occur within an individual in keeping with some defined experience is a much better test of causation than the comparison of two groups, one of whom has had the experience and the other who has not. The problem with the between-group comparison is that the differences may be the consequence of all sorts of things (many of which probably were not measured) differentiating the groups. That does not apply in the same way to within-individual changes measured longitudinally. Obviously, too, longitudinal data provide a means of sorting out time relationships. That is crucial in order to differentiate between A leading to B, rather than B leading to A. In other words, longitudinal data allow one to determine in which direction the causal arrow ran – the second requirement.

The third need is for sensitive and discriminating measures of both the risk and protective factors that are supposed to bring about the effects, and the outcomes on which the effects are supposed to operate. Unfortunately, much research relies on rather crude broad measures of both. Such research can often be highly suggestive that some kind of environmental effect has been operating but, in the absence of really good measurement, it will not be possible to determine the effects of specific environments on specific outcomes.

A fourth need is to use samples that are big enough to test for the effects that are being examined. That seems a pretty obvious requirement but it has to be said that many of the claims in the literature are based on studies that are manifestly too small for their purpose.

The fifth requirement is to use research designs that provide the possibility of pitting one hypothesis against another, rather than using a method that can only serve to show whether or not somebody's favored explanation might be correct. Thus, for example, genetic mediation needs to be pitted against environmental mediation, and child effects on the environment need to be pitted against environmental effects on the child. Lastly, it is important for studies to spell out, in an explicit way, what are the assumptions that underlie the design being used. All designs rely on particular assumptions, but all too frequently the researchers have failed to make explicit just what those assumptions are and whether or not they have tested, in their own study, whether the assumptions are justified. This applies to twin and adoptee studies, but it also applies to the whole range of natural experiments that may be employed for hypothesis testing.

Accurate identification of environmental risk factors

It ought to be self-evident that, if one wishes to examine possible environmentally mediated risk or protective effects, there must be an accurate identification of risk and protective factors. Regrettably, that has not always been the case. Three particular needs are worth mentioning. First, it is essential to differentiate between risk indicators and risk mechanisms (see Chapter 2). By indicators, what is meant is some variable that is statistically associated with some adverse outcome, but in which the actual mechanism is due to something associated with a **risk indicator** rather than any consequence of the indicator itself. For example, there is an extensive early literature on the supposed risks associated with "broken homes." Subsequent research showed that, although the break-up of the home might indeed carry some risk, the main risk effects derived from the preceding circumstances and the subsequent consequences of family break-up (such as family discord and conflict, and deleterious effects on parenting), rather than from the separation or break-up as such.[3]

The second need is to differentiate between what have come to be called distal and proximal risk factors. A distal risk factor is one that is important because it increases the likelihood of the occurrence of proximal risk factors, but which in itself does not have much of a direct risk effect. Proximal risk factors, by contrast, are those that are more directly implicated in the mechanism leading to the outcome being studied. Thus, there is good evidence that poverty is an important distal risk factor because it makes good parenting much more difficult, but low income and minimal economic resources as such do not have much of a direct effect on the psychological functioning of the children. Rather, the risk effect is, to a considerable extent, mediated by aspects of family functioning and of parent–child relationships.[4]

The third need is to consider the possibility of heterogeneity in the supposed risk variable. For example, there has long been a supposition that it is beneficial for children's psychological development that fathers be actively involved in their upbringing. That sounds unambiguously a good thing, but research has shown that whether or not fathers' involvement brings risk or protection depends on the characteristics of the fathers and on the qualities fathers bring to the children's rearing environment. Jaffee and colleagues,[5] using longitudinal data, examined the effects on children of fathers' presence in the home according to whether or not the fathers showed antisocial behavior. The findings were striking in showing that fathers' involvement in childrearing was beneficial when the fathers were not antisocial, but it was damaging when they were antisocial. Now that this has been shown, it seems pretty obvious that it was likely to be the case. However, the point is that, rather surprisingly, that was the first study to provide a direct test of the possibility that fathers' characteristics might make a difference to whether or not their presence was helpful or disadvantageous.

Designs to test for environmental risk mediation

The research strategies that can be used to test for environmental mediation include: 1) various twin designs; 2) adoptee strategies; 3) natural experiments; 4) longitudinal designs that measure within-individual change and which take account of unmeasured liability; and 5) intervention strategies.

Twin designs

Because monozygotic (MZ) twins (often termed "identical") share all their segregating genes, the examination of possible environmental risk effects within MZ pairs constitutes a powerful research strategy. Any effects that are found cannot be due to **genetic mediation** because the two twins within the MZ pair do not differ genetically. Unfortunately, most of the early research using this design suffered from two serious problems. First, in most cases the same informant provided information on the environmental risk factor and the psychological outcome. Accordingly, there is the serious possibility that any effects found were a consequence of unconscious bias in the reporting of the risks and the outcomes. In other words, because the same person was reporting on both, there was likely to be a tendency for the person to perceive a connection between the two and, because of that, unintentionally to shape their reporting to fit in with that perception. Second, because the findings were usually based on cross-sectional, rather than longitudinal, data, it was not possible to determine the direction of the causal effect. In other words, the findings showed that the two were associated with each other but they could not determine which led to the effect in the other.

These two methodological limitations do not, however, apply to the study by Caspi and colleagues.[6] They used the environmental risk (E-Risk) study based on a national sample of twins in the UK who had been studied prospectively[7] to examine the effects of maternal negative expressed emotion on children's behavioral disturbance. Negative expressed emotion means remarks exhibiting critical, hostile, or derogatory feelings that were expressed in response to neutral requests of the parents to talk about the child (in other words, these were not critical remarks in response to questions about symptoms or problems). The expressed emotion measure was based on an interview with the mother when the children were age 5 years, and the measurement of the children's disruptive behavior was based on teacher information two years later when the children were age 7. There was also a parent report measure of the children's behavior at age 5. The test of the postulated environmental risk factor was truly prospective (meaning that it was predicting on the basis of mothers' expressed negative feelings at one age what the children's behavior would be like two years later). Also, because the measures were based on different informants for the risk factor of the child outcome, this made it very unlikely that the association could simply be a consequence of biased reporting. The test, of course, was a harsh one in that it examined effects over a two-year span during which the children went through such major transitions as starting school. Despite these severe methodological constraints, substantial and significant effect of maternal expressed emotion at age 5 was found for children's behaviors measured by teachers at age 7, after controlling for the effects of children's behavior at age 5 years, as reported by the mother (see Figure 5.1). The causal inference was therefore strong – the implication being that in some way negative feelings by mothers created a risk effect for the children's behavior. It should be added that much earlier research[8] had shown that these verbally expressed feelings were a strong reflection of mothers' behavior as actually observed.

The twin design may also be used in a somewhat different way by examining the effects of the measured environmental risk variable after taking account of genetic influences on the outcome being examined. The details of the statistics that are employed for this purpose need not concern us here, but the point is that, by assessing the genetic contribution by means of the contrast between monozygotic and dizygotic pairs, it is possible to separate out the independent influence of the postulated environmental risk factor – provided a combination of research strategies is appropriately employed.[9] For example, findings have shown that there is an environmentally

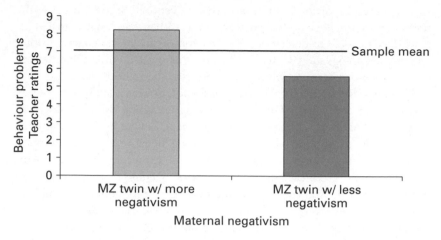

Figure 5.1   The MZ twin receiving more maternal negativism has more behavior problems, according to teachers.
Source: Caspi et al., 2004. The American Psychological Association. Reprinted by permission.

mediated effect of family negativity on adolescent depression and anti-social behavior, but that part of the mediation of risk is genetic.[10] Similarly, it has been shown that there are environmentally mediated risk effects of family maladaptation on children's antisocial behavior and of parental loss in childhood on the development of alcoholism in adult life.[11] The evidence as a whole indicates that the risk effects of some variables that seem environmental turn out to be partially genetically mediated and, conversely, that some variables that appear likely to be mainly genetic turn out to be partially environmentally mediated.

The offspring of twins design[12] provides a somewhat different opportunity to use the monozygotic–dizygotic comparison to examine environmental risk effects. The basic rationale of the design is that the offspring of two MZ twins, within the same pair, are genetically comparable but yet differ in terms of their rearing environments. Appropriate statistical analyses, therefore, provide the opportunity of detecting and quantifying environmentally mediated risk effects. Using this approach, D'Onofrio and colleagues[13] showed that, although smoking during pregnancy is influenced by genetic factors, nevertheless it has an adverse environmental effect on birth weight. Similarly, Jacob et al.[14] used the same design and found that a low-risk environment moderated the impact of high genetic risk on alcoholism. The potential of this design is great but, up to now, it has been severely under-utilized. There are, however, several studies under way that are using this design and they should be informative.

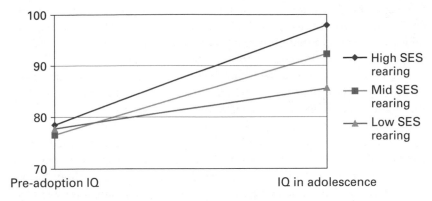

Figure 5.2   The effect of adoptive rearing environment on IQs of late adopted neglected/abused children.
Source: Duyme et al., 1999.

Adoptee designs

Adoptee designs separate genetic environmental risk mediation in a somewhat different way. There are several variations of adoptee designs that may be used for this purpose[15] but the examination of within-individual change following the adoption of children from a high-risk environment into a low-risk one constitutes a particularly useful research strategy. Duyme and his colleagues[16] used this approach to good effect in their study of the characteristics of the adoptive home environment on children's IQ (see Figure 5.2). They focused on a high-risk group – namely, children who had been removed from their parents because of abuse or neglect, and they instituted a nationwide search in France in order to identify an epidemiologically representative sample of children of this kind who had a psychometric assessment prior to adoption and who had been adopted between the ages of four and six and a half years of age. The results were striking in three somewhat different respects. To begin with, following adoption, this group of deprived children, considered as a whole, showed very substantial IQ gains. That, in itself, was not very surprising because if a really poor quality environment had indeed had appreciable effects, the transfer to a low-risk environment of a good adoptive home should provide benefits. The findings showed that it did. However, the second finding, which was really new, was that the degree of rise in IQ was a function of the qualities of the adoptive home into which the children were placed. That is, the rise in IQ was much greater in the case of children placed in highly advantaged homes as compared with those placed in less advantaged ones. As already outlined in the section above dealing with design requirements, the fact that this finding was based on within-individual change in individual children, in the context of a major change in environment, constituted powerful evidence in support of an environmentally mediated effect stemming from variations of the characteristics of the adoptive family environment within the normal range.

The third finding was different in showing that, despite this, neither the change of environment nor the characteristics of the adoptive family had much effect on the individual differences within the sample. That is to say, the children whose initial IQ was higher than most tended still to show an IQ in the upper range, and those with initially lower IQs remained below average. The finding is an important reminder that an environment may make quite a big difference on the overall level of a trait, without having much effect on individual differences on that trait. The initial IQ will have been influenced by both genetic factors and the characteristics of the early environment. These early factors continued to have a substantial effect on individual differences, despite the fact that the group as a whole had risen markedly in IQ.

A further feature of the Duyme et al.[17] study is the finding that the rise in IQ following adoption was not found for children who were already of superior IQ before adoption. Obviously, they were a highly atypical minority group, but the point is that, although the post-adoption environment may have influences on all children, it cannot be expected to bring about major gains in children who, by population norms, are already superior in their functioning.

Two findings from the study warrant particular emphasis. First, the rearing conditions that made a difference to the children's cognitive functioning reflected variations within the normal range and not extremes. Second, these rearing environments could only begin to have their effects after the age of adoption (i.e., between four and six and a half years) and, hence, do not reflect rearing influences in the infancy period.

Natural experiments

The Duyme et al. study was primarily focused on the examination of the effects of the post-adoption environment on children's psychological functioning. By contrast, the prospective longitudinal study of children adopted into UK families from grossly deprived institutional environments in Romania, undertaken by Rutter et al.,[18] focused particularly on the possible enduring effects of the pre-adoption environment. The institutional deprivation in this sample was quite extraordinarily severe, involving both nutritional and experiential deprivation of a pervasive kind. The hypothesis of an environmentally mediated risk effect could be tested in this sample in two rather different ways. First, if the institutional deprivation had truly

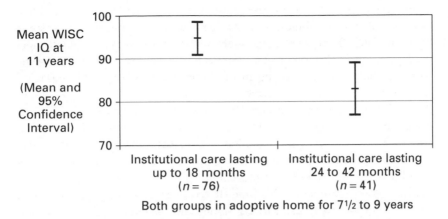

Figure 5.3 Effects of duration of privation controlling for time in adoptive home. *Source*: Rutter, in press b. Copyright © 2005 by Oxford University Press.

caused the severe developmental impairment found at the time the children left the institutions and came to the UK, it would be expected that the transfer to a somewhat above-average adoptive family environment should result in marked developmental gains. The findings showed that this was indeed the case (see Figure 5.3).

In addition, however, it was noteworthy that although the developmental gains in the sample as a whole were spectacularly great, some children were nevertheless left with deficits of one kind or another. Accordingly, the environmental risk mediation effect (with respect to the institutional deprivation) could be examined by determining whether the likelihood of deficits was systematically associated, in a dose–response fashion, with the duration of institutional deprivation. In other words, the causal inference would be supported if there were a systematic association between the duration of institutional deprivation and the likelihood of deficits. Of course, this inference would only hold if the duration of institutional care were not a function of any aspect of the child's functioning. In the case of the Romanian adoptees, that was so. That is, the duration of institutional deprivation was simply a consequence of how old the children were at the time that the Ceaucescu regime fell.

The findings from this study showed that there were four main patterns of psychological dysfunction – namely, cognitive impairment, quasi-autistic patterns, inattention/overactivity, and disinhibited attachment[19] – that did show this dose–response pattern and were quite infrequent in children who had been adopted but who did not have the same deprived background. The findings provided a dramatic demonstration of the environmentally mediated risk effects of profound institutional deprivation. However, the findings also brought out another, less expected, feature. That is, the effects of duration of institutional deprivation were just about as strong at age 11 years as they had been at six years and before that, at age four years – meaning that some environmental effects can be remarkably persistent despite very major changes in the rearing environment. The implication is that it is likely that some form of change of functioning in the brain, possibly a type of biological programming, may have occurred.[20]

Most of the designs considered so far in this chapter have used major environmental change as the prime source of research leverage for examination of environmental risk mediation hypotheses. However, an alternative approach is afforded by designs focusing on outcome differences that cannot possibly be explicable in terms of genetic effects. The twin–singleton comparison[21] is an example of this kind. It has been repeatedly demonstrated that, as a group, twins tend to lag significantly behind singletons in their language development.[22] Because there is no reason to suppose that twins and singletons differ genetically with respect to susceptibility genes for language development, the query concerns the nature of the environmental influence that accounts for this overall language delay as seen at a group level. Obviously, in both twins and singletons, genetic factors will be important in determining individual differences in language development, but what is crucial here is that there is no reason to suppose that such genes should differ between twins and singletons.

Two main alternatives with respect to possible environmental effects had to be contrasted: prenatal and perinatal biological risk factors, and postnatal differences in the upbringing of twins and singletons. In addition, various twin-specific risk factors (such as the transfusion syndrome in which the sharing of blood vessels in a common placenta means that blood can be transferred from one fetus to the other one – often resulting in one twin having too much blood in their body and the other having too little) had also to be considered. The results showed that the twin–singleton difference was largely mediated by patterns in mother–child communication and interaction (see Figure 5.4). The finding is particularly important because it concerns environmental effects that are well within the normal range.

One of the main reasons why statistical associations between a suggested risk variable and some psychological outcome cannot be assumed to reflect environmentally mediated causation is that it is usual for the supposed environmental risk factor to be associated in some way with the behavior of the individual. That is, it is well established that, to a considerable extent, people shape and select their environments.[23] Because of this, it is ordinarily quite difficult to sort out whether the apparent consequences of the risk factor are due to the effects on the child of that factor or, rather, to the person's own behavior in bringing about that environment. This type of confounding can be avoided when environmental risk factors are altered in a

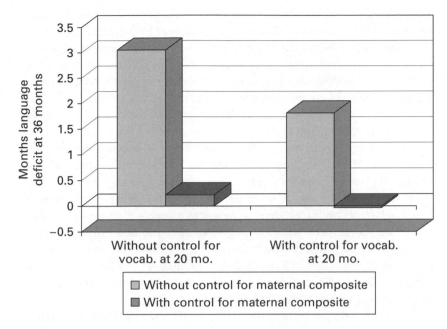

Figure 5.4 Maternal composite score at 20 months and child's language at 36 months.
Source: based on Thorpe et al., 2003.

major way by circumstances that are completely outside the control of the individuals concerned. Sometimes, the "natural experiment" arises through the external introduction of a risk factor but sometimes an even more powerful "natural experiment" arises when external forces result in the removal of a risk factor. The test in these circumstances is whether the removal of an environmental feature that is thought to carry risk results in a diminution in the rate of the adverse psychological outcome that it is supposed to cause.

Costello and her colleagues[24] used this strategy to great effect in relation to the introduction of a casino on an Indian reservation in the United States. The rules required that a proportion of the profits from the casino should be distributed to all Indians living on the reservation, irrespective of whether they were involved in any way with the work of the casino. In other words, it was a way of paying everyone for the fact that the casino was there, rather than a means of rewarding particular individuals for what they were doing. As good luck would have it, the casino was introduced in the middle of a systematic long-term total-population longitudinal epidemiological study of mental disorders in children and adolescents. Accordingly, it was possible to compare rates of disorder before and after the introduction of the casino.

The "natural experiment" was able to focus on the effects of relief of poverty because the introduction of the casino was followed by a significant reduction in the number of Indian families living in poverty. That the relief of poverty was indeed a function of the casino was indicated by the fact that this change in the rate of individuals living in poverty did not apply to White families, for whom there was no provision for the distribution of the proceeds of the casino. The findings showed that the introduction of the casino was followed by a significant reduction in the rates of disruptive behavior in Indian young people (although there was no significant change in the rate of emotional disturbance). The strong implication was that the relief of poverty had been responsible for the behavioral gains. However, the investigators went on to show that, although the benefits derived from the relief of poverty, the beneficial effects on the children were actually largely mediated by changes within the family. The evidence suggested that the key features were an improvement in parental supervision of the children and greater parental engagement with the children. In short, the findings pointed to the causal effect of a distal risk factor, poverty, with the likely proximal mediating effect of parenting qualities (influenced by relief of poverty).

A somewhat similar research strategy was used by Honda and colleagues[25] to test whether the measles–mumps–rubella vaccine was responsible for the major rise in the rate of diagnosed autism in countries around the world. The "natural experiment" was provided by the fact that, at a time when most countries were continuing with the use of this particular vaccine, Japan had decided to withdraw the vaccine because of the concerns over the possible risks associated with the mumps component of the triple vaccine. Honda and colleagues argued that, if the use of the vaccine was truly responsible for the rise in the rate of autism, the withdrawal of the vaccine should result in a fall in the rate of autism. The findings showed that, contrary to prediction, the rate actually continued to rise markedly. The findings were important in contributing to the disproof of an environmentally mediated risk hypothesis. Further, the medical doctors putting forward this particular hypothesis argued that the vaccine was particularly likely to be responsible for a form of autism that involved developmental regression. Uchiyama and colleagues,[26] again using data in Japan, showed that the withdrawal of the vaccine had no effect, one way or the other, on the rate of so-called regressive autism. Both of these studies contributed in a substantial way to the negative findings on the measles–mumps–rubella vaccine hypothesis.[27]

The same strategy was possible with respect to the parallel hypothesis that ethyl mercury in the thimerosal preservative (used in other vaccines but not the measles–mumps–rubella vaccine) was responsible for the same phenomenon of the rise in the rate of autism. In this case, the natural experiment was provided by the discontinuation of the use of thimerosal in some Scandinavian countries.[28] Once more, research leverage was provided by determining what happened when a supposed risk factor was removed. No effect was found. Of course, although the findings make it extremely unlikely that either the measles–mumps–rubella vaccine or thimerosal had a population-wide general risk effect for autism, the findings do not, and cannot, rule out the possibility of unusual idiosyncratic reactions in individuals who are especially susceptible for one reason or another. Such an unusual vulnerability could arise from genetic influences. There is no human research showing such an effect but there is one study using mice that indicates that the possibility is worth further investigation.[29]

Longitudinal designs

Although it is always advantageous, from a research point of view, to examine risk effects when the introduction or removal of risks arises through circumstances beyond the individual's control, it will always be important to be able to test the possibility that risks actually brought about by the individual's own behavior, nevertheless, have truly environmentally mediated risk or protective effects on the person's subsequent behavior or development. In these circumstances, longitudinal data are crucial in order to test whether there is in fact within-individual change, and the longitudinal data must include good measures for the risk and protective factors for the outcome being considered as well as measures on the person's own behavior prior to the environmental change. Also, of course, the appropriate statistical techniques must be employed to rule out the possibility that the supposed effects of the environmental change are brought about artifactually by unmeasured features of the person's own behavior, or of other risk/protective influences, or of measurement error.[30] Zoccolillo and colleagues[31] used this approach to test the hypothesis that a harmonious supportive marriage brought about a reduction in antisocial behavior and an improvement in overall social functioning in individuals, all of whom had shown antisocial behavior in childhood. A significant protective effect of this positive influence in adult life was found. Sampson and Laub[32] showed exactly the same thing in their long-term follow-up of the Gluecks' sample of severely delinquent adolescent boys. The statistical techniques that they employed were slightly different from those used by Zoccolillo et al.,[31] but the analytic strategies had the same purpose and, again, a substantial protective effect was found.

Two other features increase the plausibility of the environmental mediation hypothesis in these naturalistic circumstances. First, it is helpful to be able to show why it was that some individuals at high risk experienced the protective influence, whereas others did not. In relation to the Zoccolillo et al.[31] findings, the investigators were able to show that both a planning tendency (meaning a tendency to take definite decisions with respect to key life choices) and participation in a prosocial peer group made it more likely that individuals would land up in a harmonious, supportive marriage.[33] The second feature that makes the environmental mediation hypothesis more plausible is delineation of ways in which the supposed protective factor might operate. With respect to the follow-up of the Gluecks' sample, Laub and Sampson[34] were able to show, through qualitative life course interviews with a systematic planned subsample of the population, that the protective effects of a harmonious supportive marriage were likely to operate through several different routes. These included effective monitoring by the marriage partner, the obtaining of stable employment in order to maintain the family, change in peer group, and the reduction in the opportunities to engage in criminal behavior because of involvement in family and household tasks, as well as the emotional support and respect from a loving spouse and the support of the spouse's extended family.

A broadly similar approach was used by Elder[35] and by Sampson and Laub[36] to test the possible beneficial effects of army service for individuals from severely deprived backgrounds. Both sets of investigators found a significant effect, and it was apparent that this was mediated in part by the increase in educational opportunities that accompany army service, and by the postponement of marriage, so that a broadening of the social group led to a wider choice of possible partners.

Somewhat similar issues, albeit in relation to a risk rather than a protective effect, have arisen in relation to the possibility that the heavy early use of cannabis tends to have a precipitating effect on the onset of schizophrenia in susceptible individuals. Several large-scale longitudinal studies have shown the reality of a relatively strong risk effect associated with the heavy regular use of cannabis in early life but, equally, have shown that there are no risk effects associated with occasional recreational use of cannabis at a later age.[37] The causal hypothesis is also made more plausible by the finding that the risk effect cannot be accounted for by other characteristics of the individuals, and that the risk effect is found only with cannabis and not with other elicit drugs. The evidence also suggests, as hypothesized, that the risk effect is mainly (perhaps entirely) evident in the subgroup of individuals who are unusually susceptible, because of their genetic liability,[38] and who may show early indications of a schizophrenic predisposition.[39]

Finally, intervention strategies have an important part to play in the testing of environmental mediation hypotheses. If a properly conducted randomized controlled trial shows that a particular intervention brings about significant benefits, then it is reasonable to infer that the intervention caused the effect. That is a sound inference because the randomization procedure has ensured that it is purely a matter of chance whether any particular individual gets the treatment being tested. However, in order to test the environmental mediation hypothesis, two further features are crucial. First it must be possible to show, within the treated group, that a change in the postulated mediating factor was systematically associated with therapeutic benefits.[40] It is striking how few treatment studies include measurements of the postulated mediating mechanism and, hence, how few are able to contribute to the adequate testing of environmental mediation hypotheses. Nevertheless, a few studies have tested for mediation. A randomized prevention trial for rural African-American mothers showed convincingly that intervention-induced changes in parenting mediated the beneficial effects on 11-year-old children.[41] Also, treatment studies have suggested that improved parenting reduces the children's engagement in antisocial behavior.[42]

Second, although properly conducted randomized controlled trials with measurement of the postulated mediating mechanism can provide strong evidence of a causal influence, they do not necessarily show that this actually operates under ordinary conditions. Bryant[43] has argued that intervention studies must be combined with naturalistic longitudinal studies in order to meet that need. The point is that the therapeutic benefits may derive from something that plays no part in causation in normal life circumstances. Thus, for example, electric convulsive therapy (ECT) has a beneficial effect on some cases of psychotic depression, and aspirin reduces fever, but no one would suggest that a lack of electrical stimulation plays any role in the origins of depression or that fever is caused by a lack of aspirin.

Source of environmentally mediated risk experiences

There have been three main types of criticism of the claims of environmentally mediated risk and protective effects. First, it has been argued that such effects that do exist apply to extreme environments and not to variations within the range of normal environments.[44] Although, for obvious reasons, it is indeed likely that extreme environments will have greater effects, it is not true that variations within the normal range are without effects. This is evident from both animal studies[45] and from human studies. Effects within the normal range were evident, for example, in Duyme et al.'s[16] findings on the effects of variations in the educational qualities of adoptive families on children's psychological development during the years of middle childhood; and in Thorpe and colleagues'[46] finding that differences in patterns of parent–child interaction and communication between families of twins and singletons had an effect on early language development.

Second, it has been argued that, because nonshared environmental effects tend to be stronger than shared effects,[47] the differences between families and the rearing environments they provide are of negligible importance.[48] This argument, too, is mistaken (see Chapter 4). There is an important research need to focus on experiences as they impinge on individual children, but that does not mean that family-wide influences are without effects or of negligible importance.[49]

Two further points need to be made with respect to this vexed, but much misunderstood, issue of shared and nonshared environmental effects. First, as is apparent in the meaning of shared and nonshared effects, the terms concern inferences regarding the consequences of environmental influences and not the nature of environments as observed. What that means, amongst other things, is that effects that are measured in terms of their impact on the individual may actually have a predominantly shared effect if those individual impacts tend to be similar across different children in the same family. For example, that was exactly what was found with negativity in family relationships in a study by Pike et al.[50]

The second point is that it is a matter of considerable interest and importance to determine why and how family variables impinge differentially on the children. The possible explanations are many and various. For example, there is good evidence that children's own behavior elicits different reactions in the people who deal with them – both their parents and other adults or children. For example, two studies of adopted children[51] showed that children born to antisocial parents, but who were adopted outside the family, were more likely to elicit negative responses from their adoptive parents who reared them but who did not share their genes (see Chapter 9). The findings underline the likely importance of genetic influences in these interactions within families.

However, the detailed findings bring out another point, and that is that what actually induces or elicits different behavior in the adoptive parents is the disruptive behavior of the children and not their genes as such. That is to say, this effect of the children's behavior was only very partially explained by genetic risk. Studies of parent–child interactions in families where one parent is mentally ill[52] have clearly shown that parents treat their children differently. In some cases, children may be scapegoated and made the target of hostile reactions; in other cases, one of the children may be especially chosen as a source of comfort but, thereby, gets drawn into the parent's mental distress. The child's characteristics may play a considerable role in this differential treatment (and insofar as that is the case, genetic factors are likely to play a significant role) but the differences in treatment may also reflect the parent's attitudes and thought processes. The importance of gene–environment correlations and interactions is considered in more detail in Chapter 9.

In other words, we need to consider the role of genes in determining children's exposure to particular life experiences and their susceptibility to those experiences but this important issue should not get muddled up with the entirely different question as to whether the risk or protective effects are environmentally mediated. The fact that the experiences impinge on a particular child, and the fact that the child is susceptible to those risk factors, is a very important consideration, but the actual risk effects with respect to the causation of mental disorder may still be primarily environmentally mediated. Once more, it is obvious that we must be careful to avoid a simplistic subdivision of effects into those that are genetic and those that are environmental. In many instances, the effects reflect both sorts of mechanisms and the challenge is to understand how this comes about.

The third overall challenge concerns the claim that, although psychosocial experiences may be of some importance, those that matter involve the peer group rather than the family.[53] The empirical research findings do not support this claim. There are important peer group effects[54] but there are also important school effects,[55] and effects of the broader community,[56] as well as psychosocial family influences as already indicated in the examples given above.

However, it would be unduly constraining to restrict attention to postnatal psychosocial experiences. The example of cannabis as a provoking factor for the onset of schizophrenia indicates the likely importance, in some circumstances, of pharmacological drug effects. Also, attention needs to be paid to prenatal effects. These are best known, and best documented, with respect to the effects of mothers' heavy drinking in the first trimester on the development of the fetus – resulting in the fetal alcohol syndrome.[57] Maternal ingestion of opiates will result in an opiate withdrawal syndrome in the newborn baby, and there may also be more persistent effects.[58] Claims have also been made with regard to the effects of maternal smoking during the pregnancy on the children's subsequent psychological development. There is no doubt that smoking has deleterious effects on the growth of the fetus, but the effects on postnatal psychological development are not as well established (apart from effects on ADHD[59]). Smoking effects appear to be due in large part to either genetic mediation or other associated postnatal environmental risks.[60] Studies of babies who were adopted or fostered at birth have been important in showing that the ill effects are not entirely explicable in terms of the postnatal environment,[61] but this research strategy does not deal with the possibility that the supposed prenatal effects are, at least partially, genetically mediated.

It is surprising that researchers have not used the obviously relevant comparison of the effects of paternal and maternal smoking (or substance use) during the pregnancy. The point is that, whereas both could reflect either genetic mediation or postnatal effects, only maternal smoking can have a prenatal risk effect. This is certainly a design that needs to be used.

Much of the discussion in the literature on these various kinds of prenatal and postnatal experiences, within and outside the family, has tended to deal with them as if they are independent from one another. It is clear, however, that that is very far from the case. Thus, parents have influences on their children that derive from their choice of where to live, their selection of the school that their children attend, and they are likely to have some influence on their children's choice of friends and on the nature of their peer group activities. A proper understanding of psychosocial influences will need to take account of the interplay among these different settings.

Nature of psychosocial experiences that carry risk

The range of studies that has provided a really rigorous testing of environmentally mediated risk and protective effects is too small for definitive conclusions on the nature of the experiences that carry the major risks for particular psychopathological outcomes. However, three broad categories of risk experiences stand out as likely to be of particular importance.[62] First, there are substantial risks associated with the lack of ongoing, harmonious, selective committed relationships. Risks are present when there is an absence of such relationships (as there often is in most forms of institutional rearing), when the relationships are profoundly negative (as with rejection, scapegoating, and neglect), and when relationships are of a kind that engender uncertainty and insecurity. Second, social groups are influential through the ethos, attitudes, and styles of behavior that characterize them. That applies within the family, peer group, school, and community. A lack of social cohesion in any of these groups seems especially damaging, but social groups may be even more damaging as a result of the deviant values and deviant models of behavior that they provide. Third, reciprocal conversational interchange and play constitute important learning opportunities, both with respect to cognitive skills and also styles of social coping and adaptation. In addition, psychopathological risks may derive from intrauterine physical effects (such as alcohol) or postnatal pharmacological effects (as with the heavy early use of cannabis). Up to now, both types of physical influences have been rather neglected in research.

Moderation of risk effects

Much of the writing on environmental risk factors tends to imply that risk effects operate across the population as a whole. However, the evidence is clear-cut that this is rarely the case. In particular, as discussed more fully in Chapter 9, genetic influences play a major role in moderating environmental effects.[63]

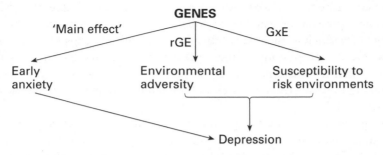

GENES

'Main effect'   rGE   GxE

Early anxiety   Environmental adversity   Susceptibility to risk environments

Depression

N.B. No significant effect of E in absence of rGE and GxE.
Little main effect of genes on depression that was independent of these 3 routes.

Figure 5.5 Genetically influenced routes to post-pubertal depression.
Source: Eaves et al., 2003.

Statistical modeling, using data from a large-scale, general population, study of twins indicated that it was likely that the important genetic effects could be subdivided into those that operated on mechanisms that did not include environmental risks to any important extent, effects that were primarily a consequence of genetic influences on people's likelihood to experience risk environments, and effects that reflected genetic influences on people's susceptibility to risk environments[64] Figure 5.5 shows a simplified version of these three pathways as shown for pubertal girls. Clearly, there is a need to replicate these findings on other samples, but the broad message of the need to consider gene–environment interplay is likely to prove correct because it is a message that is evident in research that goes well beyond the field of psychological traits and mental disorders.[65]

Of course, it should not be assumed that it is only genes that moderate environmental risk effects. Thus, for example, Conger and colleagues[66] showed that the effects of conflict between husband and wife on distress in the relationship were largely evident only when the couples had ineffective problem-solving skills. Similarly, the effects of economic pressure on emotional distress were only evident when wives were in marriages that provided low social support. Somewhat similarly, Borge and colleagues[67] found that maternal care of very young children within the home (as distinct from using some form of alternative daycare outside the home) was associated with an increased level of physical aggression by the children only within psychosocial high-risk families. Of course, the implication with these findings may be more appropriately interpreted as carrying messages about the key features that carry risk, rather than the moderation of risks as such. In other words, the proximal risk effect could be considered to derive from psychosocial adversity, ineffective problem solving, and lack of support, rather than from economic pressure or whether or not the care is in or outside the family home. Nevertheless, there is another facet to these findings that warrants attention. A further study of the Canadian data set used by Borge et al.[67] showed that non-maternal care could have either risk or protective effects according to family circumstances and the temperamental characteristics of the children.[68]

Nevertheless, even that might not be the whole story. Acutely negative life events have an important risk effect, as shown by several studies.[69] However, longstanding psychosocial adversity plays a crucially important predisposing role, both because it tends to give rise to acutely negative life events and because it increases vulnerability to those events. Thus, for example, Sandberg and colleagues[70] showed that the main risks for child psychiatric disorder derive from the acute stresses that stem from, or are otherwise associated with, chronic adversity. An earlier study had shown much the same thing with respect to the risk effects associated with hospital admission in the preschool years.[71] Similarly, Brown and Harris[72] showed that women's likelihood of developing depression following acute life events in adult life was increased if they had had various adverse experiences in childhood, such as parental loss and poor parental care.

One of the very consistent findings with respect to all types of environmental hazard is that there is huge heterogeneity in children's responses. Some succumb with disorder, but some come through relatively unscathed. The latter phenomenon has been termed resilience and the evidence suggests that, although it is a real and important phenomenon, it is not a single quality that applies to all risks and all outcomes. Also, it reflects both features within the person, including genetically influenced susceptibilities,[73] and experiential features that operate before, during, and after the risk experience.[74]

Effects of experiences on the organism

Regrettably, many studies of psychosocial influences have been undertaken and reported as if these could be considered in isolation without reference to environmental effects on the organism. Fortunately, that is changing. If experiences have enduring effects, and the evidence indicates that in some circumstances they do bring about lasting changes in function, it is necessary to ask how these changes are mediated. It is clear that a diversity of routes may be involved.[75]

These routes may be considered at various different levels. Traditionally, psychologists have tended to focus on either cognitive/affective mechanisms within the individual, or interpersonal mechanisms that involve interactions with other people. Thus, there has been a particular interest in the development of negative, or maladaptive, cognitive sets or models as possible mediators of the causal processes involved, with both antisocial behavior[76] and depression.[77] Also, the notion that such cognitive sets influence the course of psychopathology is central to the development of cognitive behavioral therapy, for which there is some evidence of efficacy.[78] However, as well as queries over whether the cognitive sets have the causal role that has been postulated, there are questions on why there are individual differences in the mental models that are formed. With respect to possible interplay with genetic influences, it is necessary to ask also about the neural changes that occur. Some studies using functional imaging have suggested that the brain changes associated with responses to cognitive behavioral therapy (CBT) and to medication were similar,[79] but a recent study of the treatment of depression suggests that they may be different.[80] There have been too few studies for firm conclusions but findings are beginning to accumulate on the brain changes associated with psychological treatments. It remains to be determined whether and how the brain changes mediate the treatment effects and, in particular, whether they account for the apparent mediating effects on psychopathological outcomes of the alteration in the mental set.

The second route of the effects of experiences in altering people's interactions with other people seems important as judged by the findings from longitudinal studies.[81] However, next to nothing is known about the biological correlates of these altered interactions.

A third route concerns the effects of stress on neuroendocrine structure and function as suggested by findings in both animals[82] and, to a lesser extent, with humans.[83] There is little doubt that there are neuroendocrine effects, but there is much more uncertainty on whether or not they mediate causal effects on psychopathological outcomes.

A fourth route concerns the adoption of maladaptive coping strategies, such as recourse to alcohol or drugs, that create their own risks for further mental disorder.[84] The cannabis example (in relation to schizophrenia) discussed in Chapter 9 is informative in showing how drug effects may interact with genetic influences.

A fifth route concerns the effects of experiences on neural structure as shown both by studies of environmental enrichment in mice and other animals[85] and by repeated parent–infant separation or deprivation[86] or unusual environmental noise.[87] Animal studies of severe stress have shown that such stress can lead to hippocampal damage[88] and there is limited evidence that the same may apply in humans.[89]

Yet another possible route concerns the effects of experience on the biological programming of the brain.[90] However, understanding of what this involves at the neural level remains quite limited.

Conclusions

It is all too obvious that much remains to be learned about the effects of experiences on the organism, and that remains a key need for the future. It is possible that a crucial mechanism concerns the effects of experiences on gene expression (as discussed more fully in Chapter 10). What the rigorous research has shown already is that there are environmentally mediated risks that apply within the normal range, as well as at extremes; that they involve family-wide, as well as child-specific, influences; that the influences extend beyond the family to include peer groups, school, and community; that some environmental effects are transitory but some are long-lasting; that there is marked individual variation in how people respond to stress and adversity; and that genetic factors are important in those individual variations in susceptibility (see Chapters 4 and 9).

Notes

See Reference list for full details.

 1   Scarr 1992; Rowe 1994; Harris 1998
 2   Rutter et al., 2001 a; Rutter, 2005 b
 3   Rutter, 1971; Fergusson et al., 1992; Harris et al., 1986
 4   Conger et al., 1994; Costello et al., 2003
 5   Jaffee et al., 2002
 6   Caspi et al., 2004
 7   Moffitt et al., 2002
 8   Brown & Rutter, 1966; Rutter & Brown, 1966
 9   See Moffitt, 2005
10   Pine et al., 1996
11   Meyer et al., 2000; Kendler et al., 1996
12   D'Onofrio et al., 2003; Silberg & Eaves, 2004
13   D'Onofrio et al., 2003
14   Jacob et al., 2003
15   Rutter et al., 1990, 1999 a, 2001
16   Duyme et al., 1999
17   Duyme et al., 2004
18   Rutter et al., 1998 a
19   O'Connor et al., 1999, 2000, 2003; Rutter et al., 2000, 2001; Rutter, in press b
20   Rutter et al., 2004, Rutter, in press b
21   Rutter et al., 2003; Thorpe et al., 2003
22   Rutter & Redshaw, 1991
23   Scarr, 1992; Rutter et al., 1997
24   Costello et al., 2003
25   Honda et al., 2005

26 Uchiyama et al., in press
27 Rutter, 2005 a
28 Stehr-Green et al., 2003
29 Hornig et al., 2004
30 Fergusson et al., 1996
31 Zoccolillo et al., 1992
32 Sampson & Laub, 1993; Laub et al., 1998
33 Quinton et al., 1993
34 Laub and Sampson, 2003
35 Elder, 1986
36 Sampson & Laub, 1996
37 Arseneault et al., 2004
38 Caspi et al., 2005 b
39 Henquet et al., 2005
40 Rutter, 2003 b
41 Brody et al., 2004
42 Snyder et al., 2003
43 Bryant, 1990
44 Scarr, 1992
45 Cameron et al., 2005
46 Thorpe et al., 2003
47 Plomin & Daniels, 1987
48 Rowe, 1994
49 Rutter & McGuffin, 2004
50 Pike et al., 1996
51 O'Connor et al., 1998; Ge et al., 1996
52 Radke-Yarrow, 1998; Rutter & Quinton, 1987
53 Harris, 1998
54 See Rutter et al., 1998
55 Rutter & Maughan, 2002
56 Sampson et al., 1997; Caspi et al., 2000; Rose et al., 2003; Jones & Fung, 2005
57 Stratton et al., 1996; Streissguth et al., 1999; Rutter, 2005 c
58 Mayes, 1999
59 Kotimaa et al., 2003; Thapar et al., 2003
60 Maughan et al., 2004; Silberg et al., 2003
61 Rutter, in press b
62 Rutter, 2000
63 Rutter, 2003 b; Rutter & Silberg, 2002; Moffitt et al., 2005 & in press
64 Eaves et al., 2003
65 Moffitt et al., 2005; Rutter & Silberg, 2002
66 Conger et al., 1999
67 Borge et al., 2004
68 Côté et al., submitted
69 Kendler et al., 1999; Silberg et al., 1999
70 Sandberg et al., 1998
71 Quinton & Rutter, 1976

72   Brown & Harris, 1978; Harris, 2000
73   Rutter, 2003 c
74   Rutter, in press c
75   Rutter, 1989
76   Dodge et al., 1990 & 1995
77   Teasdale & Barnard, 1993
78   Brent et al., 2002; Compas et al., 2002
79   Baxter et al., 1992; Furmark et al., 2002
80   Goldapple et al., 2004
81   Champion et al., 1995; Laub & Sampson, 2003; Robins, 1966
82   Hennessey & Levine, 1979; Levine 1982; Liu et al., 1997; Sapolsky, 1993, 1998
83   Gunnar & Donzella, 2002; Hart et al., 1996
84   Rutter, 2002 c
85   Cancedda et al., 2004; Greenough et al., 1987; Greenough & Black, 1992;
     Rosenweig & Bennett, 1996
86   Poeggel et al., 2003
87   Chang & Merzenich, 2003
88   Bremner, 1999; O'Brien, 1997
89   McEwen & Lasley, 2002
90   Bateson et al., 2004; Knudsen, 2004; Rutter, in press b

Further reading

Rutter, M. (2005 b). Environmentally mediated risks for psychopathology: Research
    strategies and findings. *Journal of the American Academy of Child and Adolescent
    Psychiatry, 44,* 3–18.
Rutter, M., Pickles, A., Murray, R., & Eaves, L. (2001). Testing hypotheses on specific
    environmental causal effects on behavior. *Psychological Bulletin, 127,* 291–324.

Chapter 6

Patterns of inheritance

Genes are the particles on chromosomes that carry the genetic information that is passed from parents to their offspring. The **genome** as a whole comprises the entire set of **chromosomes** for the organism, and hence all the genetic information. Every chromosome is made up of DNA, each strand of which contains many genes. Diploid organisms such as humans have two sets of chromosomes, with one copy of each chromosome inherited from each parent. Ordinarily, each gene exists in two or more alternative forms called alleles. The genetic information carried by each gene is determined by the sequence of chemical bases (that is, the particular order of the four bases that make up the genetic strand). The DNA has the form of a regular helix containing two polynucleotide chains (as discovered by Watson and Crick in 1953). It is this particular structure that allows the separation of the two strands to occur without degradation (see Figure 6.1).

There are several features of genes that are relevant to an understanding of patterns of inheritance. To begin with, a central feature is that the two strands of each parental duplex separate in order to recombine with the DNA from the other parent in order to form the DNA of the offspring. This constitutes the basis of genetic inheritance. Each parent has two copies of each gene. These separate so that one copy from the father combines with one copy from the mother to provide the two-copy duplex inherited by the offspring (see Figure 6.2). The consequence is that although the children inherit some genes from each parent, genetically they are not quite like either parent.

Another feature of genes is that, over the course of evolution, allelic variation (meaning the particular variety of the gene) arises through spontaneous **mutation**s (meaning spontaneous changes in the gene). Normally occurring allelic variations are described as "wild type," and ordinarily they code for a functional gene product. By contrast, abnormal mutations either damage or abolish gene function. However, most mutations are recessive and therefore

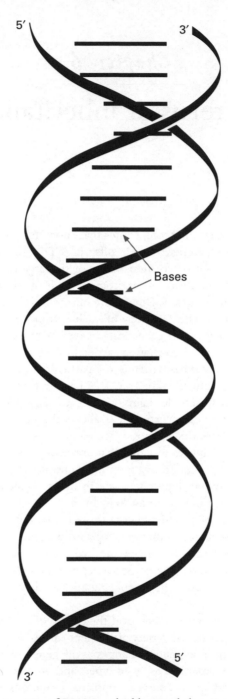

Figure 6.1   The structure of DNA is a double-stranded, antiparallel helix.
Source: based on Strachan & Read, 2004. Copyright © 2003 by Garland Science.
Adapted by permission of the publisher.

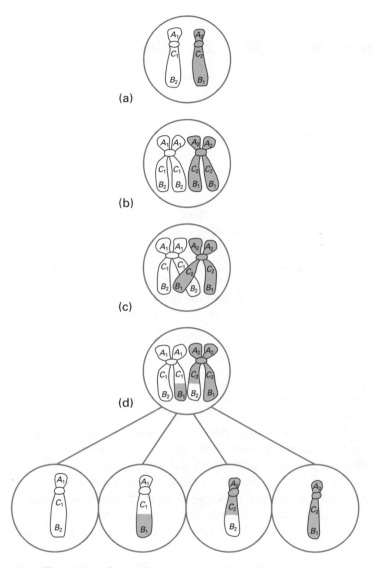

Figure 6.2 Illustration of recombination.
Source: from Plomin et al., 2001. Copyright © 1980, 1990, 1997, 2001 by W.H. Freeman and Company and Worth Publishers. Used with permission.

do not have effects that have functional consequences because the wild type or normal allele is dominant. There is a tendency to think that there must be just one wild-type allele but that is not necessarily the case. For example, the control of the human blood groups system involves several wild-type alleles.

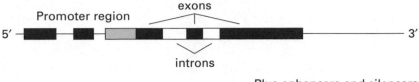

Figure 6.3   Schematic representation of gene before transcription.
Source: from McGuffin et al., 2002. Copyright © 2002 by Oxford University Press.
Adapted by permission of the publisher.

In a situation like this in which there are multiple functional alleles it is described as a polymorphism rather than an abnormal mutation.

Most genes consist of a sequence of DNA that is entirely devoted to the purpose of coding for one **protein** (although the gene will include non-coding regions as well – see below). For a long time, the dogma was that one gene led to one **polypeptide** (making up proteins). However, there are cases in which a single sequence of DNA codes for more than one protein, either because of overlapping genes or because a single gene generates a variety of messenger RNA products that have different effects (see Chapter 7).

The last point that needs to be made about genes is that they comprise an alternation of **exon**s (the bits that are represented in the final RNA product) and **intron**s (the bits that are removed by a process called RNA splicing during the phase of **transcription**) (see Figure 6.3 and Chapter 7). Only mutations in exons can affect the protein sequence but mutations in introns can affect the processing of the RNA and, thereby, prevent the production of proteins. Accordingly, although the central dogma that DNA leads to RNA that leads to the production of polypeptides and therefore to proteins remains true, it is not as narrowly determinative as used to be thought and it is probably best conceptualized as a dynamic system in which various features influence the end result.

Up to this point, genetic inheritance has been discussed entirely in terms of genes that are on the nuclear chromosomes. However, there is, in addition, the rather different mitochondrial genome that is situated in the extranuclear portion of the cell. **Mitochondrial inheritance** is distinctive in terms of two main features. First, the inheritance is entirely through the mother because the sperm does not contribute mitochondria to the zygote. A mitochondrially inherited condition can affect either males or females but it is passed on only by mothers who are affected. The second distinctive feature is that cells contain many mitochondrial genomes and that in some cases there can be a mixed population of normal and mutant genomes seen within each single cell (described by the technical term heteroplasmy). In other words, there is genetic mosaicism. That can also apply to the DNA in the nucleus of the cell but that arises post-zygotically, that is, at a later stage in development. A third feature is that mitochondrial DNA replication tends to be much more error prone than nuclear DNA replication. Much less is known about mitochondrial diseases and, although they are responsible for various neurodegenerative conditions, so far as it is known they do not account for mental disorders or psychological traits.

Different patterns of inheritance

Although there are more than two varieties of inheritance, as discussed below, the main distinction is between Mendelian, single-gene, inheritance and multifactorial inheritance. Mendelian inheritance reflects the situation whereby a particular **genotype** at one **locus** is both necessary and sufficient for the character to be expressed, given the ordinarily expectable human genetic and environmental background. Over 6,000 Mendelian characters are known in humans[1] and these generally reflect disorders that are closely related to the primary gene action.

By contrast, multifactorial inheritance depends, not on just one gene, but on several (or many) genes. With multifactorial inheritance, the effect of any one gene is not sufficient to account for the trait or disorder. There will be environmental influences that may be of major, or minor, effect and the **phenotype** (meaning the manifestation of the genetically influenced trait) will be dependent on multiple genes. When only a small number of loci are implicated, inheritance tends to be called **oligogenic**, and when there are many loci each of which, when considered separately, has only a very small effect, the inheritance is described as **polygenic**. In addition, there may be a single major locus with the involvement of a polygenic background. When the trait involves a characteristic that is categorical so that you either have it or you do not have it, the loci affecting the underlying liability are described as susceptibility genes. This probably applies, for example, to conditions such as schizophrenia. When, however, the characteristics are ones that are quantitative or continuous, the variation is reflected in how much of the characteristic you have, and the loci that influence the trait are described as **quantitative trait loci (QTLs)**. This clearly applies to features such as height and weight and presumably it does too to features such as intelligence or temperamental traits such as emotionality or sensation seeking. Although genetic texts tend to consider susceptibility genes and QTL genes as different (because they are analyzed in different ways), there is no evidence that they operate via different genetic mechanisms. In both cases the assumption is that the genetic liability is dimensional. The only difference is that this is assumed in the case of susceptibility genes, whereas it is measured in the case of QTL (see below).

Mendelian pedigree patterns

There are five basic Mendelian **pedigree** patterns classified on the basis of whether or not the loci are on an **autosome** (meaning any chromosome other than X or Y) or on a **sex chromosome** (X or Y) and, then, according to whether or not the trait is dominant or recessive. A trait is dominant if it is manifest in the **heterozygote** (meaning that the individual has only one allele with the relevant mutation) and recessive if the individual has to have *both* alleles with the mutation in order to be affected. The terms dominant and recessive apply to the traits and not to the genes themselves, although the two usually go together.

With autosomal **dominant inheritance**, the affected individual will ordinarily have at least one affected parent. The trait or disorder can affect either sex and can be transmitted by either the father or the mother. A child who is born to one parent who is affected and one who is unaffected has a 50 percent chance of being affected themselves. The best known example that is relevant to psychiatry is Huntington's disease, a rare adult-onset disease involving progressive neurological deterioration and dementia.

Autosomal recessive inheritance means that the individuals who are affected are usually born to parents who are not affected, the parents generally being asymptomatic **carrier**s of the relevant gene. Because, in order to show the trait, the person must have both alleles with the mutation, there is an increased incidence of parental consanguinity (meaning that the mother and father are biologically related to each other). Again, as with autosomal dominant inheritance, either males or females can be affected. After the birth of a child, each subsequent child has a 25 percent chance of being affected (on the assumption that both parents are asymptomatic carriers). Several diseases associated with mental retardation represent autosomal recessive conditions. **X-linked** recessive inheritance mainly affects males who are born to two unaffected parents. Because the X chromosome is the one that is implicated in being female, at first sight one might suppose that X-linked recessive inheritance ought to apply to females. However, the key point is that females have two X chromosomes whereas males have only one. This means that if there is a mutation on that single X chromosome possessed by a male, it will lead to the recessive trait, whereas that will not be so for females (because they will have two X chromosomes, only one of which will have the mutation). The X chromosomes in a male always come from the mother; therefore there can be no father-to-son transmission in the family tree. X-linked recessive inheritance applies to several mental retardation syndromes,[2] as well as to the bleeding disease hemophilia.

X-linked dominant inheritance can affect either sex but usually it affects females more than males. That is because females are often more mildly and more variably affected than males and conditions in males may be sufficiently severe to lead to death before birth. **Rett syndrome** is probably the best known neuropsychiatric condition that involves sex-linked dominant inheritance.[3] Before Rett syndrome became better understood, the social impairments seen in the early stages of the disease were sometimes confused with autism.

Y-linked inheritance can affect only males because it is only males who have a Y chromosome. Unless the trait is due to a new mutation, affected males will always have an affected father, and because the Y chromosome is always passed on by the father, this means that all sons of an affected man will be affected. The Y chromosome contains rather a small number of genes and there are no known examples of Y-linked inheritance that apply within the field of mental disorders and psychological traits.

Complexities in Mendelian inheritance

The rules of Mendelian inheritance are straightforward and this means that genetic counseling can be based on what is known about the different patterns of Mendelian inheritance. However, for quite some time, it has been evident that there were some puzzling anomalous patterns associated with conditions that were, with good reason, regarded as Mendelian. Over recent years there have been important discoveries that have identified the reasons for many of these anomalies and there is better understanding of how these come about.

Incomplete penetrance

To begin with, it has long been known that dominant conditions may be only partially penetrant. Thus, with conditions known to be dominant, there are occasional instances in which the inheritance skips a generation. This must mean that in the skipped generation there will be someone who carries the mutant gene but nevertheless appears normal. At first sight, this seems to contradict the rule that with Mendelian inheritance, the mutant gene constitutes both a necessary and a sufficient cause of the condition. Actually, incomplete **penetrance** does not contravene that rule in that it is still the

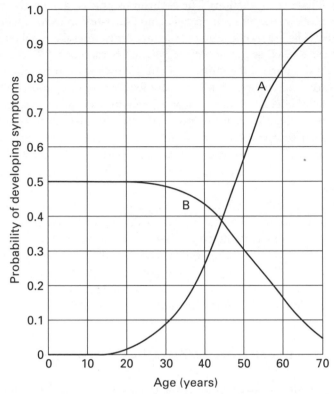

Curve A: probability that an individual carrying the disease gene will have developed symptoms by a given age. Curve B: risk that a healthy child of an affected parent carries the disease gene at a given age.

Figure 6.4 Age of onset curve for Huntingdon disease.
Source: from Harper, 2001. Copyright © 1998 by P.S. Harper. Reprinted by permission of Elsevier.

case that the development of the condition does not depend at all on any particular environmental factor, and it does not depend on the presence of another gene. However, that does not mean that manifestations cannot be influenced both by other genetic influences and by environmental circumstances. Ordinarily, the degree to which the manifestation is affected by these other features is quite small but in some instances it could be clinically meaningful. The best known example of age-related reduced penetrance is that provided by late-onset diseases such as Huntington's disease. This can arise even in childhood but in most cases the manifestations are only evident in middle age, and occasionally it has an onset even in old age. In the case of Huntington's disease, good data are available on the probability that an individual carrying the disease gene will have developed symptoms by a given age, and this is of considerable help in relation to genetic counseling[4] (see Figure 6.4). What it is about advancing age that causes the disease to become manifest is not well understood.

Variable expression

Variable expression is a phenomenon that is closely related to non-penetrance but it is much more frequent. What this means is that, although all individuals with a mutant gene show the condition, they show it in markedly varied ways and with striking variations in severity. For example, that is the case with tuberous sclerosis, a neuropsychiatric condition that is associated with mental retardation, epilepsy, and a substantially increased risk for autism.[5] The range of expression in this condition is extremely wide. At one extreme, the affected individuals may show only very minor spots on the skin that are likely to be picked up only by an expert and sometimes only through the use of Wood's light, an ultraviolet light torch that highlights the skin features. At the other extreme the individuals are severely handicapped and have large tubers (a type of abnormal growth) in their brain. As with reduced penetrance, other genes, environmental factors, or pure chance may be what is influencing the development of symptoms. For obvious reasons, it is very important for clinicians to be aware of the importance and strength of variable expression because, unless the right steps are taken to detect the condition (as for example through the use of Wood's ultraviolet light), the condition may be missed.

For the most part, the statement that variability in Mendelian conditions is brought about, in some instances, by modifier genes is an assumption that is based on what is known about genetics. However, mouse genetics has provided definitive evidence of examples where this is the case.[1] Thus, it has been observed that the expression of a mutant gene can change when it is bred onto a different genetic background. Also, a statistical analysis of the variation and the clinical picture within large families can provide human evidence for modifier genes – as shown, for example, with neurofibromatosis (a condition that has some similarities with tuberous sclerosis[6]). Nevertheless, it is likely that pure chance also plays a significant role in variable expression.

Anticipation

For many years, clinicians had observed a tendency for some Mendelian conditions to become more severe, or to have an onset at an earlier age, in

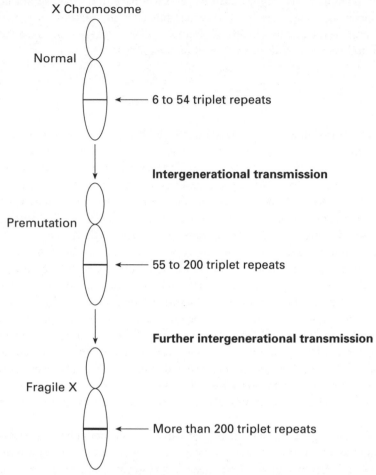

The Fragile X anomaly involves a triplet repeat sequence of DNA on the X chromosome that expands over the generations – first from a normal chromosome to a permutation with an increased frequency of triplet repeats and then finally through a further intergenerational transmission to a much increased number of triplet repeats, which is associated with the handicapping syndrome.

Figure 6.5　The Fragile X anomaly.
Source: based on Plomin et al., 2001. Copyright © 1980, 1990, 1997, 2001 by W.H. Freeman and Company and Worth Publishers. Used with permission.

successive generations. For quite a while, most geneticists were skeptical that this was a real phenomenon because of the numerous biases that could lead to this pattern. However, the discovery in 1991 of unstable expanding **trinucleotide** repeats demonstrated an entirely novel and, up to that time, unprecedented, disease mechanism.[7] The psychiatric conditions where this phenomenon applies include the Fragile X anomaly (an important cause of mental retardation and an occasional cause of autism) and Huntington's disease. What happens in these conditions is that stable repeat sequences occur at low rates in individuals without any symptoms but that, over the course of successive generations, these can increase to much higher levels of repeats and then they do lead to the handicapping condition (see Figure 6.5). In the Fragile X syndrome, the enormously expanded repeat causes a loss of gene function by abolishing transcription. However, the effects are not exactly the same in each of the diseases showing unstable expanding repeats. It is striking that each of the diseases showing this pattern is either a neurological or a neuropsychiatric condition. Whether that says something about the meaning of the phenomenon, or rather it simply reflects the diseases where people have been looking for it, is not clear at the moment. The expanding repeats and their frequency are diagnosable now by molecular genetic methods. An understanding of the patterns of inheritance is important for genetic counseling.

Parental imprinting

Ordinarily, genetic effects are basically the same irrespective of whether the gene comes from the father or the mother. However, genomic or parental imprinting describes the situation in which there is non-equivalence in the expression of alleles at certain genetic loci, dependent on the parent of origin. When there is imprinting, the expression of either the paternally inherited allele or the maternally inherited allele is consistently suppressed, resulting in monoallelic expression. This pattern of monoallelic expression is transmitted to the daughter cells following cell division but the nucleotide sequence of the suppressed allele is not altered. The best known neuropsychiatric example is provided by the **Prader-Willi** (PWS) and **Angelman (AS) syndromes**.[8] Both PWS and AS are caused by problems with differentially imprinted genes at the same particular location on chromosome 15. PWS is a condition characterized by mental retardation, floppy muscles, and gross obesity amongst other things and it is caused by a lack of function of genes that are expressed only from the paternal chromosome. AS also involves mental retardation but its characteristics are otherwise quite different in involving overactivity and inappropriate laughter. It is due to the lack of function of a closely linked gene that is expressed only from the maternal chromosome. In about three-quarters of cases the event that leads to the lack of the relevant chromosome 15 sequence is a de novo deletion at the relevant spot on the chromosome. However, it can also come about because a person with apparently normal chromosomes has inherited both copies of a particular pair from the same parent. In addition, it can happen that something has gone wrong with the mechanism of imprinting. As noted in Chapter 7, imprinting constitutes an example of epigenesis.

X *chromosome inactivation*

X chromosome inactivation is another example of epigenesis; it is a normal process that occurs in all mammals. It involves the selective inactivation of one of the two X chromosomes possessed by females. It thereby provides a mechanism for dosage compensation to overcome sex differences in the expected ratio of autosomal gene dosage to X chromosome gene dosage. This inactivation takes place early in life and the choice of which X is inactivated appears to be largely random. This means, however, that there will be variability in the proportion of X chromosomes that are normal and the proportion carrying the mutant gene. If most of the chromosomes are normal, the woman may show few, if any, indications of having the condition. Conversely, if most of the cells in some critical tissue have inactivated the normal X, the women may be unusually severely affected.

At the very early stages in development, both X chromosomes are active but inactivation is initiated as the cells begin to differentiate. It has been shown that there is an **X inactivation** center on chromosome 13 that controls the initiation and propagation of X inactivation and an X-controlling element that affects the choice of which X chromosome remains active and which inactivated. In all usual circumstances, it is of no consequence which X chromosome is inactivated, but it does become very important if one of the X chromosomes carries a gene mutation that is associated with some kind of phenotypic abnormality. Thus, for example, the rare condition Rett syndrome, which leads to impaired brain growth, mental retardation, epilepsy, and a most characteristic stereotyped hand-wringing mannerism, is due to a mutant gene on the X chromosome (see Chapter 8). The resulting phenotype varies, however, from this classical pattern to much more atypical, and milder, varieties of phenomena that have some similarities with the full syndrome, but also key differences. It appears that this variation in expression of the phenotype is explicable to a large extent by the pattern of X inactivation.

New mutations

Mendelian conditions vary in the frequency with which the mutant gene is transmitted across the generations and the frequency with which a new mutation arises in an individual from a family without a history of the

Mendelian condition. For example, new mutations account for about half the cases of tuberous sclerosis.

Mosaicism

Mosaicism means that individuals have a mixture of genes, some of which are normal and some of which involve the mutant gene. This is actually a very common phenomenon so that nearly everybody is likely to be a mosaic for innumerable genes. However, in the great majority of instances, this is of no particular significance. It will only matter if the mutation causes abnormal proliferation of the cell that would normally replicate slowly or not at all (as exemplified by cancer) or the mutation occurs in an early embryo affecting a cell that is the progenitor of a significant fraction of the whole organism. When that is the case, the mosaic individual may show clinical signs of the disease. Mosaicism can give rise to very confusing family histories but molecular studies can often be helpful in indicating what is happening.

Genetic heterogeneity

Genetic heterogeneity is the rule, rather than the exception, in medicine. This may take the form of locus heterogeneity in which the same clinical condition results from mutations at one of several different loci. This is the case, for example, with tuberous sclerosis, which arises from a mutant gene either on chromosome 9 or on chromosome 16. **Allelic heterogeneity** is where there are many different mutations within a particular gene, all of which give rise to the same genetic condition. For example, that has been demonstrated to be the case with cystic fibrosis, which arises from several hundreds of different mutations of the same gene, and also with the breast cancer genes.[9] Clinical heterogeneity is the term describing the situation when mutations in the same gene produce two or more different diseases. This can come about in several different ways but one way is that the same gene may give rise to either loss of function or gain of function and, for obvious reasons, that will have different effects. Rarely, individuals may have mutations that bring about both loss of function and gain of function in different cell types in which the gene is expressed.

It might be thought that if a child inherits one mutant gene from the father and another mutant gene from the mother, both of which lead to the same recessively inherited characteristic, the effects would be cumulative, but that is not necessarily the case. For example, when two individuals with autosomal recessive profound congenital deafness marry, most of the children tend to have normal hearing. That is because there is complementarity, with different genes being involved in pathways leading to the same rather general function such as hearing or intelligence.

Lack of specific correspondence between a mutant gene and a clinical syndrome

Over half a century ago, genetic understanding was greatly aided by the hypothesis that one gene had effects on only one enzyme. In general, that is still the case but there are numerous exceptions. To begin with, genetic mediation is not confined to enzymes. In addition, it is obvious that there cannot just be one effect of each gene because there are about 6,000 known Mendelian conditions and it is implausible that these will be tied specifically to the same number of DNA coding sequences. The same gene may sometimes produce multiple enzyme defects; the mutations may affect only a subset of the tissues in which the gene is expressed (as is the case with Huntington's disease); and mutations leading to a deficiency of a protein are not necessarily in the structural gene encoding the protein (for example, that is so with the genes causing immunodeficiency).

Heterozygote advantage

When a mutant gene leads to a condition that is usually fatal before maturity, it might be expected that it would die out unless there was a very high rate of spontaneous new mutations. Thus, up until a few years ago, very few people with cystic fibrosis lived long enough to reproduce and the implication was that there must be an amazingly high new mutation rate. In fact, the evidence indicated that new mutations were actually quite rare.[1] In such a situation, it is quite likely that the explanation lies in heterozygote advantage. That is to say, the people who carry the mutant gene, but who have only one copy of the mutation giving rise to the recessive condition, have some really important advantage over individuals without the mutant gene. There are suggestions as to what this advantage might consist of in the case of cystic fibrosis, but it is not really properly understood. The general point, however, is that the heterozygote advantage need not be very great for it nevertheless to have a quite major effect on gene frequency.

Overview of Mendelian inheritance

Most mental disorders do not show Mendelian inheritance. Accordingly, it might be thought that an understanding of such inheritance is needed only for specialized experts. That is not the case, because clinicians will encounter Mendelian conditions in their ordinary clinical practice and because the genetic mechanisms may have a broader applicability. Thus, child psychiatrists need to have an awareness of Mendelian conditions such as the Fragile X anomaly and tuberous sclerosis because it is essential to consider them as possible causes for both mental retardation and autism and it is necessary to be aware of the clinical tests (such as the use of Wood's ultraviolet light) or the laboratory tests (as in the case of Fragile X) needed to make the diagnoses.

Chromosome abnormalities

Chromosome abnormalities provide a somewhat different way in which genetic differences can arise.[10] Ordinarily, they arise in an individual through something going wrong in the course of normal chromosomal mechanisms, rather than anything that is inherited. Broadly speaking, chromosomal abnormalities can be subdivided into two main types. First, there are those that are present in all cells of the body – generally termed a constitutional abnormality. Abnormalities of this kind must have been present very early in development (in order for them to apply to all cells) and in most cases this will have come about as a result of an abnormal sperm or egg, or possibly some form of abnormal fertilization, or an abnormal event in the very early embryo. The second type of abnormality is one that is present in only certain cells or certain tissues – generally called a somatic or acquired abnormality. These differ from constitutional abnormalities in the crucial respect that they will give rise to cells with two different chromosome constitutions, meaning that there is mosaicism (i.e., a mixture of two different types within the same individual).

In most cases, chromosomal anomalies have been produced by a misrepair of chromosomes that have been broken during cell division, by improper recombination of chromosomes, or by their malsegregation during cell division. These can arise either by chance (given the very high frequency of cell divisions, it is scarcely surprising that occasionally the process goes awry), or chromosome breaks may derive from damage to the DNA from factors such as irradiation or chemicals. Certain sorts of anomalies are also more common in fertilization of an old egg, as will be the case with older mothers (because all of the eggs in the ovary are already present before birth; unlike sperm, they are not made throughout life). Not surprisingly, older eggs will tend to be of less good quality than younger ones. This means that they are less likely to be fertilized but, also, it may mean that the fertilization process involves errors. The most notable example of this is Down syndrome in which the individuals have an extra chromosome 21, which has resulted from a failure in chromosomal division.

Broadly speaking, there are two main types of chromosome abnormalities: those that involve an extra chromosome or a missing chromosome, and those that involve structural abnormalities of one kind or another. Extra or missing autosomal chromosomes (meaning any chromosome other than the sex chromosomes X and Y) are generally incompatible with development; the chromosome 21 trisomy that gives rise to Down syndrome is the only major exception to that generalization. Interestingly, extra or missing sex chromosomes have far less serious consequences. In the case of the Y chromosome, that is almost certainly because it carries so few genes. In the case of the X chromosome, the protective mechanism probably lies in X-chromosome inactivation, which controls the level of gene products encoded on that chromosome, independently of the number of X chromosomes present in the cell. Turner syndrome is the one example of a missing sex chromosome (Skuse & Kuntsi 2002). The females with this syndrome have just one X chromosome rather than the usual two. However, about half possess part of the second X chromosome. Individuals with an XO anomaly show a relative failure of development of secondary sexual characteristics and there are some other physical features (such as a webbed neck). There is reduced fertility in Turner syndrome but affected women can occasionally become pregnant and, when they bear children, their offspring do not show the XO anomaly. Most individuals with Turner syndrome are of normal intelligence but they tend to be impaired in their handling of visual-spatial information and in their numerical skills. There are also more subtle anomalies in their social functioning.

Klinefelter syndrome is caused by an extra X chromosome in males that can be either maternal or paternal in origin.[8] It is the commonest of the sex chromosome anomalies, accounting for about one in 500 male live births. The affected men are usually particularly tall and there is inadequate development of the testes, with a majority of affected men being infertile. As with Turner syndrome, the men are usually of normal intelligence and there are only subtle effects on specific aspects of cognitive and social functioning. An extra Y chromosome in males (i.e., XYY) occurs in about one in 1,000 births.[11] Affected individuals generally have an IQ within the normal range but they do show a somewhat increased rate of specific learning difficulties and an increased rate of overactivity and impulsivity. An early report based on a biased sample claimed that the XYY led to marked physical aggression but it is now clear that that is not the case. Probably, as a consequence of the combination of hyperactivity and learning difficulties, there is a significant increase in antisocial behavior, but it is not particularly of an aggressive variety.[12]

There are several different types of structural abnormalities. These may involve deletion (in which a large stretch of DNA is lost); inversion (whereby a piece of chromosome breaks and becomes reattached the wrong way round); duplication (in which a segment of the chromosome is duplicated); and translocation (in which segments from one chromosome become attached to another). The most important distinction is between abnormalities that are balanced in the sense that there is no overall net gain or loss of chromosomal material and unbalanced if there is gain or loss. Ordinarily, balanced abnormalities have few clinical effects but they may be important if the break disrupts an important gene or affects the expression of a particular gene.

The importance of chromosome anomalies in connection with the topic of genes and behavior derives from three main considerations. First, they give rise to several uncommon, but nevertheless important, syndromes that involve mental retardation, which is often associated with a relatively distinctive pattern of behavior. Williams syndrome (occurring in some one in 20,000 live births) is an example of this kind and so are both the Prader-Willi and Angelman syndromes. Williams syndrome is associated with deletions on chromosome 7 and the other two syndromes are a consequence of deletions or disruptions on chromosome 15 – which syndrome it is being a function of genomic imprinting. The second reason for interest derives from the light that their study may throw on the nature of genetic mechanisms of one kind or another. The third reason is that chromosome anomalies may sometimes provide useful leads with respect to the possible location of susceptibility genes for mental disorders. In practice, this has not been as helpful as might have been hoped. There have been several false leads. Nevertheless, there are examples of instances where it was relevant. For example, the evidence that individuals with Down syndrome had a much increased rate of Alzheimer's disease suggested the possibility that there might be a mutated gene on chromosome 21. In the event, that did indeed turn out to be the case. Also, the association between the velo-cardio-facial syndrome (VCFS) and schizophrenia pointed to the possibility of a susceptibility gene on chromosome 22 because VCFS is due to a small interstitial deletion there. The COMT gene, which may be relevant for schizophrenia (see Chapters 7 and 9), is found in the VCFS region.

Multifactorial inheritance

Although there are many complexities and anomalies, Mendelian disorders can be studied by means of family pedigrees dealing with qualitatively distinct characteristics that people either have or do not have. However, it has been obvious for a very long time that most physical and most psychological traits concern dimensions, with the variability among people lying in the degree to which they exhibit the trait, rather than whether they have it at all. In the psychological arena, this clearly applies to features such as intelligence or temperament. It has long been evident that these dimensional traits tend to run in families. This led to the conclusion that genetic factors were likely to be implicated in the variation but, for many years, it was not obvious how this could be made compatible with Mendelian notions of the inheritance of discrete characteristics that were either present or absent. The initial breakthrough in the resolution of this apparent problem was the demonstration by the statistician R.E. Fisher[13] that traits governed by a large number of independent Mendelian factors would display continuous quantitative variation, together with the familial correlations that had been found. It came to be accepted that these dimensions were influenced by multiple genes and that the genetic principles were compatible with what had been described in relation to Mendelian inheritance.

That seemed to provide resolution with respect to traits like intelligence and temperament but did not solve the problem with respect to disorders such as schizophrenia or autism or bipolar disorder that clearly ran in families but which did not seem to follow Mendelian patterns of inheritance. The breakthrough here was provided by Falconer's extension of polygenic theory to categorical traits that were present or absent, rather than dimensional.[14] Falconer postulated that even with multifactorial categorical variables, the genetic liability might well be dimensional. Whether or not a person showed the characteristic then depended on whether or not their genetic liability exceeded a particular threshold (see Figure 6.6). The theory helped to explain how recurrence risks might vary among families. The individuals affected with the characteristic would be those who had many high-susceptibility alleles. Their biological relatives, with whom they shared some of their genes, would also, on average, have a raised susceptibility but they would tend to have fewer high-susceptibility alleles. The extent to which relatives diverged from the mean in the general population would depend on the proportion of their shared genes and, hence, the polygenic threshold characteristics would tend to run in families.

The notion has come to be generally accepted as likely to be true, although it is difficult to put it to the test in a rigorous empirical fashion when the susceptibility genes are unknown. One way in which the theory can be tested out is by determining what happens with conditions that are supposed to follow the Falconer threshold model but which have different rates in the two sexes. The reason why this provides a test is because it would seem to follow that the thresholds must differ between males and females. Congenital pyloric stenosis (a relatively common condition giving rise to projectile vomiting in babies) constitutes a good example. It is about five times as common in boys as in girls. The implication, therefore, is that the threshold must be higher for girls than boys. If that is the case, it should then follow

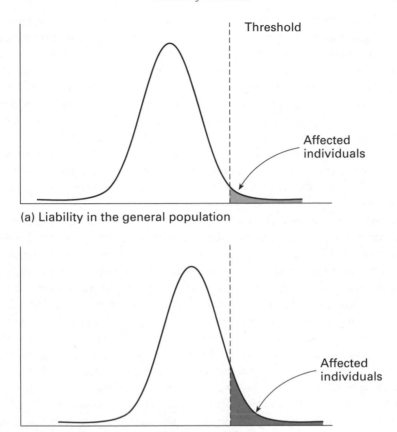

(a) Liability in the general population

(b) Liability for relatives of affected individuals

Figure 6.6 Liability threshold model of disorders.
Source: Plomin et al., 2001. Copyright © 1980, 1990, 1997, 2001 by W.H. Freeman and Company and Worth Publishers. Adapted with permission.

that the relatives of a girl with congenital pyloric stenosis would have a higher average susceptibility than relatives of an affected boy. Research findings have shown that that seems to be the case.[15]

Regression to the mean

There are many poorly understood, and some controversial, aspects of polygenic theory. Perhaps the one that goes back furthest is that of regression to the mean. This refers to the fact that the children of parents who are unusually high or unusually low on some characteristic will tend to be similar to their parents but will have levels of the trait that are not so extreme as their parents and which are closer to the mean for the general population. The misconception has been that this regression reflects a genetic principle, but it does not. Thus, for example, it was argued years ago that because the IQs of children in certain ethnic groups regressed to a mean that was below that in White populations, this meant that the mean differences in IQ among the ethnic groups was genetic in origin.[16] The wrong assumption, that regression derives from a genetic mechanism, was made, whereas in fact it is a purely statistical phenomenon. It will be found for any multifactorial trait in which the same mix of causal influences applies across the population. The regression to the mean will be found irrespective of the extent of genetic influence.[16]

Nevertheless, if properly handled, the degree of regression to the mean can constitute a most useful measure in genetic analyses.[17] The details need not concern us here but the key point is that the analyses are useful because the quantification of regression to the mean, when comparing monozygotic and dizygotic twin pairs, can provide a good measure of the strength of the genetic influence and also a measure of the extent to which an individual showing an extreme on some characteristic shares the same genetic liability as their relatives (see Figure 6.7). Figure 6.7 illustrates the point by comparing the IQ distributions of the siblings of individuals with severe mental retardation (with an IQ below 50) and the siblings of individuals with mild mental retardation (with an IQ in the 50 to 69 range). The former show a normal IQ distribution with a mean of 103 whereas the latter show a depressed IQ distribution with a mean of 85. In short, the latter tend to resemble their mildly retarded brother or sister but with some regression back to the general population mean of 100. The former show no similarity to their severely retarded sibling. The implication is that the causes of mild retardation (both genetic and environmental) are likely to be similar to those influencing variations of IQ within the normal range, whereas that is not the case with severe retardation (which is usually due to gross brain abnormalities). These distributions on their own do not indicate whether the familial resemblance is genetic in origin but quantification of the degree of regression to the mean in MZ and DZ co-twins will make that possible. All of this is possible because the statistic can be used to test genetic hypotheses and not because the regression as such is due to a genetic influence.

An example of a condition that is genetically determined but yet does not reflect the genes running in the family is provided by severe mental retardation and particularly by Down syndrome. Down syndrome is due to a chromosomal abnormality that ordinarily arises de novo and therefore has not been inherited from the parents. The chromosomal anomaly is crucial for the resulting mental retardation but it is probably of no relevance for

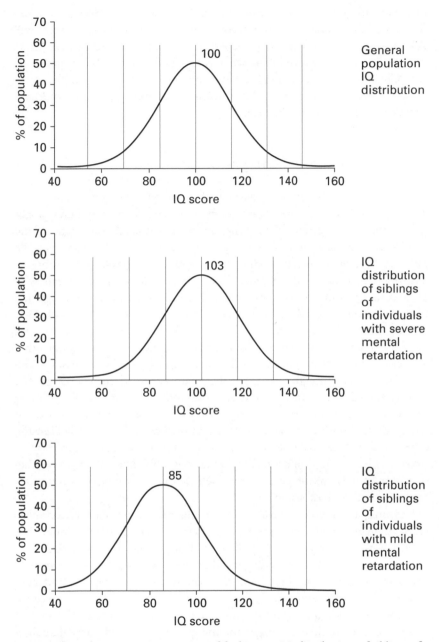

Figure 6.7 Schematic representation of findings on IQ distribution of siblings of individuals with either severe or mild mental retardation.
Source: from study by Nichols, 1984.

variations in IQ within the rest of the family (because they do not have the chromosomal anomaly), although, of course, everyone in the family will share the many genes that act polygenetically to influence intelligence. These genes will not make much difference in the individual with Down syndrome (although they will make some difference) because the effect of the chromosomal anomaly is so great that it ordinarily outweighs all the ordinary genetic influences on intelligence.

Susceptibility genes and quantitative trait loci

At the moment, it is not at all clear whether susceptibility genes and quantitative trait loci concern the same or different genetic features. Operationally, the distinction is provided by whether or not the characteristic being considered is measured as a category or as a dimension. For example, the molecular genetic research looking for susceptibility genes for schizophrenia has been concerned with categorical distinctions between individuals who do and those who do not have schizophrenia. By contrast, although the research interest focused on dyslexia as a categorical condition, the molecular genetic research actually measured reading skills as a dimension. In both cases the research has been positive in showing genes or gene locations that are very likely to be implicated in the causation of the characteristics. The difference is that although there is an inferred underlying dimension of genetic liability for schizophrenia, there is no established measure at the moment that can quantify this in terms of features that can be validly assessed and quantified with respect to variations in the general population. On the other hand, reading skills can be measured as a quantified dimensional trait. Accordingly, the question has to be whether this difference reflects something that is meaningful in the genetics or whether it is no more than a reflection of the current state of knowledge.

How might it matter? Autism and schizophrenia can be taken as examples. Up until relatively recently, most people would have had little doubt that autism constitutes a qualitatively distinct disorder that does not blend into normal variations. Autism as diagnosed in the 1960s and 1970s was usually associated with a degree of mental retardation, about a quarter of affected children developed epileptic seizures (most typically in late adolescence or early adult life), a substantial minority of the children never developed a useful level of spoken language, and many of the features seemed qualitatively, and not just quantitatively, different from normality.[18] However, that separation from normality does not seem quite so obvious and clear-cut today. Genetic studies were important in indicating that the genetic liability extended much more broadly than this seriously handicapping disorder. Thus autism spectrum disorders include a broader range of social, communicative, and behavioral abnormalities that are qualitatively very similar to those seen in autism as traditionally diagnosed, but are much milder and which often occurred in individuals of normal intelligence who were able to function in the community.[18] Together with clinical and epidemiological research evidence that pointed in the same direction, this led to a substantial broadening of the diagnostic concept of autism. Of course, that does not necessarily mean that it is meaningful to talk about normal variations in autistic tendencies in the general population. On the other hand, that no longer seems quite as ridiculous as it did some time ago. Accordingly, many research groups around the world are now seeking to develop measures of autistic features that can be applied in the general population. It remains to be seen quite how well this will work but present indications are that dimensional measures may be possible and can be used for quantitative trait loci genetic analyses.

On the other hand, there are also differences that seem important. Thus, the much milder manifestations of autistic features that are so common in the relatives of individuals with autism seem to differ from autism "proper" in two key respects. First, they are usually associated with normal levels of intelligence and, secondly, they seem not to be associated with epilepsy. Of course, that could simply reflect the effects of variations in genetic liability but differences also raise the possibility that some kind of "two-hit" mechanism is involved. In other words, what is required for autism "proper" to develop are the susceptibility genes and some other risk factor that could be either genetic or environmental in origin. The implication, if it is a two-hit process, is that the genes underlying the broader phenotype may not be exactly the same as those involved in the transition to the handicapping disorder.

Somewhat comparable issues apply to schizophrenia. There is good evidence that the genetic liability extends beyond schizophrenia as traditionally diagnosed. It includes so-called schizotypal personality disorder and paranoid conditions but does not include a broad range of other psychiatric disorders.[19]

Perhaps surprisingly, the group of disorders outside the genetic liability for schizophrenia seems to exclude schizoid personality disorder which, on the face of it, would seem to have much in common with schizophrenia.[19] Recent research investigating the families of individuals with schizophrenia, using a range of clinical measures, imaging, and other approaches, has confirmed the abnormalities in relatives. However, as with the broader phenotype of autism, it has not proved quite so straightforward to determine the boundaries of milder abnormalities and, in particular, how to decide whether the personality features that lead on to schizophrenia differ from those that lead on from autism, as well as those associated with other forms of psychopathology. Progress has been made in identifying the childhood precursors of schizophrenic psychoses that generally develop in late adolescence or

early adult life.[20] The findings have yet to be tied up with the relevant
susceptibility genes.

Specificity or non-specificity of genetic effects

Psychiatric classification systems have been based on longstanding
assumptions about the specificity and separateness of different psychiatric
disorders. For example, from the time of Kraepelin onwards, clinical studies
of the course and characteristics of schizophrenia and of bipolar psychoses
have led to a general acceptance that these two conditions are quite separate
and were likely to reflect different genetic liabilities. Recent genetic research,
both quantitative and molecular, raises questions about this assumption
(see Chapters 4 and 8). Although there are differences, there seems to be
substantial overlap as well. The feature that more clearly differentiates the
two types of psychosis is the much stronger association with neurodevelopmental abnormalities in the case of schizophrenia.[21] What is less
clear as yet is whether these neurodevelopmental abnormalities are part of
the genetic liability or represent a separately determined environmental
risk factor. It is obvious that once the susceptibility genes have been clearly
identified, it will become much easier to obtain research leverage on the
determination of the non-genetic risk factors for schizophrenia and a better
understanding of how they operate. The same applies in the case of autism.

   Much the same message about the limited specificity of genetic liability
derives from research into other forms of mental disorder and of other
psychological features. Thus, although psychiatric classification separates
anxiety disorders from depressive disorders, the genetic liability appears
to be much the same for the two sets of disorders, at least with respect to
generalized anxiety disorders.[22] In part, this is because the personality trait
of neuroticism constitutes a genetically influenced risk factor for both and,
in part, it comes about because anxiety disorders in childhood tend to lead
on to depressive disorders in adolescence and early adult life, with the two
sharing the same genetic liability.[23] Of course, the fact that the genetic liability
spans the two does not necessarily mean that it is mistaken to diagnose
them separately. There is a limited amount of evidence, for example, that
the types of life stresses that tend to precipitate anxiety disorders are somewhat
different from the sort that tend to precipitate depression. There are also
treatment implications that may matter. Thus, drugs with a specific effect on
anxiety (such as the benzodiazepines) have no place in the treatment of
depression. Because of their addictive qualities, they are now no longer the
mainstay of treatment of anxiety disorders but they do have a limited place
for acute, rather than chronic, use. The converse, however, is less the case.
That is to say, the selective serotonin re-uptake inhibitors (the SSRIs) such as

"Prozac" may have beneficial effects in the treatment of anxiety as well as depression. The particular SSRI drugs, however, vary in the extent to which they are useful in the treatment of anxiety.

Twin and family studies have been important in suggesting that the same genetic liability that applies to the relatively rare condition of Tourette syndrome (a disorder characterized by compulsive uttering of obscenities) extends to include chronic multiple tics and some cases of obsessive-compulsive disorder.[24] The evidence is persuasive but it is not definitive because, as yet, no susceptibility genes have been identified. Also, probably, the evidence is stronger in the case of the extension to chronic multiple tics than it is to obsessive–compulsive disorders. The limited available evidence suggests that the overlap applies only to some forms of obsessive–compulsive disorder, although it is not clear how these may be clinically differentiated. Twin findings on specific developmental disorders of language[25] indicate that the genetic liability extends more broadly than the traditional diagnostic categories would suppose. The same applies to the disorder of dyslexia.[26] It is important to note, however, that the findings do not suggest a complete lack of specificity. That is to say, although the genetic liability for either dyslexia or specific developmental language disorders includes a somewhat broader range of cognitive impairments, this does not mean that it accounts, for example, for the whole of mild mental retardation. That is partly because, insofar as a few susceptibility gene loci have been identified, they have been specific to dyslexia or developmental language disorders rather than encompassing the whole of cognition. Moreover, although there is a substantial overlap between language impairment and reading difficulties, the susceptibility gene loci of the two are not quite the same (but see Chapter 8). The systematic comparisons across the range of general and specific cognitive difficulties have yet to be undertaken. The evidence to date is more in keeping with a degree of specificity than with total generality.

Developmental pathways

Although genes are, of course, present from the very beginning, it is quite frequent for their effects not to be manifest until adolescence or adult life. In some cases, the delayed onset of the genetically influenced disorder is apparent rather than real. For example, it is now well established that, although schizophrenic psychosis does not usually have an onset until late adolescence or early adult life, there are nevertheless precursors that are identifiable from early childhood onwards. Apparently, how they are shown varies by age. Thus, in early childhood the features include neurodevelopmental impairment, social problems, and some kinds of disruptive behavior. At this early age, the connection with the later development of schizophrenia cannot be determined at an individual level. For quite a while, there was skepticism, too, about their identification in later childhood and early adolescence, but findings from the Dunedin study are very persuasive in indicating that these can be identified.[27] Three main queries arise, however. First, although the childhood precursors have been well demonstrated, they are not so clearly distinctive at an individual level that it is possible to use any of the features as a way of specifying which children are going to go on to develop schizophrenia in later life. Second, there is the query as to why, if there are manifestations even in early childhood, does the psychosis not develop until a much later age? There are several alternative possible explanations. Thus, psychotic manifestations could be dependent upon changes in the brain that do not occur until late adolescence. Certainly, brain development does continue until this age and it is quite likely that is part of the explanation. Also, it could be that maturational changes are required in order for the relevant genes to be, in effect, "switched on." A third possibility is that the transition from the precursors to a frank psychosis depends on environmental factors. The risk factor for which there is the most evidence is the heavy early use of cannabis.[28] In that connection, it is necessary to ask whether the risk effects of cannabis are dependent upon a combination with genetic liability. Recent research, focusing on the COMT gene, suggests that they are. There is a significant gene–environment interaction (as discussed more fully in Chapter 9).

Conclusions

The traditional dichotomous distinction between single-gene Mendelian disorders following just one of five patterns of inheritance and polygenic multifactorial disorders has turned out to be a considerable oversimplification, quite apart from the complicating role of chromosomal abnormalities. Mendelian disorders are meaningfully different from multifactorial disorders in that the responsible genetic mutation constitutes both a necessary and sufficient cause. However, as shown by the phenomena of incomplete penetrance and variable expression, the manifestations of the disorder may be considerably affected by other background genes, by chance, and by environmental circumstances (even though none of these influence the mutation as such). Also, there are important oddities in inheritance pattern (as shown, for example, by genomic imprinting and transgenerational trinucleotide repeat expansion). Less is known about the details of multifactorial inheritance but what is clear already is that its manifestations depend not just on the separate additive effect of genes and environment but also on their joint co-action as brought about through gene–environment correlations and interactions (discussed in Chapter 9) and through environmental effects on gene expression (discussed in Chapter 10).

Notes

See Reference list for full details.

1 Strachan & Read, 2004
2 Sutherland et al., 2002
3 Shahbazian & Zoghbi, 2001; Zoghbi, 2003
4 Harper, 1998
5 Harrison & Bolton, 1997
6 Huson & Korf, 2002
7 Margolis et al., 1999
8 Skuse & Kuntsi, 2002
9 Collins, 1996; Cutting, 2002
10 Rimoin et al., 2002; Skuse & Kuntsi, 2002; Strachan & Read, 2004
11 Allanson & Graham, 2002
12 Rutter et al., 1998
13 Fisher, 1918
14 As reviewed in Falconer & Mackay, 1996
15 Passarge, 2002
16 See Rutter & Madge, 1976
17 DeFries & Fulker, 1988
18 Rutter, in 2005 a; Rutter, 2005 d
19 Kendler et al., 1995
20 Cannon et al., 2002; Poulton et al., 2000
21 Keshavan et al., 2004
22 Kendler, 1996
23 Eaves et al., 2003; Kendler et al., 2002
24 Leckman & Cohen, 2002
25 Bishop et al., 1999; Bishop 2002 a & 2003
26 Snowling et al., 2003; Démonet et al., 2004
27 Poulton et al., 2000
28 Arseneault et al., 2004

Further reading

Plomin, R., DeFries, J.C., Craig, I.W., & McGuffin, P. (Eds.) (2003). *Behavioral genetics in the postgenomic era.* Washington, DC: American Psychological Association.

Plomin, R., DeFries, J.C., McClearn, G., & McGuffin, P. (Eds.) (2001). *Behavioral Genetics* (4th ed.). New York: Worth.

Rimoin, D.L., Connor, J.M., Pyeritz, R.E., & Korf, B.R. (Eds.) (2002). *Emery and Rimoin's principles and practice of medical genetics* (4th ed.) (vols. 1–3). London: Churchill Livingstone.

Strachan, T. & Read, A.P. (2004). *Human molecular genetics 3* (3rd ed.). New York & Abingdon, Oxon: Garland Science, Taylor & Francis.

Chapter 7

What genes do

Popular science writers (and, unfortunately, some scientists) often make reference to genes "for" schizophrenia, intelligence, or depression. Of course, geneticists are well aware that genes are not "for" any of those traits.[1] Some might well argue that it is simply a convenient shorthand meaning genes that play some contributory role in influencing individual variations in liability for these traits. Nevertheless, this shorthand creates the highly misleading impression that there is a more or less direct genetic influence on these features. In fact, that is not the case. At first sight, it might seem that this is no more than semantic pedantry. After all, no one seems quite so bothered about referring to genes "for" cystic fibrosis, or tuberous sclerosis, or achondroplasia. One key difference is that each of these is a Mendelian disorder in which the abnormality is wholly due to some genetic mutation without the need for involvement of any environmental risk experience. However, even with these conditions, the genes do not actually cause the phenotype (meaning the overt manifestations of the genetic liability). Rather, genes are involved in the causation of some specific biochemical consequence that serves to give rise to the phenotype. That brings us back to the question of what genes do.

The genetic code

It is necessary to start with a reminder of how DNA codes its genetic information (see Chapter 1). The key constituents of DNA are the four **base**s made up of rings of carbon and hydrogen atoms constituting **nucleotide**s – **adenine** (A), **cytosine** (C), **guanine** (G), and **thymine** (T). These four bases are organized in triplets called "**codon**s." The genetic information is provided by the specific sequence the codons form – such as ATC CGA CTT ACC etc. These lie on very long chains distributed on a double helix in which the two strands constitute a kind of spiral staircase.

Mutations cause a change in the gene sequence and it is this change that brings about the genetically influenced effects.

It might be thought that it would make biological sense for the DNA sequence to be an uninterrupted chain, but that is not the way it is. Basically, there are *"exons"* (occurring as several separated segments) that constitute the sequences represented in the mature RNA, which is what codes for the polypeptides that make up the proteins that bring about the real biological "action." *"Introns"* are intervening sequences that do not code for proteins and which are removed during the process of *transcription* to produce DNA.

The central dogma

The so-called "central dogma" of molecular biology is that the expression of genetic information in all cells is a one-way system. It begins with the DNA (which carries the inherited genetic information). The DNA, in turn, specifies the synthesis of **mRNA**, and then the mRNA specifies the synthesis of polypeptides, which ultimately go on to form proteins.

Transcription and translation

The first part of the causal chain involves processes known as transcription and **translation**. *Transcription* is the process by which the DNA directs the synthesis of mRNA molecules (see Figure 7.1). This is followed by *translation*, which is the process by which the transcribed mature mRNA is translated into a polypeptide. However, only a small proportion of all DNA in cells is ever transcribed. Furthermore, only a small proportion of the mRNA made by transcription is translated into a polypeptide. There are several different reasons why this is the case but it is crucial that only part of the mature mRNA is translated, and hence it is necessary to consider the causal chain effects that go beyond genes coding for some protein product. The first step is the pretranscription phase in which the DNA leads to an mRNA replica that differs from DNA only in the loss of the **promoter region** (i.e., the section that regulates the transcription process (see below).

Various elements influence the series of steps involved in transcription. The process of transcription is influenced by transcription factors that collectively constitute the "promoter." Some of the factors are distant from the genes that they are influencing; they are called *trans*-acting because they have to migrate to the site where they act. In addition, there are other factors that are said to be *cis*-acting because their function is local and limited to the DNA duplex on which they reside. In addition, there are enhancers that, as might be expected by their name, enhance the transcriptional activity

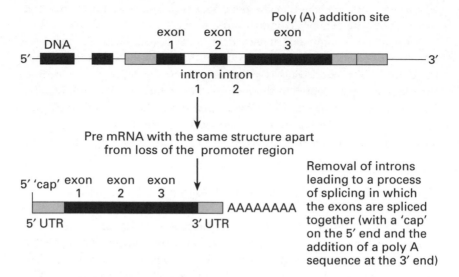

Figure 7.1   Process of transcription.
Source: from McGuffin et al., 2002. Copyright © 2002 by Oxford University Press. Adapted by permission of the publisher.

of specific genes, and silencers that inhibit the transcriptional activity of specific genes. Although, by convention, these various transcriptional factors are not usually termed genes, they are made up of DNA sequences and will be inherited along with the rest of the DNA.

The second transcription phase involves the removal of all the intron segments and the splicing together of the exons to produce a continuous segment of end-to-end exons (see Figure 7.1). Many genes in humans show **alternative splicing** whereby different exon combinations are represented in transcripts from the same gene during RNA processing. The key implication is that this constitutes a way in which the same gene may give rise to multiple different proteins with different effects. Only a small proportion of all the DNA in cells is ever transcribed and not all the transcribed RNA is translated into a polypeptide. These other different types of RNA have other functions – including influences on translation.

Transcription mainly takes place in the nucleus of cells. By contrast, translation (the process by which mRNA specifies the production of poly-peptides) occurs in **ribosome**s, which are large RNA-protein complexes found outside the nucleus in the surrounding cytoplasm, but also in mitochondria. There are the various post-translational modifications that include chemical alteration of some **amino acid**s and polypeptides, each of which can be subjected to post-translational modification. The protein structure is highly varied and not easily predicted from the amino acid sequence.

The conversion of polypeptides to proteins involves the folding of proteins, which is crucial for their effects. The precise mechanisms involved in this folding process are unclear. To a major extent they are driven by genes, but also they are influenced by the environment of the cell and, especially, the confining cell membranes. However, the effects of these proteins are also influenced by the interplay among different protein products. Again, the factors shaping such interplay remain ill-understood. Further down the causal chain, these proteins play a role in the liability to genetically influenced traits; however, in most instances we do not know just how and why they lead to the outcome behaviors. This last set of steps is crucially important for any understanding of how genes might influence behavior but we are only just beginning to appreciate the steps involved. The "central dogma" provides a reasonable enough succinct shorthand summary of how genes "work" but it is not quite as straightforward as that. The message is that the ultimate behavioral outcome of gene action is a complicated process that is systematic and organized in a regular set of steps, but it is not directly determined by the inherited DNA in a single causal cause that can be understood as the gene "for" any psychological characteristic or mental disorder.

The first key message of all that is involved in transcription is that although, traditionally, the main interest has been in the DNA that has a specific codon sequence that codes for a particular protein product specified by the mRNA, numerous other DNA elements play crucial roles. In a real sense, therefore, a single gene effect is actually a consequence of the action of several inherited DNA elements. The second key message is that much of the DNA is not used in the production of proteins; hence it is necessary to consider what else it does. This is discussed further below in relation to so-called "junk DNA."

Gene expression

The complexities do not end there. The DNA content of all cells in the same organism is much the same. What makes the various cell types different (meaning whether or not they are liver cells or brain cells or blood cells) is that only a proportion of the genes in any one cell are significantly "expressed" (meaning that they are functionally activated) and that the pattern of expressed genes varies between different cell types. Accordingly, there have to be features that control this selective activation of specific genes in different tissues.

Basically these are the transcriptional and translational elements noted above, plus **epigenetic** mechanisms involving methylation (see Chapter 10). Some genes, known as housekeeping genes, need to be expressed in all cells because they deal with general functions such as protein synthesis. On the other hand, many genes are expressed only in body tissues or only during a particular developmental phase. It is important that some genes can have different functions in different tissues as a result of tissue-specific promoters or tissue-specific alternative splicing. The implication is that the differential patterns of **gene expression** provide another way in which a single gene can have multiple effects.

A key feature of expression is that is can be altered in a reversible way by extracellular signals. DNA methylation and histone **acetylation** (two linked chemical processes) are involved in the epigenetic mechanisms by which environmental influences can affect gene expression. The process is both dynamic and open to multiple influences. For example, Diamond et al.[2] studied gene expression in mice as it operated in the effects of glucocorticoids (a type of steroid hormone that is much involved in both responses to stress and in social interactions). These hormones regulate a particular gene, proliferin. It was found that two different transcription factors influenced hormone responsiveness, but depending on the pattern of activity of these factors, the effect could be either positive or negative – thus providing a potential mechanism for the influence of stress, via hormones.[3]

At the very early stages in development, both X chromosomes are active but inactivation is initiated as the cells begin to differentiate. It has been shown that there is an X-inactivation center on chromosome 13 that controls the initiation and propagation of X inactivation and an X-controlling element that affects the choice of which X chromosome remains active and which inactivated. In all usual circumstances, it is of no consequence which X chromosome is inactivated, but it does become very important if one of the X chromosomes carries a gene mutation that is associated with some kind of phenotypic abnormality. Thus, for example (as noted in Chapter 6), the rare condition Rett syndrome, which leads to impaired brain growth, mental retardation, epilepsy, and a most characteristic stereotyped hand-wringing mannerism, is due to a mutant gene on the X chromosome. The resulting phenotype varies, however, from this classical pattern to much more atypical, and milder, varieties of phenomena that have some similarities with the full syndrome, but also key differences. It appears that this variation in expression of the phenotype is explicable to a large extent by the pattern of X inactivation.

As implicit in this account of what genes "do," a key feature concerns gene expression. Although DNA starts off the causal chain, what really matters is the expression of the genes (in terms of mRNA). There are no genetic effects without this expression. Unlike the operation of DNA, which is active in all cells, gene expression tends to be specific to particular body tissues and to particular phases of development. The class of mechanisms involved has been called epigenesis. They are distinctive in that they concern heritable states that do not depend on the DNA sequence. In other words, they do not alter the DNA sequence that constitutes the genetic code that is relevant for a particular trait. That is why the mechanisms are called epigenetic rather than genetic. Nevertheless, the genetic changes are potentially heritable, meaning that they could be passed on to the next generation. In most cases, however, this does not happen, because they are canceled. It has been found that the epigenesis involved in influencing gene expression comes about through a chemical process called DNA methylation[4] In Chapter 6, the consequences of epigenetic mechanisms were illustrated by reference to the two best established examples; namely, genomic imprinting and X chromosome inactivation. However, epigenesis is also influenced by environmental features; these are considered further in Chapter 10.

Up to now, there has been little research in humans that has examined the consequences of epigenetic effects, but a study by Petronis et al.[5] indicates the possibilities. They compared the DNA methylation patterns in blood cells of one pair of twins concordant for schizophrenia and one pair discordant, focusing on the promoter region of the dopamine D2 **receptor gene**. This is concerned with neurotransmitter functions thought to be important in schizophrenia. The results showed that the epigenetic patterns were more different in the discordant pair than in the concordant pair. In the case of peripheral blood cells, it is likely that the differences in methylation arose from chance effects rather than environmental influences but the latter will be important in other circumstances. The point of this small study, however, is that it emphasizes the possible importance of differences in gene expression in accounting for differences in outcome among individuals with the same susceptibility genes for some disorder or trait.

It should be added that, although ordinarily both the paternal and maternal alleles are expressed, this is not always the case. This provides the mechanisms for parental imprinting of genes (see Chapter 6). Similarly, X chromosome inactivation involves active repression of gene expression (see Chapter 6).

"Junk" DNA

The traditional concept in molecular biology was that, although DNA provided the starting point for the sequence of processes leading to protein production, it was the proteins that constituted the workhorses that brought about the genetic "action." The implication was that the key to understanding the mechanisms involved in the multistage pathway that ends up with some normal or abnormal phenotypic trait would be heavily dependent on determining what proteins "did," how they interacted with other proteins, and how all of this resulted in some endpoint of interest. That is indeed the case but this view has left behind many puzzles about the role of genes, with many of these puzzles only partly resolved.

Most strikingly, there is the observation that only about 2–3 percent of the DNA gives rise to messenger RNA. That raises the question of what on earth the remaining 97–98 percent of the DNA does? Until relatively recently it was generally dismissed as "junk" DNA that may have had a role in an earlier stage of evolution but no longer had any functional purpose. That assumption is now increasingly being called in doubt.[6] To begin with, it seems that a much higher proportion of the DNA is transcribed than had been originally envisaged. Although protein-coding sequences constitute a small minority of the human genome, a much larger proportion of the genome is in fact expressed, but it is expressed in terms of non-protein-coding transcripts. The issue then is what these expressed RNAs do if they are not making proteins. It seems now that they probably comprise a most important part of the regulatory system. It has been suggested that complex organisms require two rather different levels of programming; the first specifies the functional components of the system (mainly proteins) and the second involves the control of developmental programming and the regulation of transcription. In other words, the non-coding RNAs do seem to have a crucially important role in the transcriptional process. Thus, for example, non-coding RNA plays a key role in X chromosome inactivation and it may well play a role in genomic imprinting (see below and Chapter 6). Perhaps, even more surprisingly, non-coding RNA genes play a crucial role in disease. For example, it has been found that a particular form of short-limbed dwarfism, first identified more than three decades ago, is attributable to a non-coding RNA gene and the same applies to a particular form of their autosomal-dominant skin disease.

A **pseudogene** is a gene copy that does not produce a functional full-length protein. Nevertheless, such genes may be expressed and a recent study by Hirotsune et al.[7] suggests that they may have effects on disease-inducing genes. This was shown in a study of transgenic mice in which mice with the gene suffered from failure to thrive and severe bone deformities. The results showed that the mutated gene was regulated by imprinting. It is not known as yet whether such a mechanism applies in human diseases, but the finding opens up the possibility of a greater role for pseudogenes than used to be considered to be the case.

All of this is too new for there to be any definitive conclusions. However, what is clear already is that genetic influences reflect a much more dynamic process than used to be considered the case and that there are, therefore, many more potential influences that can impinge on the process. DNA is what constitutes the message of the genes but it is DNA expression that leads (indirectly) to the phenotype. Because allelic variations are so many, and because the interplay among genes is much greater than used to be thought, and because epigenetic mechanisms are probably very influential, and because genes probably lead to several protein products and not just one, there is much more scope for a single gene to have multiple diverse actions. But, even more basically, this dynamic process forces one to reconceptualize just what is meant by a gene. These new findings in no way undermine the evidence of the crucial pervasive importance of genes but they do undermine any notion that genes are determinative in a simplistic fashion favored by the genetic evangelists.

Why so few genes have so many effects

One of the findings from the "sequencing the genome" project that was surprising to many people was that the number of genes seemed so small. The exact number remains a bit uncertain but the most recent estimates place it within the range of 20–25,000. That may sound a lot but when you consider that genes have to play a part in the construction and functioning of the whole of the human body and that the workings of the mind, based on the structure and functions of the brain, are so amazingly complex, it does seem rather a few. It could not possibly be the case that there is a gene to determine the actions of each neurone. There are far more neurones than there are genes so that could not conceivably be the case.

Considerations such as these led Ehrlich and Feldman[8] to attack claims regarding the importance of genetic influences on behavior on three main grounds. First, they argued that there are not enough genes to account for the large variation among individuals in an enormous range of behavioral traits. However, that both presupposed specific links between individual genes and individual behaviors (which is a mistaken view) and it completely failed to take into account the importance of the interplay among multiple genes. Second, they argued that it was impossible to separate the influences of genes and environments because of the interplay between them. However, there are reasonable designs that allow an approximate estimate of the relative influence of genes and environments on individual variations in particular populations at particular times (see Chapter 3). They were correct in arguing that even a high heritability does not rule out hugely important environmental effects, but that is accepted by all geneticists. They were also correct in arguing that many behavioral geneticists severely underplay the importance of gene–environment interactions and correlations (see Chapter 9) and they also tended to ignore the epigenetic effects of environmental influences (see Chapter 10). Third, they argued that heritability figures cannot deal with causal processes. That is correct insofar as knowing the proportion of population variance accounted for by genes does not, in any way, indicate how the genes work. However, that is where molecular genetics can be informative (see Chapter 8). It is certainly necessary to move from quantitative genetics to molecular genetics in order to begin to have a research lever for the elucidation of causal processes.

The Ehrlich and Feldman general dismissal of genetic influences is not well based. Nevertheless, the query as to whether humans have "enough" genes to account for all the effects attributed to genes does require an answer.

Several considerations are relevant.[9] To begin with, ordinarily, genes are not determinative. Rather, they work in a probabilistic fashion specifying processes and methods but not determining precise outcomes. This is evident in the whole of biology. For example, it is well known that construction of the brain involves an initial overproduction of neurones followed by a selective pruning in order to provide the fine-tuning required to bring about the right input.[10] In other words, the general pattern is set by the genes, but the expectation is that it gets it only approximately right and that there are equally genetically influenced regulatory processes to correct, as it were, the initial mistakes and to ensure that the final biological product is more or less as it should be.

Yet another feature is that the phenomena of differential tissue-specific gene expression and alternative splicing (see above) mean that each individual gene is able to lead to the production of several different but related proteins. In other words, by this means, there is a greater range of proteins than there is of genes.

It is also clear that, in most cases, genes work in combination. All the genetic findings that are available so far have shown that each individual identified gene actually accounts for only a small proportion of the variance on whatever trait it influences. The implication is that many genes are involved. Sometimes they may work in an additive fashion and sometimes in a synergistic pattern and sometimes requiring particular combinations of genes. However, whatever the details, the fact is that most susceptibility genes have a role in multiple causal pathways.

A related, but somewhat different, point is that each gene expressed in the brain tends to be expressed in multiple locations. Each location subserves a somewhat different function and the consequence is that each gene plays a contributory role in a wider range of functions than might have been thought to be the case.

It is also relevant that what is usually meant by the number of genes is the genes that are involved in the causal sequence that determines the production of proteins. However, this is the misleadingly oversimplified way of thinking about gene action. That is because for each gene of that kind there are several, sometimes many, other genes that serve to influence gene translation, transcription, and expression. What this means is that for each single gene involved in the pathway leading to protein production, there are other genes that will influence what happens. It is clear that that immediately leads to a far greater number of genetic permutations.

Finally, so far as the brain is concerned, it differs from almost all other organs in having the expression of a majority of genes. The effects of genes are brought about by gene expression, and gene expression tends to be both tissue specific and developmental timing specific. Most genes are expressed in only a minority of tissues, presumably because they have such specialized functions. By contrast, at least 60 percent of genes are expressed in the brain. Accordingly, the complexity of the brain is paralleled by it having the influence of a much larger proportion of genes than most other body organs.

Accordingly, although at first sight the argument that there are too few genes seems plausible, the argument is actually mistaken. There is no direct connection between the number of genes and the number of functions they affect – for the reasons already given.

Humans, chimpanzees, mice and fruit flies

Another puzzle has been how to conceptualize the genetic similarities and differences across diverse species.[11] To begin with, there does not seem to be any clear correspondence between the number or size of genes in a genome and the complexity of the species. We come back to the question of whether humans have "enough" genes for the purposes that they are supposed to control. It is interesting in that connection to note that there seems to be a somewhat stronger association between the complexity of an organism and the size of that portion of the gene that does not directly code for proteins. It may be that this functional complexity comes from all these other genes that promote, enhance, and regulate processes leading to gene expression; the focus only on genes leading to proteins is much too narrow.

However, that does not deal with the question about genetic similarity across species. Two rather different sorts of statement tend to be made. On the one hand, there is the well-known statement that monozygotic twins share 100 percent of their segregating genes, whereas dizygotic twins share only 50 percent (see Chapter 3). On the face of it, that statement seems incompatible with the rather different statement that human beings share 98 percent of their genes with chimpanzees. How can people be more similar to chimpanzees than brothers (or non-identical twins) are to each other? The answer is that, although the two statements sound alike, they refer to quite different things.

The 100 percent versus 50 percent contrast is concerned with allelic variations – that is, the particular genetic variant of a specific gene. These are what differ among individuals and that is why they are referred to as segregating genes. It is what the genetic basis of individual differences is all about (through inherited genes that are identical by descent). However, there are lots and lots of genes that all human beings have in common. Thus, there are genes that are concerned with walking upright, being able to develop spoken language, and having a thumb that moves across the palm in such a manner as to allow a grip.

The statement about 98 percent of genetic similarity is concerned with something that is entirely different from the allelic variation concerned with individual differences (which will apply between chimpanzees as well as between humans), and is not quite the same as the statement that there is 100 percent sharing of genes that are essential to what is distinctive about being human. Rather, it is recognizing that not only are there very striking similarities among divergent species in the way that genes work, but that there is a surprisingly high degree of similarity in what specific genes do. It is that similarity that makes it possible to make extensive use of mice in studying genetic effects of one kind or another. That is so despite the fact that mice and human beings are so obviously different in crucially important ways. The similarities do not stop with mice. There are also similarities with fruit flies, which are even more different from us. It has proved very helpful in genetics to be able to move across species in this way. The lessons learned in one species are very often applicable to other species. Nevertheless, there are differences, and such differences may be crucial. Thus, care is always needed when studying the genetic influences on behaviors that are supposed to be comparable in, say, mice and humans. That is most obviously the case, of course, when considering characteristics that involve language, or thought patterns that are obviously not within the repertoire of other species. Thus, it is not likely that one could find a really satisfactory mouse equivalent for disorders such as schizophrenia or autism. On the other hand, it may still be possible to examine in mice the effects of genes that play a part in susceptibility to these disorders because it will often be the case that the genes involved are found in other species.[11]

Conclusions

Seven key points derive from what is known about how genes work. First, genes do not have direct effects on any trait or disorder. The DNA specifies the mRNA which, in turn, specifies the proteins that are produced. The actions of the protein depend on their folding and on their interactions with other proteins. So far, little is known on just how these protein products lead to phenotypes involving behavioral traits or disorders. Second, through several different mechanisms, a single gene can have several quite diverse effects (**pleiotropy**). Third, the processes of transcription and translation involve several different inherited DNA factors. They do not, themselves, code for proteins but they influence the expression of genes that do code for proteins and, thereby, they can have quite important effects of genetic influences. Fourth, the effects of genes are dependent on gene expression, which is often specific to particular body tissues and/or particular phases of development. The process of gene expression is influenced by a range of other DNA factors and by both physical and psychosocial experiences or environments (see Chapter 10). Fifth, as discussed in Chapter 9, some (possibly many) genetic effects operate through effects on both exposure and susceptibility to risk environments. Sixth, although little is known about possible synergistic effects among genes, it is probable that such effects may be important. Seventh, the major similarities in the genetic organization found in different animal species means that much can be learned from their study, as well as from the study of human genetics.

Notes

See Reference list for full details.

1   Kendler, 2005 c
2   Diamond et al., 1990
3   Meaney, 2001
4   Jaenisch & Bird, 2003
5   Petronis et al., 2003
6   Eddy, 2001; Felsenfeld & Groudine, 2003; Gibbs, 2003 a & b; but see Nóbrega et al., 2004. The view that "junk DNA" may actually have an important functional role has been queried by Nóbrega et al. (2004) on the basis of their finding that large-scale deletion of non-coding DNA in mice appeared to have no effects. Clearly the issue is far from settled and it is important to bear in mind that there could be important species differences in the role of genes that do not code for proteins.
7   Hirotsune et al., 2003
8   Ehrlich & Feldman, 2003
9   Marcus, 2004
10 Curtis & Nelson, 2003; Huttenlocher, 2002
11 Marks, 2002

Further reading

Lewin, B. (2004). *Genes VIII*. Upper Saddle River, NJ: Pearson Prentice Hall.
Strachan, T. & Read, A.P. (2004). *Human molecular genetics 3* (3rd ed.). New York & Abingdon, Oxon: Garland Science, Taylor & Francis.

Chapter 8

Finding and understanding specific susceptibility genes

Quantitative genetics is concerned with the basic question of measuring the relative strength of genetic and non-genetic influences on the population variance for particular traits and disorders. The findings are not particularly interesting in terms of the precise quantification of those estimates but they have been extremely useful in using such data as a jumping-off point to examine more interesting and important questions that aid our understanding of the operation of traits and disorders. Molecular genetics is quite different in being concerned, not with the quantification of genetic and environmental influences but, rather, with the completely different task of identifying the actual individual genes that underlie the overall genetic effects.

Linkage designs

The two main research strategies that have been employed are linkage designs and association designs.[1] They work on quite different principles and have very different patterns of strengths and limitations. Linkage strategies basically ask whether there is systematic co-inheritance between a **gene locus** (meaning a particular segment of a chromosome) and the trait being studied. Usually, the focus is on sib pairs both of whom have the trait or disorder that is being studied. However, the same strategy may be applied between a broader range of relative pairs.[2] The method involves a minimum of assumptions. That is, clearly it is necessary that both of the relatives indubitably have the disorder that is being investigated. On the other hand, there is no need to take decisions on uncertain cases; they are simply excluded from the analysis. Statistics then determine whether the extent to which two affected sibs share genetic alleles that are identical by descent exceeds the probability of the sharing that would be expected on the basis of chance alone. The rationale is if there is a significant tendency for the locus to be co-inherited with the trait, then linkage between the two may be inferred. The statistical term used to determine linkage is called a **LOD score** (log odds). By convention, a score of at least +3 is generally regarded as showing significant linkage and one of −2 as excluding linkage. Because such coinheritance will occur by chance alone, rather large samples are needed in order to determine whether or not the linkage exceeds chance levels to a sufficient extent to have confidence that it is real. Accordingly, there has been increasing use of combining samples across different research groups.[3] Compared with association studies (see below), affected sib pair linkage studies are robust to differences in the genetic composition of the study populations. However, it is important to ensure that an adequate number of genetic markers is used to ensure that false negative findings do not result from gaps in genome coverage.

Ordinarily, the procedure involves a scan of the whole genome without the need to focus on any specific regions. Three technological advances have made this a practical proposition (as noted in Chapter 1). First, there was the discovery of thousands of polymorphic genetic markers (meaning markers that varied across individuals in any population). At first, restriction fragment length polymorphisms (RFLP) were used. Since then, however, microsatellites, which comprise repeated units of a single DNA sequence, have become the standard tool. More recently, single nucleotide polymorphisms (SNPs) have provided a further advance.

The second technological development concerned robotic methods of analysis. At first, the identification of genetic markers had to be undertaken by very time-consuming laboratory methods. These have now been replaced by highly efficient automated fluorescence-based systems using robots that can undertake simultaneous analysis of multiple markers. As a consequence, it is now possible to undertake total genome scans of large samples, and to do so relatively quickly. The third development was provided by the **polymerase chain reaction** (**PCR**) that allows sequences of interest to be amplified selectively.

The affected relative design has several very important strengths. As already noted, it does not require any assumptions about mode of inheritance or degree of penetrance and it can focus on traits that can be reliably and validly measured, without the need to take difficult decisions about uncertain cases. The second crucial strength is that the scan of the entire genome can be undertaken with just several hundred genetic markers. That is possible because linkage can be detected with markers that are quite some distance away from the actual susceptibility gene.

Unfortunately, there are two compensatory disadvantages of substantial importance. First, the susceptibility genes must have a relatively strong effect if they are to be detectable with samples that are likely to be feasible with most psychiatric disorders. Thus, a decade ago it was estimated that to detect a susceptibility gene causing a five-fold increase in risk to a first-degree relative would require some 200 sib pairs and that 700 pairs would be needed for one causing a two-fold increase in risk. Given the very high heritability of disorders such as autism, schizophrenia, and bipolar disorder, it might be thought that that should not be a problem because the increase in risk for a first-degree relative, as compared with the general population, is well in excess of five fold. Unfortunately, the overall increase in risk is not the key statistic. That is because what matters is the increase in risk that is attributable to any one susceptibility gene. Because it has been an almost universal finding that the susceptibility genes in multifactorial disorders involve quite a small increase in risk (usually well short of 2-fold, and mostly less than $1^1/_2$ times[4]) the disadvantage of needing huge samples is real. The overall increase in risk is high but it is made up of the effects of multiple genes, not just one. The second disadvantage is that the method can only localize the susceptibility gene to quite a large area. In other words, having shown the likelihood of a locus containing a susceptibility gene, the finding applies to areas that will include a very large number of genes, making the task of identifying the relevant susceptibility gene quite a formidable one.

Nevertheless, at first sight, it might seem reasonably straightforward to confirm a positive finding once evidence of linkage has been found in one sample. It is dispiriting and frustrating, therefore, to realize that the literature is absolutely full of positive findings either that have not been replicated or where the replication is weak and uncertain. Why should that be? After all, if there is a true susceptibility gene that has been localized, why would it not be equally evident in some other sample? There are three main sources of difficulty. It might be thought that once a positive finding has been obtained, a rather smaller sample would be all that is needed to confirm it, because you know what you are looking for. Unfortunately, as it happens, for strong statistical reasons, the samples required to replicate a finding need to be much larger than those acquired with the original observation.[5] Accordingly, many attempted replications may fail because of a lack of statistical power (meaning that the samples were not big enough). Second, even within a single population of relatively homogeneous composition, individuals will vary as to which susceptibility genes have given rise to a disorder in their case. That has been evident even with respect to single-gene disorders where, for example, tuberous sclerosis may be due to a gene on either chromosome 9 or chromosome 16. When dealing with multifactorial disorders involving complex patterns for multiple genes, this problem is multiplied many times. In other words, the situation is one in which genetic heterogeneity must be expected. The third problem is that, when dealing with populations that differ in either their genetic makeup or their life circumstances, or both, the findings may not be the same. For example, for reasons that remain ill-understood, the ApoE-4 gene, which plays a major role in liability to late-onset Alzheimer's disease, carries with it a particularly strong risk effect in Japanese, an intermediate risk in Caucasians, but a much weaker risk in people of African background.[6]

What is the solution? As in the rest of science, the true test lies in replication – that is, different groups of investigators finding substantially the same finding in a different sample. That is far more important than the statistical significance of a finding in any single study. Alternatively, much the same purpose may be served by meta-analyses in which multiple samples are combined in a systematic fashion to see whether the effect holds up when all the evidence is combined.

For many years, psychiatric molecular genetics was mainly made up of strings of unreplicated findings. Fortunately, the tide is beginning to turn in an important way and there is the beginning of findings that have held up under rigorous scrutiny (as discussed below).

Association strategies

The second major research design is provided by **association strategies**. These work on an entirely different principle. Basically they determine whether individuals with a particular trait (or disorder) are more likely than appropriately chosen controls to have some particular genetic allele. In other words, the method is to test whether a particular allele is associated with a trait and not whether it is co-inherited with it. The method has a quite different set of advantages and disadvantages as compared with linkage strategies. The main strength is that it allows the detection of susceptibility genes of relatively small effect, a crucial consideration in the study of multifactorial disorders.[7] The association can arise either when the marker is extremely close to the susceptibility gene or when the marker itself is involved in predisposition to the disease. Given the knowledge that most susceptibilities do indeed have only quite small effects, that is an important advantage. Unfortunately, there are four compensatory disadvantages. The first is that the association can be detected only if the marker is very close indeed to the susceptibility gene. The practical consequence of this consideration is that systematic mapping by association requires a marker map that is some 10–100 times as dense as that needed with the sort of linkage mapping involved in an affected sib-pair design.

Second, because of this need for a huge number of markers, there is a major statistical problem in knowing what threshold to set to statistical significance, particularly as there is no straightforward way to determine the prior probability of association with which the association found in any study needs to be compared.[3] Accordingly, there is a considerable danger of false positive findings.

Third, association can readily arise as a result of what is called **population stratification**. That is to say, population groups frequently differ in allele frequencies for reasons that have nothing whatsoever to do with the disease being studied. Accordingly, if cases and controls are drawn from somewhat different populations, entirely spurious associations may readily be found. There has been considerable discussion in the literature on how serious a problem this is in practice and opinions differ on this point. Nevertheless, there are examples where false findings have arisen from **population stratification**.[8] For example, that seems to have been the case with the claimed association between the dopamine-receptor D2 on chromosome 11 and alcoholism.[9]

The most satisfactory way of dealing with possible stratification biases is to analyze trios of two parents and one affected child. The rationale is that by comparing the proportion of parental alleles that are transmitted and the proportion that are not, association can be detected in a way that is based on three individuals who all have the same population of origin. The first approach of this kind was the haplotype relative risk (HRR) method devised by Falk and Rubinstein[10] but this was largely replaced by the transmission/ disequilibrium test (TDT) because this can detect both linkage and association (provided the parents are heterozygous).[11] Further new methods are also coming to be adopted in order to serve the same purpose.[12]

DNA pooling

Because associations require a far larger set of genetic markers for a genomic screen than is the case with affected sib-pair linkage designs, the resource implications have been formidable. A parallel consideration is that the statistical problems are also considerable. The use of pooled DNA for genomic screening has been put forward as a possible solution.[13] What this involves is putting together the DNA of all members of the sample with the trait under investigation and analyzing this as a single data set, apart from the fact that, of course, parents and offspring need to be dealt with separately in order to deal with stratification biases. The method has various technical difficulties that are still being sorted out but it may prove to be a promising way forward. However, one important limitation is that it necessarily presupposes that any allelic difference will apply to the trait or disorder as a whole, and not to subcomponents. Thus, for example, if the genetic liability to autism involved susceptibility genes some of which were relevant for the language and communication abnormalities, different susceptibility genes for the social interaction problems, and a different set of genes for repetitive and stereotyped behaviors, that would not come out of an analysis in which all cases of autism are combined. The same would apply to any other trait or disorder. At the moment, it simply is not known whether the susceptibility genes do operate on different facets or components of a disorder, but it is certainly a possibility that will have to be considered. Similarly, DNA pooling cannot deal with effects that involve combinations of genes operating at several different loci.[14]

The first three disadvantages of association methods are mainly likely to lead to false positive findings. The fourth disadvantage, by contrast, causes the danger of false negative findings. The comparison of cases and controls works well if the same allele is always associated with the outcome being studied. However, it will not work well if there is substantial allelic heterogeneity – meaning that different allelic variations have effects in different populations. It is known already that that is unfortunately often the case.

Quantitative trait loci (QTL) studies

A further development that may be advantageous is the extension of both linkage and association methods to the study of continuous variables, for which the relevant susceptibility genes have come to be termed quantitative trait loci (QTL).[15] The reasons for developing QTL approaches are conceptual, empirical, and statistical.

The conceptual reason is that many psychiatric disorders seem to represent quantitative, rather than qualitative, departures from normality. This is an issue already discussed in Chapter 2, but with respect to the definition of a phenotype. In addition, however, even when a disorder represents a qualitatively distinct category because of its severity and need for treatment, it may still be based on continuously distributed dimensional risk factors. Thus, for example, myocardial infarctions (heart attacks) clearly represent a qualitatively distinct category because they involve structural damage to the heart and indeed often result in death. On the other hand, it is most unlikely that there will be a gene for heart attacks as such. Rather, the genetic influences are much more likely to apply to continuously distributed dimensions such as cholesterol level, blood-clotting tendencies, raised blood pressure, and so forth. Exactly the same consideration probably applies to many mental disorders.

The empirical reason suggesting the value of QTL approaches is that the genetic findings indicate that some disorders are mediated through a temperamental trait. For example, that applies to the role of neuroticism in the liability to generalized anxiety and depressive disorders.[16]

The statistical reason favoring a QTL approach is that, in general, the analysis of continuous variables provides greater statistical power than the analysis of categorical ones. Of course, that advantage is crucially dependent on the validity of the basic assumption of a dimensional liability and on the availability of a reliable and valid measure of the dimension. For example, there are continuing efforts to devise appropriate dimensional measures of the problems in reciprocal social interaction that characterize autism. As discussed in Chapter 4, that there is good evidence of the existence of a valid concept of a broader phenotype but it remains uncertain how far that extends into normality and we have not yet got really satisfactory ways of differentiating social difficulties of an autistic type from, say, the social difficulties associated with schizophrenia or antisocial behavior or social anxiety. Nonetheless, the problem is intrinsically soluble and, once appropriate reliable validated measures have been devised, QTL approaches may come into their own.

The rationale for linkage and association methods as applied to QTLs is basically the same as that applied to categories but the details are different in one crucial respect. That is, the optimal design for a QTL **sib-pair linkage study** is to use pairs of sibs that are extremely *discordant* for the trait, rather than pairs in which both sibs are affected.[17] The method seems to have had some success in the realm of reading disabilities (see below) but it is, as yet, too early to know how far this approach will pay off in a broader range of mental disorders.

Haplotype methods

Haplotypes are sets of closely linked genetic markers present on a single chromosome that tend to be inherited together; that is, they are not easily separable by the recombination that takes place as a result of inheritance. It has been suggested that genetic susceptibility may be indexed more solidly through haplotypes than through single genetic alleles and that case–control differences in association studies may be easier to detect.[18] The pros and cons of haplotype methods have still to be sorted out but it is clear that the dangers of false positive findings are particularly great.

Some methodological hazards with respect to all molecular genetic studies

As noted above, there is a long history of failed replications in the search for susceptibility genes for multifactorial traits and disorders. There are numerous reasons why this has proved such a difficult field of investigation. To begin with, it is necessary to consider the possibility of genotyping errors. There is a tendency to assume that laboratory measures are always reliable and valid, but that is not a safe assumption. The few studies of genotyping errors have shown that the error rate is by no means trivial, and modeling has shown that these can lead to a surprisingly high, and troubling, frequency of false findings on a commonly used test (the haplotype-sharing TDT).[19] With respect to linkage studies, Cardon[20] showed that an error rate of only 0.5 percent would result in a drop in the LOD score in 1,000 sibling pairs from 3.0 to about 2 and a 1 percent error rate would result in a drop of more than half. At an error rate of 2 percent, a true genetic locus would almost certainly escape detection.

A second problem concerns statistical power. As already noted, replications always require much larger samples than the original positive study[5] and it is obvious that many investigations involve samples that are much too small. One solution is provided by the combining of multiple samples through some form of meta-analysis.

A third problem stems from genetic heterogeneity. As discussed above, this is the usual situation. Not only may several different genes, or multiple alleles of the same gene, lead to the same trait, but which ones do so may vary geographically.

A further consideration concerns the possibility that the traits being investigated have been conceptualized or measured in different ways in the various studies.

Lastly, the field of molecular genetics has been bedeviled by unwarranted claims that some particular method is the *only* acceptable research strategy and, moreover, that it will solve all the key problems. Spence et al.[21] cautioned against the acceptance of these myths, or "pseudo-facts," and urged the need to retain a healthy skepticism regarding the claims of experts, to encourage innovation, and to recognize the value of multiple complementary research strategies.

Despite these, and other, methodological hazards it remains the case, as it is throughout science, that there can be confidence in any finding only when it has been confirmed by other researchers using independent samples. Accordingly, in the summaries of findings that follow, emphasis is placed on results that have been confirmed. However, even this is not sufficient on its own. Findings have real meaning only when the protein products of genes have been identified and, preferably, with demonstrations in animal models that there are effects on a phenotype that seems likely to provide a parallel to what is found in humans. These are tough requirements and it is only quite recently that they are beginning to be met.

Single-gene disorders

In the early days of the application of molecular genetics to the study of psychiatric disorders, the usual expectation was that a substantial proportion of psychiatric disorders would prove to be due to a single major gene exhibiting Mendelian inheritance. That always seemed an implausible assumption[22] and it has now become accepted that the research strategies that were applicable in the case of single-gene disorders need considerable modification when applied to the inheritance of multifactorial disorders, which represent nearly all psychiatric conditions. Nevertheless, there are a few instances of mental disorders that are due to a single gene. Accordingly, it may be instructive to consider them before turning to the much more frequent situation of multifactorial disorders.

Rett syndrome

Rett syndrome first came to general notice as a result of an important paper by Hagberg et al.[23] reporting a series of cases, although the condition had actually been described in 1966 in a German paper that was rather neglected. Rett syndrome is a most unusual condition because it almost always occurs in girls, and it rarely runs in families. The babies appear normal at birth but at some point, usually between the ages of 6 and 18 months, there is a marked reduction in head growth, a progressive loss of purposive hand movements, a diminution in social engagement (which at first seemed to bear some resemblance to autism), and the development of stereotyped movements – particularly a very characteristic hand-washing movement and bouts of over-breathing. There is marked intellectual impairment followed by loss of muscle power (of variable degree) and the development of epileptic attacks. Although the great majority of cases of Rett syndrome are sporadic, arising anew without a family history, there are occasional familial cases. Careful analysis of four families in which this was the case led Huda Zoghbi and her colleagues to focus their search for the relevant gene on the X chromosome. Their search was successful and a paper announcing the finding was published in 1999.[24] Other investigators quickly confirmed the finding and it was also shown that the same abnormal gene was responsible for the sporadic cases, as well as the familial ones. The next need was to determine the actions of the gene and the process by which it led to this particular disease manifestation. Successful animal models that closely mimicked the human condition were developed and these were important in showing how the gene knocked out a key biological function.[25]

As is the way in science, this crucial discovery led on to a further set of questions. Thus, one query was whether this was truly a wholly genetic condition that was not in any way contingent on interplay with environmental hazards. The animal models were instructive in showing that, provided the knockout was complete, the syndrome invariably resulted. That was consistent, too, with the human findings. On the other hand, there were occasional instances of women who had to have the genetic mutation because they had passed it on to their children but who nevertheless did not seem to have the usual manifestations of Rett syndrome themselves. The answer was found to lie in X inactivation. That is to say, ordinarily, in all females, one of the X chromosomes is inactivated or shut off (see Chapters 6 and 7). It turned out that these apparently unaffected women were ones in whom most of the inactivated X chromosomes were the ones carrying the mutation, leaving a high proportion of normal X chromosomes. Subsequent research has shown that variations in the severity of the clinical condition are explicable, to a large extent, by the pattern of X inactivation. That was associated with an appreciation that, although the genetic mutation usually led to the very characteristic severe neuropsychiatric condition, there were many more atypical varieties than had at first been appreciated.[26] Thus, in some instances, the syndrome would look like more ordinary varieties of mental retardation and occasionally it looked like autism. The question then arises as to whether the findings in this rare and unusual condition might have a broader relevance for other disorders. The answer to that question is not yet clear but the possibility needs to be further studied. Molecular genetic studies of large samples of individuals with an autism spectrum disorder have shown that very few have the genetic mutation leading to Rett syndrome, but that does not necessarily mean that there may not be similarities in the causal mechanisms.[27]

Early-onset, autosomal-dominant Alzheimer's disease

Although typically Alzheimer's is a disease of extreme old age, it has been known for a long time that it can have an onset in much earlier life – in the 40s or 50s or early 60s. These rare early-onset varieties include cases showing an autosomal dominant pattern – meaning that they are wholly genetic, single-gene disorders following a particular pattern of inheritance.[28]

The researchers, in this case, focused their search for the relevant pathological gene on ones that are connected with the pathophysiological processes that are involved in the disease. However, there was also another clue and that is the observation that individuals with Down syndrome have a much increased rate of Alzheimer's disease. The clue here is provided by the knowledge that Down syndrome is associated with an abnormality on chromosome 21. In the event, three genes have now been identified: an amyloid precursor protein gene on chromosome 21 and two presenilin genes, one on chromosome 14 and one on chromosome 1. These are indeed genes that affect the pathophysiological processes involved in Alzheimer's disease. As with Rett syndrome, this was confirmed by transgenic mouse models. In other words, when mice with the relevant genetic mutation were created, they showed some of the relevant pathological effects. As with Rett syndrome, the next question was whether these genes might also be responsible for the much more common multifactorial variety of the disease that affects such a high proportion of the population in extreme old age. It has been found that they do not, but, nevertheless, because the brain pathology of the rare early-onset variety of Alzheimer's disease seems to be so comparable to the much more frequent late-onset variety, it probably is relevant that the general message with respect to the underlying pathophysiological processes applies to the late-onset, as well as the early-onset, varieties.

It should be noted that, even with wholly genetic disorders, it is usual to find that the diseases are caused by more than one gene mutation. Thus, tuberous sclerosis, a neurological condition that is often associated with psychiatric problems, is known to be due to a mutation that can be on either chromosome 9 or chromosome 16. The clinical picture seems very similar regardless of which mutation is present. Because one of the psychiatric complications is the development of an autism spectrum disorder,[29] researchers wondered whether this meant that the susceptibility genes might be located on either chromosome 9 or chromosome 16. On the evidence available so far, that seems not to be the case. That is probably because the development of autism is a consequence, not of the gene location, but rather of the effects of tuberous sclerosis on the brain. Thus, it has been found that the development of autism usually arises in tuberous sclerosis only if the tubers (the abnormality that characterizes the disease) are found in the temporal lobes of the brain, if the individuals show mental retardation, and if there is the early onset of epileptic seizures.[30] Accordingly, in the case of tuberous sclerosis, the location of the genes probably will not prove to be useful to the search for susceptibility genes for autism spectrum disorders, but they might have been helpful.

Multifactorial disorders

Alzheimer's disease

The findings from studies of the rare autosomal dominant, early-onset type of Alzheimer's disease (see above) are of interest, not because they account for many cases of Alzheimer's disease (which they do not), but because they are illuminating with respect to the hypothesis that amyloid deposition is part of the cause of Alzheimer's disease. That it does contribute to an understanding of the basic causation is also suggested by the evidence from transgenic mouse models. They do not exactly parallel what is seen in humans but they are supportive in tying the brain changes to the adverse effects on memory. These three genes do not seem to play any role in susceptibility to the very much more common variety of later-onset Alzheimer's disease. On the other hand, so far as is known, the basic brain changes in the two varieties of Alzheimer's disease are pretty much the same and so the findings do contribute to an understanding of the later-onset variety.

So far as late-onset Alzheimer's is concerned, it is not directly genetically determined in the way that the early-onset type is. Rather, it is a multifactorially determined disorder in which genes play an important, but contributory, role. In 1993 it was found that a gene associated with lipid metabolism was associated with late-onset Alzheimer's disease.[31] Specifically, a particular gene variation (ApoE-4) is associated with a much increased risk. This association has now been confirmed many times over by other investigators. However, for reasons that are not well understood, the risk effect of the ApoE-4 variant differs by ethnicity – being particularly strong in Japanese and much weaker in African Americans.[6] Exactly how the ApoE-4 influences the development of Alzheimer's disease is not known, but it does appear likely that it is implicated in the process leading to the brain changes. Interestingly, the ApoE-4 seems to be associated with an increased risk of poor recovery from a variety of forms of injury to the brain.[32] In other words, the genetic risk seems to involve non-specific adverse responses to brain injury, and not just a particular form of dementia.[33]

In addition, the ApoE4 has been associated with the process of cognitive decline in normal ageing and in altered magnetic resonance imaging in asymptomatic individuals.[34] In other words, despite the well-demonstrated risk effect with respect to Alzheimer's disease, it is probably not really best conceptualized as a susceptibility gene for that disease as such. For that, and other, reasons there is no acceptable role for ApoE4 genotyping in risk assessment for Alzheimer's disease.[35] There would be far too many misleading findings for this to be acceptable.

Schizophrenia

For a long time, progress was slow in identifying susceptibility genes for schizophrenia, but there are now replicated findings with respect to the neuroregulin 1 gene, and the dysbindin gene, and possibly for a particular gene protein regulator gene (RGS-4) and possibly a gene for catechol-O-methyl transferase (COMT).[36] Moreover, there is a relevant transgenic mouse phenotype for three of these. In addition, there are several other genes that may be associated with schizophrenia but for which the evidence is less solid as yet. In each case, the identified genes account for quite a small proportion of the variance in the liability to schizophrenia and there are remaining queries about some of the findings. Nevertheless, it now seems very likely that the findings will hold up.[37] What is interesting and important about the findings is that the evidence indicates that the genes are involved in neurotransmitters that are thought to play a role in the causation of schizophrenia. It is the promise that the genetic findings will be informative about the biochemical pathways and the molecular mechanisms that make the findings so important. Two additional points, however, need to be made. For a long time, schizophrenia was thought to be an entirely distinct condition that had nothing to do with bipolar affective disorders. The evidence now is beginning to point to the likelihood that there may be overlap in the genetic liability for these two serious conditions.[38] The differences between the two conditions may come about through the stronger association with neurodevelopmental abnormalities in the case of schizophrenia and, possibly, the difference between the two disorders with respect to environmental influences.

Attention deficit disorder with hyperactivity

The evidence from twin studies that there is a strong genetic influence on ADHD (see Chapter 5), together with the usually beneficial response to stimulants, has encouraged the search for susceptibility genes that are implicated in some way in the dopaminergic neurotransmitter system. There is now replicated evidence from both association and linkage studies that two genes probably provide an increased susceptibility for ADHD.[39] They are DRD4 (a dopamine receptor gene) and DAT-1 (a dopamine transporter gene). The first genome-wide scan that was published[40] was negative for both genes, but the replications and the meta-analysis (i.e., the statistical bringing together of findings from multiple studies) indicate that the findings were probably solid. Two further whole genome scans[41] have suggested that there may be gene loci on chromosomes 16, 17, 5, 7, and 9, but the findings of the two scans did not agree well with each other. A joint association analysis of multiple samples showed a significant, but weak, association with a microsatellite near to the DRD5 gene; this seemed to apply only to the predominantly inattentive and combined types of ADHD – i.e., *not* the predominantly hyperactive/impulsive.

The findings appear promising, but several points need to be made. To begin with, the genetic variants account for quite a small proportion of the population variations in the liability to develop ADHD. Second, the genes are associated, not only with ADHD, but with addictive behavior and with various personality features.[42] Most particularly, the gene loci suggest that there may be a partially shared genetic liability with reading disability and with autism spectrum disorders. Third, the precise role of these genes in the causal pathways leading to disorder has yet to be delineated. Castellanos and Tannock[43] have suggested that the limited experimental evidence available indicates that ADHD may reflect cognitive deficits associated with the dopaminergic system and that this may constitute the route by which genetic influences operate. The suggestion is plausible and warrants further exploration but it has yet to be tested in rigorous fashion.

Dyslexia (specific reading disability)

Dyslexia was one of the first psychological features for which a gene location was identified – by Smith and colleagues.[44] There are now similar findings from several different research groups in both Europe and North America, with positive findings at some 6 different gene locations. For some 20 years there was frustration that this did not lead to actual identification of any specific susceptibility gene, but the situation may now be changing. A study from Colorado[45] showed that the QTL on chromosome 6 was more strongly linked to dyslexia when IQ was above average; in these circumstances the QTL appeared to influence a wide range of components involved in reading. A larger-scale association analysis of two sibling samples in the UK together with twin-based sibships in Colorado[46] showed a QTL risk haplotype on chromosome 6, occurring in about 12 percent of the sample, that influences a broad range of reading-related cognitive abilities (particularly in the severe range) but which had no significant impact on IQ. Interestingly, the haplotype was not distinguished by any protein-coding polymorphisms (i.e., gene variants) and it may be, therefore, that the functional effects of the haplotype concern gene expression.

Autism spectrum disorders

The situation with respect to susceptibility genes for autism spectrum disorders is at about the same stage as with dyslexia. That is, there are replicated findings of likely gene locations on several different chromosomes, but the actual genes themselves have yet to be identified.[47] There are findings that may identify particular genes that play a part in the causation of autism[48] but they have yet to be confirmed. Potentially, they are of interest in that, in one case, the gene is involved with cerebellar development (as shown by mouse studies) and, in the other case, the gene is involved in the production of ATP that is thought to be involved in the functioning of brain cells.[49] In both cases, the genes regulate the function of other genes rather than bringing about function or dysfunction directly themselves.

Specific developmental disorders of language

Specific developmental disorders of speech/language concern delays in the growth of language skills when development is proceeding normally in other respects and when there is no obvious explanatory factor for the language delay (such as hearing loss, global mental retardation, or some acquired neurological disorder).[50] There is the practical problem of differentiating these disorders from normal variations in the timing of language acquisition. However, that there are clinically significant disorders is clear from the evidence from long-term follow-up studies showing the substantial deficits that frequently persist into adult life.[51] Nevertheless, although the disorders are described as "specific," the evidence indicates that, at least with the more severe developmental disorders, the deficits in psychological functioning extend beyond language. Also, it is clear that this is not a single disorder. In particular, it seems important to differentiate between disorders that involve only the production of spoken language and those that also involve the child's understanding of spoken language. In addition, there is an important sub-group of disorders where the main problem is the child's ability in contextualizing language usage. In this group, the problem lies less in the use of the words as such, but rather in terms of problems in social communication.

The first major genetic breakthrough concerned a most unusual family in which there were multiple examples of a severe and uncommon form of speech/language disorder associated with problems in pronunciation and with poor coordination of tongue and face.[52] Inheritance in this case seemed to follow an autosomal-dominant mode of transmission and it was found that a mutation of a Fox protein gene (labeled *FOX-P2*) was responsible. It seems likely that the disorder in this family resulted in a lack of sufficient functional protein at a key stage in fetal brain development. For obvious reasons, there was a lot of interest as to whether this gene might be more broadly responsible for specific developmental language disorders, or indeed for autism. In the event, early research showed that it was not. Rather, a genome-wide scan indicated highly significant linkage with loci in particular regions of chromosomes 16 and 19.[53] What is particularly interesting is that the linkage on chromosome 16 also applied to three reading-related measures, suggesting that there may be a partially shared genetic liability between specific language impairment and reading – a finding in keeping with the epidemiological evidence on the connections between the two. As yet, the genes themselves have not been identified.

Personality features

In 1996 there were two studies showing, for the first time, an association between a specific genetic variant and a personality trait; these concerned the dopamine D-4 receptor gene and novelty seeking. Since the first reports,[54] some investigations have confirmed the association and some have failed to do so. This inconsistent mixture of findings is typical of molecular genetic studies dealing with quite small effects on multifactorial traits. Nevertheless, the finding may still be valid and meaningful.[55] What is also characteristic is that the findings apply not just to the sensation-seeking trait but to ADHD and addictive behavior. In the same year (1996) there was also a report of an association between the serotonin transporter promoter region affecting transcription of that gene and emotionality or neuroticism.[56] Again, this was followed by an inconsistent mixture of confirmations and failures to replicate. However, this may well be because the effect of the gene is dependent upon interaction with environmental risk factors[57] – see Chapter 9. A more surprising finding may be the association reported between the DRD4 gene and disorganized attachment.[58] It is surprising because this feature in young children has been associated with risk factors in the rearing environment. A different research group[59] failed to replicate the finding. Uncertainty arises from the fact that a further study by the Lakatos group failed to show the effect on disorganized attachment, although it did show a significant non-transmission of the relevant allele in relation to secure attachment[60] – the supposedly normal variety of attachment behavior. It is too early at this stage to know whether the finding will hold up and, equally, it remains uncertain whether or not the genetic effect is dependent upon interaction with some sort of risk environment. Other findings on genes relevant for neurotransmitters and various personality features provide other promising leads.[55] However, apart from the serotonin transporter gene finding, doubts remain because a meta-analysis failed to show significant effects.[61] In principle, the genetic effects on personality features are likely to be of importance in relation to risks for mental disorder but the findings to date remain rather uncertain and account for a tiny proportion of the individual variations on the traits being studied. It may well be that future progress will be dependent on a better understanding of gene–gene and gene–environment interactions.

Substance misuse

The best established genetic influence on substance misuse is provided by the finding that a gene concerned with alcohol metabolism plays a major role in variations in risk of alcoholism in people of Chinese and Japanese origin.[62] A particular mutation in the gene for aldehyde dehyrodenase (*ALDH-2*) leads people with this mutation to have a very characteristic and unpleasant flushing response after ingestion of alcohol. Individuals with this gene have a very low risk of becoming alcohol dependent. This gene does not seem to be found in individuals of purely European ancestry and therefore it is not contributory to the genetic risk of alcohol dependence in European origin populations. However, the mechanisms are more generally applicable in terms of the implications. To begin with, this is an example of a mutation that provides a protective effect and not a risk effect.

It is important to appreciate that genes may be involved with either protection or risk. For example, in the field of cancer, disease is influenced by the absence of genes that suppress the development of cancer, as well as by genes that lead to cancer. It is also noteworthy that the genetic effects seem to interact with environmental influences. Thus, Japanese women without the flushing response are much less likely than men to become alcoholic because of the heavy social pressures on Japanese men to drink together, in contrast to the non-acceptance of this pattern in women. A further interesting feature is that genetic effect seems to vary by the stage in the process leading to alcohol dependence. Thus, individuals with the mutation associated with a flushing response are much less likely than other people to consume large quantities of alcohol (because the effect is so unpleasant) but among those who do drink heavily, the mutation is associated with an increased (rather than a decreased) risk of medical complications.[62]

There have been many studies trying to identify genes implicated in alcohol dependence in non-Asian populations and there is probable evidence of linkage with respect to particular regions on chromosomes 4 and 11.[63] However, the actual susceptibility genes have yet to be clearly identified, although they are certainly likely to be found.

It makes sense to suppose the genetic influences might operate through effects on the ways in which individuals metabolize and respond to particular drugs (whether they be nicotine, alcohol, or cocaine). Animal models of substance misuse have similarly focused on sensitivity to specific drugs.[64] However, it is extremely unlikely that sensitivity to specific drugs will prove to be the whole story. That is because most people with a drug problem take multiple drugs and not just one. Accordingly, it will be important in looking to susceptibility genes that focus on risk taking and other more general features, not just on response to specific drugs. That is where studies of personality features are potentially relevant.[55]

Social bonding

There are no confirmed findings of susceptibility genes for social bonding or for parenting in humans. However, animal studies have provided import-ant leads. Tom Insel and his colleagues used the interesting strategy of comparing montane voles, which are polygamous, and prairie voles, which are monogamous.[65] They showed that the key difference between the two lay in the pattern of gene expression (see Chapter 7) in the molecular receptors for oxytocin and vasopressin. They went on to knock out the oxytocin gene of mice before birth and found that this led to an inability to remember other animals; an inability that could be reversed by hormone injections into the appropriate part of the brain in adult life. The genetic differences lay in the promoters of the genes for hormone receptivity and not in the genes themselves, and even within prairie voles there was individual variation in the relevant genetic promoters. Of course, key questions remain about the applicability of this to selective attachments and couple bonding in humans and it is quite uncertain whether individual differences in the ability to acquire social memories has anything to do with social behavior in humans. Nevertheless, the research was highly innovative in moving well beyond molecular genetic differences related to social bonding to the identification of one of the possible mediating mechanisms involved. The research indic-ates one of the ways in which genetic research needs to proceed to the understanding of the biological underpinning of the effects on behavior (a topic discussed further in Chapter 9).

Pharmacogenetics

A consistent finding with respect to almost all medical treatments is that, even with the most effective drugs, there is substantial individual variation in response – both with respect to beneficial effects and also adverse side effects. During the past decade, there have been many molecular genetic studies testing for the effects of specific genes on this individual variability in response.[66] Basically, the genes involved may be concerned with either the metabolism of the drugs (which is very relevant to considerations of the desirable dosage) or the effects of the drugs on particular neurotransmitters of relevance to mental disorders (with implications for which drug may be most appropriate for an individual patient). The potential, therefore, lies in the possibility of individualizing treatment in a way that has not been possible up to now. There are some replicated findings in this field (particularly with respect to the metabolism of the drugs) but the evidence is only just beginning to approach the stage when it may be applied in clinical practice.[67]

Endophenotypes

The early molecular genetics research in the field of mental disorders assumed that the genes would act on the liability for specific psychiatric categories. As we have seen, that simplistic assumption has had to be modified. It is more likely that genes will influence biochemical pathways that play a role in the causal mechanisms leading to mental disorder. Hence, the interest in genes that appear to be implicated in neurotransmitter functions. Some psychiatric geneticists have argued that it might be helpful for molecular genetics research to focus on "endophenotypes."[68] This is a term that is used to apply to specific functions that are thought to be closer than diagnoses to genetic effects, but which are part of the liability for some diagnostic category. Possible endophenotypes include specific cognitive, or specific physiological, functions. The suggestion is a useful one, but it is too early to know how helpful it will prove to be in practice.

Conclusions from molecular genetic studies

It is all too tempting to conclude that once there is a solid confirmed finding on a gene that is associated with some behavioral trait or disorder, then that gene is necessarily involved with the cause of that feature. In a sense, that is probably correct, but the connections may be both less specific and more indirect than they seem at first sight. It is necessary to keep firmly in mind that genes do not code for any particular behavior[4]; rather, they code for specific polypeptides, which provide the basis for proteins which are the chemical products that have possible effects on the pathways leading to a behavioral characteristic of mental disorder (see Chapter 7). The identification of individual susceptibility genes constitutes an essential step in what is needed to gain an understanding of the causal pathways and, therefore, the positive findings that are now beginning to appear and to be confirmed will be hugely helpful. It is appropriate to be enthusiastic about both the achievements and their potential, but five cautions are necessary. First, the genes may code for some polypeptide that is indirectly relevant but yet not involved in the main causal chain. Second, not only are multiple genes affecting proteins involved, but also there are multiple genetic elements that influence the operation of any single gene affecting proteins (see Chapter 7). Third, there are environmental influences on gene expression – the key process that determines the functional operation of genes (see Chapter 10). Fourth, some genetic effects are contingent on an interaction with specific environmental features (see Chapter 9), so that any understanding of the causal pathway must incorporate identification of the mechanisms underlying that interplay. Fifth, even after the main genetic pathway has been fully identified, there will be influences operating on the pathway to the behavior or disorder that involve thought processes.[69] Of course, they too will be subject to genetic influence but their understanding will depend on much more on that of cell chemistry.

Notes

See Reference list for full details.
 1 Freimer & Sabatti, 2004; McGuffin et al., 2002; Plomin et al., 2003; Rutter et al., 1999 a
 2 Davis et al., 1996
 3 Freimer & Sabatti, 2004
 4 Kendler, 2005 c
 5 Suarez et al., 1994
 6 Farrer et al., 1997
 7 Risch & Merikangas, 1996
 8 Ardlie et al., 2002; Cardon & Palmer, 2003; Hirschorn & Daly, 2005
 9 Kidd et al., 1996
10 Falk & Rubinstein, 1987
11 Spielman & Ewens, 1996
12 Hirschorn & Daly, 2005; Wang et al., 2005
13 Barcellos et al., 1997; Daniels et al., 1998
14 Hirschorn & Daly, 2005; Sham, 2003; Wang et al., 2005
15 Plomin et al., 1994, 2001
16 Kendler, 1996
17 Eaves & Meyer, 1994; Fulker & Cherny, 1996; Risch & Zhang, 1995
18 Sham, 2003
19 Cardon, 2003; Knapp & Becker, 2004
20 Cardon, 2003
21 Spence et al., 2003
22 Rutter, 1994
23 Hagberg et al., 1983
24 Amir et al., 1999
25 Shahbazian et al., 2002; Guy et al., 2001

26   Shahbazian & Zoghbi, 2001

27   Zoghbi, 2003

28   Liddell et al., 2002

29   Smalley, 1998

30   Bolton et al., 2002

31   Strittmatter et al., 1993

32   Saunders, 2000

33   Freimer & Sabatti, 2004; Liddell et al., 2002

34   Bretsky et al., 2003; Small et al., 2000

35   Scourfield & Owen, 2002

36   Glatt et al., 2003

37   Elkin et al., 2004; Harrison & Owen, 2003; O'Donovan, Williams & Owen, 2003

38   Badner & Gershon, 2002; Cardno et al., 2002; Levinson et al., 2003; Hattori et al., 2003

39   Asherson et al., 2004; Faroane et al., 2001; Thapar, 2002

40   Fisher et al., 2002

41   Bakker et al., 2003; Ogdie et al., 2003

42   Reif & Lesch, 2003

43   Castellanos & Tannock, 2002

44   Smith et al., 1983

45   Knopik et al., 2002

46   Francks et al., 2004

47   Folstein & Rosen-Sheidley, 2001; Rutter, 2005 d

48   Gharani et al., 2004; Ramoz et al., 2004

49   Ramoz et al., 2004

50   Bishop, 2001; Bishop, 2002 a, b

51   Howlin et al., 2000; Clegg et al., 2005

52   Fisher, 2003

53   SLI Consortium, 2004

54   Ebstein et al., 2003

55   Reif & Lesch, 2003

56   Lesch et al., 1996

57   Caspi et al., 2003

58   Lakatos et al., 2002

59   Bakermans-Kranenburg & van IJzendoorn, 2004

60   Gervai et al., 2005

61   Munafò et al., 2003

62   Heath et al., 2003

63   Ball & Collier, 2002

64   Crabbe, 2003

65   Insel & Young, 2001; Young, 2003; Young et al., 1999

66   Kerwin & Arranz, 2002; Aitchison & Gill, 2003

67   Nnadi et al., 2005

68   Gottesman & Gould, 2003

69   Kendler, 2005 b

Further reading

Freimer, N., & Sabatti, C. (2004). The use of pedigree, sib-pair and association studies of common diseases for genetic mapping and epidemiology. *Nature Genetics*, *36*, 1045–1051.

McGuffin, P., Owen, M.J., & Gottesman, I.I. (Eds.) (2002). *Psychiatric genetics and genomics*. Oxford: Oxford University Press.

Plomin, R., DeFries, J.C., Craig, I.W., & McGuffin, P. (Eds.) (2003). *Behavioral genetics in the postgenomic era*. Washington, DC: American Psychological Association.

Wang, W.Y., Barratt, B.J., Clayton, D.G., & Todd, J.A. (2005). Genome-wide association studies: Theoretical and practical concerns. *Nature Reviews – Genetics*, *6*, 109–118.

Chapter 9

Gene–environment interplay

At least as viewed by non-geneticists, the old-fashioned view tended to consider genes as if there were a relatively direct connection between a particular genetic mutation and development of some undesirable condition or trait. Even with single-gene disorders wholly attributable to a genetic mutation, this was always an oversimplification. As discussed in Chapter 7, the operation of genes is a complex dynamic process in which the outcomes are affected by a range of background genes and by non-coding parts of the genome that do not produce proteins. There is a surprising degree of variability in the expression of even these single-gene disorders, as we have already noted in Chapter 4. Phenotypic effects are dependent not just on the inherited DNA but also on the timing and pattern of genetic expression in specific tissues of the body (see Chapter 7). Such expression can be influenced by environmental experiences in a manner that can have profound and lasting effects on function (discussed in Chapter 10). These epigenetic effects do not change the basic DNA sequence but they do alter its expression and, hence, its effects. However, in this chapter, attention is turned to a broader range of different kinds of gene–environment interplay.

Concepts of interplay and interaction

Before considering the research findings on gene–environment interplay, it is necessary to note that the terms "interplay" and "interaction" have been used in several quite different ways, with much resulting confusion and pointless controversy. Some scientists have criticized all behavioral genetics attempts to quantify the separate effects of genes and environment on the grounds that both are necessarily involved in all effects.[1] They rightly point out that genetic influences have to operate in some environmental context and, therefore, that the very notion of a genetic effect that is entirely independent of the environment is a nonsense. By the same token, environments have to impinge on an organism, and the make-up of the organism is bound to be influenced by genetic effects on organismic characteristics. As we saw in Chapter 3, behavioral geneticists accept these points, and are well aware that heritability estimates are necessarily specific to particular populations at a particular time in history. Nevertheless, within that crucial constraint, it is possible, and meaningful, to quantify the strength of genetic influences on individual differences with respect to psychological characteristics or mental disorder as they occur in the populations studied. Some key findings on the results of twin, adoptee, and family studies seeking to partial (separate) and quantify the relative strength of genetic (G) and environmental (E) influences on the population variance of selected important traits were discussed in Chapter 4.

Nevertheless, a word of caution is required in view of the evidence that inbred strains of animals (with, therefore, specific differing genotypes) may show behavioral differences as a result of either differences in the background of other genes[2] or laboratory conditions[3] or of strain differences in experiences.[4] Thus, in one study it was found that a period of food shortage altered genetic strain differences in response to stimulant drugs. The implication is that both gene–gene and gene–environment interactions may be influential.

Given that there are both genetic and environmental effects, the next question is whether the effects of the one are independent of the other in the sense that the impact of genes is not contingent on there being a particular environmental context; and that the impact of the environment is not dependent on the presence of a particular genetic susceptibility. When that is the case, the effect is said to be "additive," meaning that the combined effects of G and E are no more, and no less, than the sum of the two when considered separately. Until relatively recently, most researchers expected that this would be the usual state of affairs, and the research findings seemed to bear that out. As we shall see, that now seems much more doubtful than used to be thought.

The most obvious, and straightforward, alternative to additive effects is the occurrence of *synergistic interaction* (or its opposite – meaning that the effects of one are reduced by the presence of the other) by which the effects of G are greater, or lesser, in the presence of a particular environment, and similarly the effects of E are influenced by the presence or absence of some specific genetic susceptibility. During the 1970s there was much controversy over the statistical issues involved in the study of such interactions.[5] This primarily arose from a clash between those who conceptualized *interaction* biologically and those who wanted the term to apply only to the statistical interaction term in multivariate analyses.[6] In addition, however, there was confusion through a failure to appreciate that the statistical interaction terms could refer either to *multiplicative interactions* or what were misleadingly termed *additive interactions*, the former considering interactions as measured on a logarithmic scale. The practical implications of the statistical considerations are discussed below. In the meanwhile, let me simply note than in this chapter synergistic gene–environment interaction is discussed in terms of a biological concept. The reasons for wanting to differentiate this from a statistical interaction are discussed in more detail below. Moreover, because the focus is on possible biological implications, the main focus will be on the interaction between some identified and measured genetic allelic variation and some identified and measured environmental risk factor. This approach[7] stands in sharp contrast to the traditional behavioral genetics strategy of considering possible interactions between G and E as anonymous "black box" variables (meaning that their effects are inferred from twin or adoptee or family study findings and therefore apply to general overall genetic influences rather than the effects of individual genes).

Population variability in heritability

A rather different type of gene–environment interplay concerns population variability in levels of heritability. Thus, during recent years there have been several studies finding that the effects of genetic influences are greater in individuals from advantaged backgrounds and, conversely, that they are less in the case of those from disadvantaged backgrounds[8] Figure 9.1 shows the type of pattern found, using the data from Rowe et al. as illustrative. This sort of variability is sometimes described as a gene–environment interaction (misleadingly in my view). The statistical analysis does indeed show a statistically significant interaction, but the interaction is between overall heritability and some environmental feature. It does *not* refer to an interaction involving any specific identified gene and it does *not* necessarily mean that the genetic influences operate on environmental susceptibility.

Nevertheless, the findings are truly important as a reminder that heritability estimates are population specific. In many circumstances, as we saw in Chapter 4, such estimates do remain remarkably stable across different environments, but certainly there are situations in which there is a major variation in the strength of overall genetic effects in different environments. There have been too few studies examining the possibility for any overall conclusion on population variability in heritability, but it is important to study it and to understand what it means.

So, let me consider a few possibilities. First, the variability may come about because the effects of genes are so strong that they predominate over environmental influences except in the case of extreme environments. A

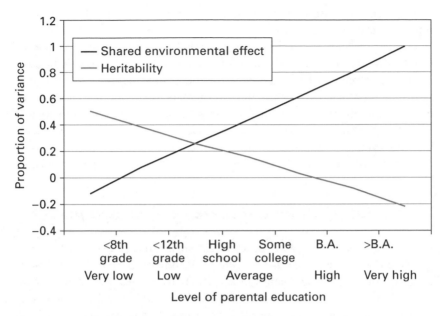

Figure 9.1 Relations between genetic and shared environmental variance components by level of parental education.
Source: from Rowe et al., 1999. Copyright © 1999 by Child Development. Reprinted by permission of Blackwell Publishing Ltd.

possible example might be the evidence (albeit rather limited) that, in the case of Down syndrome and of autism, there is little variation in IQ level as a result of the quality of the rearing environment as indexed by the educational level of the parents.[9] The point is that the chromosomal anomaly leads to an average reduction of IQ in the region of about 60 points. Of course, the IQ of individuals with Down syndrome (or autism) will be influenced to some degree by the polygenic and environmental influences that affect IQ variations within the normal range. Indeed, studies of institutional-reared children with severe mental retardation (of whom the largest group will be those with Down syndrome) have shown environmental effects.[10] The interaction here concerns the variation in environmentality (i.e., the environmental effects of heritability) according to the presence/absence of the chromosomal anomaly leading to Down syndrome.

A second possibility is that the effects of serious environmental risks are so strong that they predominate over ordinary polygenic influences. A possible example of this kind might be the lack of genetic influence on cognitive level in children who had been born extremely prematurely (at least 8 weeks early) as studied in the UK National Twin Sample.[11] The analyses showed that extreme prematurity had such a strong environmentally-mediated negative effect on early cognitive performance that genetic influences were minimal, in contrast to their considerable importance in children born normally at the expected time.

A third possibility is that the variability in heritability according to environmental circumstances might be no more than a consequence of variations in the effective range of either the genes or the environments.

It may be concluded that the finding of marked variations in heritability according to environmental circumstances (if confirmed by the research of other investigations) emphasizes the need to investigate the possible mechanisms involved. The interaction finding on its own, however, does not point unambiguously in any particular direction with respect to causal mechanisms.

Effects of specific environments on gene expression

One of the most exciting and important findings in recent years has been the growing body of evidence that specific environments have major effects on the expression of specific genes in specific body tissues, including specific parts of the brain.[12] Many of the scientists working in this field, as well as reviewers from other disciplines,[13] have discussed the effects in terms of gene–environment interaction. The effects are clearly biological and they involve individual genes (in specific parts of the brain in the case of effects on behavior) and specific environments at a specific phase in development. The importance of these findings is enormous and the evidence is considered in more detail in Chapter 10. Nevertheless, the findings (and the concept) are more meaningfully understood as the effects of experiences on genes, rather than an interaction in which an environmental effect is moderated (meaning in this instance altered) by a specific genetic polymorphism (meaning allelic variation in gene variant). The effects on gene expression are not directly concerned with specific allelic variations, and they do not affect the genomic sequence. They are therefore epigenetic rather than genetic. The effect of the environment in these circumstances is, therefore, not dependent on the presence or absence of a particular allelic variation. Rather, it is an effect on gene expression. This is a crucially important, relatively new, field of research that has enormous consequences for the ways in which we think about the effects of environments on the organism and, therefore, about the biological processes that may be involved in the long-term effects of early experiences. Some of the key findings are discussed in Chapter 10.

Genetic influences on exposure to specific environments

Yet another type of gene–environment interplay is provided by the evidence that there are genetic influences on exposure to particular risk or protective

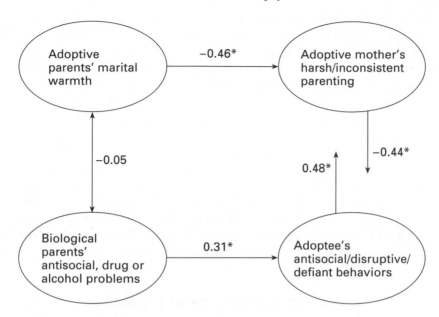

Figure 9.2 Effects of disorder in biological parent on disciplinary practices of adoptive mother – mediated by biological effects on child behaviour.
Source: based on Ge et al., 1996.

environments.[14] Behavioral geneticists tend to discuss these gene–environment correlations as if the genes were having effects on individual differences in environments experienced. That is, however, rather a misleading way of thinking about things in biological terms. That is, what the findings show is that the mediation of the genetic effect is through the behavior of either the parents or the children.[15] Figure 9.2 illustrates the effects with respect to the findings of Ge et al.'s[16] study of adoptees. Adopted children whose biological parents showed antisocial personality disorder or drug dependency or alcoholism were more likely to have *adoptive* parents who showed a high level of harsh, inconsistent parenting. The detailed findings showed that this came about as a result of the children's disruptive behavior, which served to elicit negative parenting. In this case, the effect was a consequence of the child's biological background. Note, however, that the harsh parenting was also influenced by the parent's marital relationship and note, too, that the mothers' parenting both influenced and was influenced by the children's behavior.

Something comparable occurs when the parents' genes influence their behavior in ways that shape the rearing environment that they provide for their children. The distinction between genetic effects on behavior and genetic effects on environments is an important one because the effect comes about as a result of the ways in which genes influence behaviors that, in turn, serve to shape or select different environments. This is a most important indirect route of gene action and it warrants much more serious attention than it has received up to now. The topic is considered in more detail below under the heading of "gene–environment correlations." People sometimes express surprise that, in view of the extensive evidence of genetic effects on individual differences in environmental risk exposure, there are no known identified genes shown to have a link with particular environments.[17] The question is a reasonable one but the answer is that genes do not affect environments as such; rather, they influence behaviors that serve to shape or select environments. It would make no sense to search for genes that code for particular environments, because there are none. Instead, the research needs to focus on the parent and child behaviors that influence the environments experienced. The gene hunting, then, needs to be focused on the susceptibility genes for those behaviors and not for the environments as such.

Statistical gene–environment interactions

In the field of behavioral genetics the dominant concept of interaction has been that of a descriptor for a particular statistical finding – namely, what has usually, if a bit misleadingly, been called a "departure from additivity."[18] The term is misleading because it concerns departures only on a multiplicative model that uses a logarithmic scale.[19] The point is most easily illustrated by taking an actual example, using a finding from Brown and Harris[20] – see Figure 9.3.

The data dealt with a postulated interaction between two environmental variables (a vulnerability factor and a provoking agent) but the statistical point applies in exactly the same way to gene–environment statistical interactions. As shown in Figure 9.3, the base rate for depression (which was what was being studied) in the absence of either the vulnerability factor or a provoking agent was less than 2 percent. A provoking agent on its own (i.e., without a vulnerability factor) increased the rate to 17 percent. By contrast, the vulnerability factor on its own had a zero effect. On a simple additive model, therefore, the two in combination would be expected to lead to a depression rate of 17 percent (i.e., 17 percent + 0 percent). However, the combination actually led to a rate of 43 percent, well above the actual rate found. Brown and Harris[20] used an appropriate statistical test and found that this interaction was statistically significant. Their critics[21] used a different test for a multiplicative interaction (based on ratios and a logarithmic scale) and found that this was not statistically significant, although, as shown in Figure 9.3, it is obvious that the vulnerability factor had no effect on its own

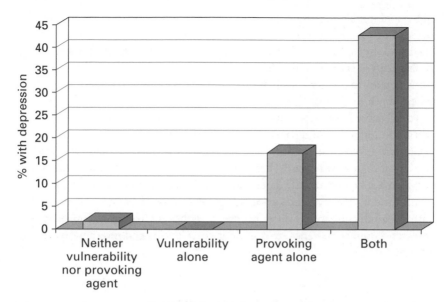

Figure 9.3 Interaction of vulnerability factors and provoking agents in the risk for depressive disorders in women.
Source: data from Brown & Harris, 1978.

but increased the effect of the provoking agent. The extent to which this interaction has been confirmed by other investigators need not concern us here, as the relevant point applies to the statistics. The argument generated much heat at the time, but most of the argument missed the key point that two different types of statistical interaction were being used. Both are perfectly reasonable on statistical grounds but they differ conceptually and require different statistical approaches.[6] From a methodological point of view, however, the dispute serves as a useful reminder that statistical interaction effects tend to be greatly influenced by changes in the way variables are scaled (i.e., what sort of measurement scale is used).[22]

The traditional multiplicative model[23] approach to gene–environment interactions has another crucial flaw. That is, it specifies that there must be variation in *both* the genes and the environment; without both there can be no interaction.[24] On the face of it, that sounds reasonable but it is inappropriate in relation to the biological concept. That is because some biological gene–environment interactions involve pervasive environments that do not vary across individuals to any substantial extent. For example, much the most striking medical example of gene–environment interaction is provided by the metabolic disorder phenylketonuria (PKU). This is an entirely genetic Mendelian disorder in which the genetic mutation renders the individual unable to handle the dietary phenylalanines present in all ordinary diets. The result is severe mental retardation. The genetic risk is entirely mediated by a biological gene–environment interaction but there is no multiplicative statistical interaction because there is no variability in E. The same applies to the genetically moderated susceptibility to malaria in regions where the infection is endemic.[25]

For all these reasons, it is unsatisfactory to conceptualize gene–environment interaction in terms of a particular specific statistic. Of course, the biological concept has to be tested statistically but the testing must be made appropriate to the biological concept.[6] That concept is concerned with an interaction between a specified identified genetic allelic variation and a specific measured environment. The evidence on this topic is discussed below. Following that rather lengthy preamble on concepts of gene–environment interplay, the research findings on gene–environment correlations and interactions can be considered.

Gene–environment correlations

In Chapter 4 the important role of genetic influences in bringing about individual differences in the likelihood that people will experience risky or protective environments of various kinds was noted. This effect comes about in two main ways – both of which involve gene–environment correlations.[26] Such correlations have traditionally been subdivided into those that are "passive," those that are "active," and those that are "evocative."[27] Passive correlations mean that, on the whole, the parents who pass risky genes on to their children are the same parents who tend to create risky rearing environments for the same children. The situation is probably most easily illustrated by considering the situation first in terms of behaviors before considering the evidence on genetics. For example, some years ago, my colleagues and I compared families in which one or both parents had some form of mental disorder with a non-patient community sample of families living in the same geographical area.[28] What we found was that the parents with some form of mental disorder were much more likely to have families characterized by discord, disharmony, and conflict and also more likely to show a focused high level of criticism, or hostility, to one or more of their children. In other words, the presence of parental mental disorder was associated with an increased rate of seriously risky environments. What these findings (and others like them) show is that parental qualities are quite strongly associated with the rearing environments that they provide for their children. Of course, the parental qualities were not entirely determined by genes. On the other hand, the mental disorders associated with family discord and conflict were ones in which much other evidence has shown that genetic influences play a substantial and significant role (see Chapter 4). The implication is that gene–environment correlations are involved.

In order to test more specifically that there is indeed a gene–environment correlation, some form of genetically sensitive design must be employed. Several are available and the findings from each of these all tell much the same story. For example, an extended twin-family design has shown that there is a genetic association between antisocial behavior in the parent and maladaptive family function, but that there is also an environmentally mediated effect of such family adaptation of the children's risk for antisocial behavior.[29] In other words, what is happening is that the parental genes are increasing the likelihood that the children will experience a risk environment but such risk environments then involve an environmentally mediated risk for the children. These findings illustrate one of the indirect ways in which genetic factors can operate. In these instances they are not influencing the children's behavior directly but they are influencing it indirectly by their effect in making it more or less likely that the children will experience environments that carry environmentally mediated risk or protective effects.

Active and evocative gene–environments correlations work in a somewhat different way, although again the genetic effects are indirect, even though they may be quite strong. What is meant by an active correlation is that the child's genetically influenced behavior has effects on the environmental situations that the child grows up in.[30] It is fairly obvious why this is likely to come about. Thus, a child who spends a lot of time on reading will have much more opportunity of learning from books than some other child who spends an equivalent amount of time on the sports field or practicing on the piano. The fact that the children choose to spend their time in these ways will, of course, be influenced by their genes (as well as by their upbringing); their genetically influenced propensities and interests will cause them to have distinctive experiences.

Evocative gene–environment correlations operate in a somewhat comparable fashion, the difference being that the effect is not on the selecting of environments, but rather it is on the responses induced in other people. Children, like adults, vary in their ability to get on well with other people, to show humor and compassion, to express interest and concern for other people, and in their tendencies to quarrel, provoke, or reject others. These tendencies will, of course, influence not only their ability to make friends but also the likelihood that such friendships will last rather than break down rapidly as a result of conflict and rejection. From the point of view of considering the role of gene–environment correlations, it is convenient to consider active and evocative correlations together, if only because they are not always easy to separate.

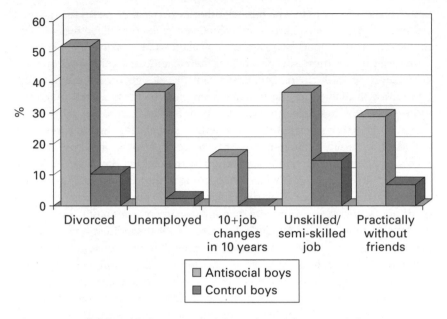

Figure 9.4 Childhood behavior and adult psychosocial stressors/adversities. *Source*: data from Robins, 1966.

Longitudinal studies well illustrate the pervasive and long-lasting effects of children's behavior on the environments that they experience in adult life. For example, in a pioneering, now classical, long-term longitudinal study, Lee Robins[31] compared the outcome in mid-adult life between children who had attended a child guidance clinic when young and children living in the same geographical area who had not. One key comparison was between the boys who had shown antisocial problems when young and those who had not (see Figure 9.4). The results were dramatic. The boys who had been antisocial when children had a much higher rate of both acute and long-term environmental stressors in adult life. These included features such as repeated frequent changes of job, rebuffs from friends, multiple divorces, unemployment, and lack of social support. Note that these are the sort of stress experiences in adult life that other research has shown are powerful provoking agents of the onset of depression.

The same story is evident in an 18-year follow-up from age 10 to age 28 undertaken by Lorna Champion and her colleagues[32] in London. The children's behavior at age 10 was measured through a standardized teacher questionnaire. The adult environments focused on acute life events that carried long-term threat plus long-term difficulties of a similar kind. The measures used were based on those pioneered and developed by George

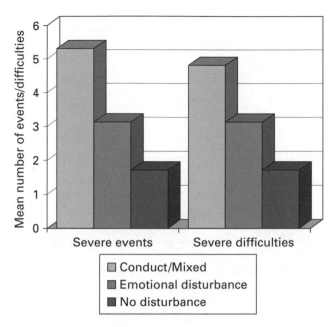

Figure 9.5 Severe events and difficulties in early adult life and types of disturbance at 10 years in females.
Source: Champion et al., 1995.

Brown and Tirril Harris and, again, these are the life stressors (both acute and chronic) that have been shown to have a powerful provoking role on the onset of depression. What was found was that the children's behavior at age 10 showed a strong association with these negative life experiences in adult life. The effect was most marked in connection with the children's antisocial behavior, but, to a lesser extent, it was also evident in relation to emotional difficulties (see Figure 9.5).

As with the passive gene–environment correlations, these findings show the powerful effect of children's behavior on the environments that they experience but they cannot quantify the extent to which the behavior is genetically influenced. Once more, genetically sensitive designs were needed in order to do that.

Adoptive studies provide the most straightforward approach because of their clear separation between the biological parents who provided the genes but who did not rear the children and the adoptive parents who did not provide the genes but who did provide the rearing environment. O'Connor et al.[33] used the Colorado Adoption Project to examine the effect of the children's biological parentage on the rearing environment provided by their

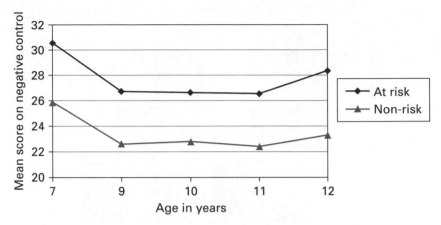

Figure 9.6 Adoptive children's genetic status and adoptive parents' negative control.
Source: based on O'Connor et al., 1998. Copyright © 2004 by the American Psychological Association. Adapted with permission.

adoptive parents. What was found was that the children born to antisocial mothers were substantially more likely to experience negative parenting from their adoptive parents (see Figure 9.6). How could that come about? The finding showed that the mediating influence was provided by the children's own disruptive behavior. That is, children born to antisocial parents were more likely to behave in disruptive ways and it was this disruptive behavior that evoked or elicited negative parenting from their adoptive parents. It is important, however, not to overplay the role of genetics in this effect. The findings showed that there was the same evocative effect deriving from the children's disruptive behavior even within the group of children who did not have antisocial biological parents. In other words, the driving force stemmed from the children's behavior and this behavior was only partially influenced by the genes. Other studies have shown a broadly similar set of findings.[16]

There is a danger, too, in assuming that this effect is much more determinative than is actually the case. For example, Riggins-Caspers and colleagues[34] showed in one study that there was no evocative effect of children's problem behavior in low-risk environments but there was a significant effect in high-risk circumstances. It seems that when biological risk (meaning in this case, deviance in the biological parents) predisposes to problem behavior in the away-adopted children, the adoptive parents respond to the problem behavior with harsh discipline only when they themselves show deviance or experience difficulties (thereby providing an environmental risk). Replication of this finding is needed before too much weight is placed on it but the implication is that social context may well influence evocative effects.

Before leaving the topic of gene–environment correlations, it is necessary to consider how pervasive and how important they are likely to be. The evidence is clear-cut that virtually all environments over which people have some choice or control are genetically influenced to a significant degree (see Chapter 4). This would be true, for example, for the likelihood of experiencing divorce, the presence of family discord, negativity shown to the children, and a wide range of acute and chronic life stressors. Of course, there are some life experiences that are outside people's control. For example, that would apply to the death of people in their social network and, as one would expect, there is little or no genetic effect on events of this kind. Of course, too, there are natural and man-made disasters of various kinds and, although little studied, it may be assumed that genetic factors play a minor role in exposure to such extreme unexpected events. On the other hand, the effect may not be zero in that people do have some choice in the situations in which they put themselves.

It is important, too, not to overstate the genetic effects on individual differences in environmental risk exposure. The genetic effects are far from determinative and, in most instances, they account for only a minority of the population variance. On the other hand, they do have effects that are not only statistically significant, but are strong enough to make a difference. Two implications arise immediately from the findings. First, it is likely that an important part of genetic effects on multifactorial traits comes about through indirect influences on effects on individual differences in environmental risk exposure. In other words, the effects of the genes on the traits are mediated by the environments they influence, rather than reflecting any kind of more direct influence on the traits themselves. Second, just because a risk factor is clearly environmental in its characteristics does not necessarily mean that its effects on any trait or disorder will be environmentally mediated. Indeed, numerous studies have shown that part of the risk effects associated with features such as negative life experiences, of family conflict, or parental divorce are genetically mediated. In many cases, environmental mediation predominates but, nevertheless, genetic mediation is quite substantial.

Gene–environment interactions

Gene–environment interactions refer to situations in which the effects on health of exposure to an environmental pathogen are conditional upon a person's genotype; or, to put the same point the other way round, when environmental experiences moderate genes' effects on health or disorder. In other words, what this means is that the genes are not affecting the trait in any kind of direct fashion, but rather are having influences as a result of their effects on susceptibility to some environmental hazard. For a long time, many behavioral geneticists argued that gene–environment interactions were sufficiently rare and sufficiently unimportant to make it safe to disregard them in studying genetic effects.[35] However, this was a fundamentally misguided assumption for several different reasons. Most crucially, it focused on the implicit hypothesis that there might be a simple unified interaction between all the anonymous genes relating to a disorder and all the anonymous environments that played a role in its causation. This is obviously biologically implausible[6] and it is not therefore surprising that the data seldom supported it. The second reason is that the statistical testing for gene–environment interactions in behavioral genetics has been based on detecting statistically significant multiplicative interaction terms. As already noted, that is much too limiting.

Are there positive reasons, however, for expecting gene–environment interactions? There are. Four stand out as particularly important.[17] First, there is the basic underlying evolutionary concept of natural selection which argues that genes are involved in the adaptation of organisms to their environment, that all organisms in a species will not respond to environmental change in the same way, and that this within-species variation in response involves individual differences in genetic endowment. In short, genetic variation in response to the environment is the raw material for natural selection.[36]

Second, biological development at the individual level involves adaptations to the environmental conditions that prevail during the formative period of development.[37] The literature on biological programming as a result of early experiences provides relevant examples.[38] Given that human development is an environment-dependent process, it is implausible that genetic factors do not play a role in moderating that process.[39] It is even more implausible that the process does not include mental health and mental disorder among its outcomes.

Third, both human and animal studies consistently reveal great variability in individuals' behavioral responses to a variety of environmental hazards. Heterogeneity in response characterizes even the most overwhelming of traumas, including all known environmental risk factors for psychopathology. To argue that such response heterogeneity is not influenced by genes would require the assumption that, although genes influence all other areas of biological and psychological function, responsiveness to the environment is uniquely outside the sphere of genetic influence. That is clearly implausible and the evidence contradicts it.[40] Moreover, against any such assumption, research guided by resilience concepts shows that individual variation in response to environmental hazards is associated with preexisting individual differences in temperament, personality, cognitive functioning, and psychophysiology, all of which are known to be under a degree of genetic influence.[41]

The fourth reason for expecting gene–environment interactions in the field of behavior and mental disorder is that there is a rapidly growing body of evidence of their importance in somatic medicine. For example, in the study of cardiovascular disease, subjects in the Framingham Heart Study who had high dietary fat intake developed abnormal HDL cholesterol concentrations, or did not, depending on their genotype on the polymorphic hepatic lipase (HL) gene promoter.[42] This HL GxE has been replicated.[43] A separate study showed that tobacco smokers developed coronary heart disease, or did not, depending on their lipoprotein lipase genotype[44] and their apolipoprotein E4 (APOE4) genotype.[45] The APOE4 GxE has been replicated.[46] In the study of stroke-prone hypertension, rats exposed to a high-salt diet developed elevated systolic blood pressure, or did not, depending on their genotype on the polymorphic angiotensin-converting enzyme (ACE) gene.[47]

In a study of low infant birth weight, women who smoked tobacco during pregnancy gave birth to underweight infants, or did not, depending on their genotype with respect to two polymorphic metabolic genes, CYP1A1 and GSTT1.[48] In the study of dementing illnesses, patients with a history of head injury developed Alzheimer's dementia, and increased beta-amyloid deposition in the brain, or did not, depending on which allele of the polymorphic apolipoprotein (APOE) gene they possessed.[49] This GxE pattern also applied when instead of head injury, the environmental influence on cognitive decline was estrogen therapy.[50] In the study of dental disease, heavy tobacco smokers developed gum disease, or did not, depending on their genotype on the polymorphic interleukin 1 (IL1) gene.[51] This GxE has been replicated.[52]

In summary, the traditional notion was that additive effects for genetic environmental influences would constitute the norm and it is now apparent that this assumption must be rejected. Of course, that is not to deny that, in some (perhaps many) instances the environmental influences on psychopathology will operate through different causal pathways than those involved in genetic effects. On the other hand, it is unlikely that that is generally the case. Accordingly, it has become appreciated that research must take on board, in serious fashion, the possibility of influential gene–environment interactions and the research must be designed accordingly.[53]

The starting point here, as with gene–environment correlations, involves the evidence on individual variation in response to serious environmental hazards, using non-genetic designs. The findings from both human and animal studies are entirely consistent in showing huge individual variation with respect to environmental hazards of all kinds – infections, physical extremes, malnutrition, and psychosocial stresses and adversities.[41] Moreover, this variation has been found with even the most serious and damaging of experiences. For example, our study of children adopted into UK families from profoundly depriving Romanian institutions well illustrated this variation. The adoption into UK families was associated with a dramatic degree of developmental recovery but, nevertheless, in those who had experienced at least two years of profound institutional deprivation, there was a lasting substantial deficit in cognitive functioning. Nevertheless, even in this extreme group, there was marked individual variation. A few children continued throughout childhood to function in the severely retarded range but there were some, too, who exhibited superior cognitive functioning. Of course, it could be that this huge individual variation reflected independently operating genetic influences that had got nothing to do with responsivity to a depriving environment. On the other hand, that does not seem very likely in view of the finding that the spread of IQ scores at age 11 (as at earlier ages) was as great in the children who experienced the most prolonged deprivation as in those who experienced only a few months in early infancy. The more likely role of genetics is through influences on individual differences in vulnerability to institutional deprivation.

Still, rather than debate plausibility or otherwise of different explanations, we need to turn to quantitative genetic research strategies. Kendler et al.[54] devised the ingenious strategy of using twin data to infer genetic liability at the individual level. The logic ran something along the following lines (applying it to the outcome of depressive disorder in early adult life). The highest genetic liability could be inferred in cases where the co-twin of an index twin with depressive disorder had also suffered from a depressive condition. That is, because they shared all their genes, it seemed reasonable to conclude that the occurrence of the depressive disorder in the co-twin was strongly influenced by genes. Conversely, the lowest genetic liability was inferred in the case of a monozygotic co-twin of an index twin with depressive disorder who did not have a history of a depressive disorder. The argument here is that, if despite being a member of a monozygotic pair the co-twin had escaped developing depression, the genetic liability was likely to be low. Using similar logic, dizygotic pairs could be inferred to be somewhere in the middle. What the results of that study showed (see Figure 9.7) was that the likelihood that a co-twin would develop the onset of a new depressive disorder following a serious negative life event was greatest when there was a high genetic liability and lowest when there was low genetic liability. The clear implication is that at least part of the genetic effect was likely to be operating through effects on susceptibility to risk environments.

Jaffee and colleagues used basically the same design to examine the comparable issue with respect to child maltreatment and the development of antisocial behavior.[55] Again, the same pattern of findings was evident (see Figure 9.8). Once more the implication was that part of the genetic effect operated through influences on susceptibility to environmental hazards.

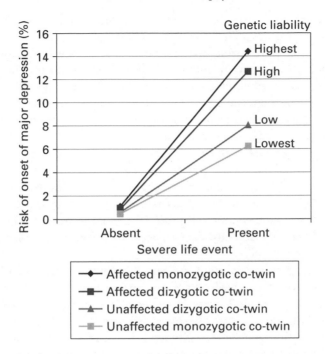

Figure 9.7 Response to life events as a function of genetic liability.
Source: from Kendler et al., 1998. Copyright © 1998 by Pharmacopsychiatry.
Reprinted by permission of Thieme New York.

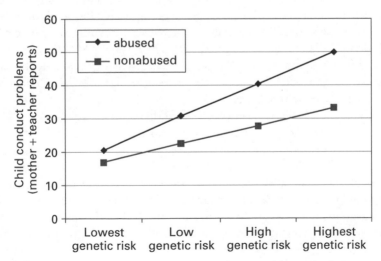

Figure 9.8 Child conduct problems as a function of genetic risk and physical maltreatment.
Source: from Jaffee et al., 2005.

Adoption studies, too, have produced evidence of gene–environment interactions.[56] The design involves a comparison of the effects of measured aspects of the adoptive rearing environment in individuals without a biological parent with the genetically influenced trait being studied. The rearing environment is not confounded with a genetic influence, and the biological parent risk factor is not confounded with the rearing environment (although the biological risk will include prenatal, as well as genetic, influences). Cadoret et al.[57] found that adversities in the rearing environment had no effect on aggression or conduct problems on those without a biological risk, the interaction being statistically significant. The implication is that genetic factors played a role in responsivity to environmental hazards. Similar findings have been evident in the Tienari studies of schizophrenic-spectrum disorders in the adopted-away offspring of biological parents with schizophrenia.[58] Longitudinal study data all tend to point to the likelihood of gene–environment interactions.[59]

These findings were important and persuasive but, inevitably, they suffered from the disadvantage of having to rely on an inferred genetic liability, rather than a measured genetic liability in relation to an identified susceptibility gene. This limitation has now been remedied in three important findings deriving from the Dunedin Longitudinal Study. In the first study, it was hypothesized that a functional polymorphism in the promoter region of the gene encoding the neurotransmitter-metabolizing enzyme monoamine oxidase A (MAOA) would moderate the effect of child maltreatment in predisposing to antisocial behavior (see Figure 9.9). The findings showed that maltreatment in children whose genotype conferred low levels of MAOA expression more often developed conduct disorder, antisocial personality, and adult violent crime than children with a high activity MAOA genotype.[60] This finding has now been replicated by the genetics group in Richmond, Virginia, using a different sample and measures that differed in detail but kept the same basic constructs.[61]

In the second study, it was hypothesized that a functional polymorphism in the promoter region of the serotonin transporter gene would moderate the influence of both maltreatment and stressful life events on depression. It was found (see Figures 9.10 and 9.11) that individuals with one or two copies of the short allele version of this gene exhibited more depressive symptoms, diagnosable depression, and suicidality than individuals who were homozygous for the long allele; that is, they had two copies.[62] Again the findings have been replicated by half a dozen other research groups,[63] although there is one negative study.[64]

Several findings are noteworthy about this pair of studies. First, there was no main effect of the gene in the absence of the environmental hazards. There was a small main effect of the environmental hazards, but much the

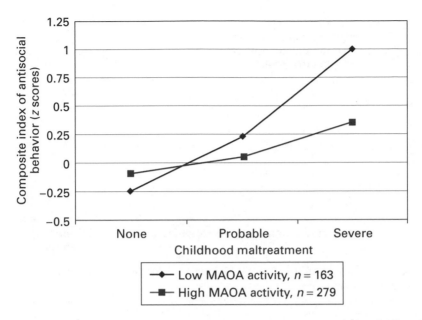

Figure 9.9 Antisocial behavior as a function of MAOA activity and a childhood history of maltreatment.
Source: from Caspi et al., 2002. Copyright © 2002 by Science. Adapted by permission of Science.

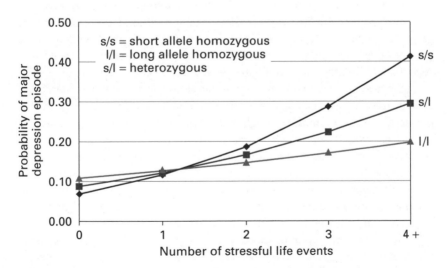

Figure 9.10 Effect of life stress on depression moderated by 5-HTT gene.
Source: from Caspi et al., 2003. Copyright © 2003 by Science. Adapted by permission of Science.

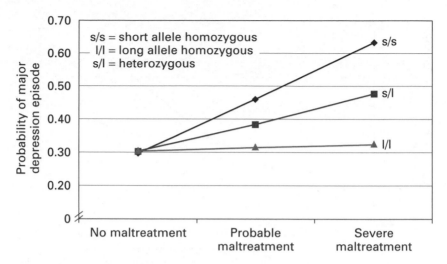

Figure 9.11 Effect of maltreatment in childhood on liability to depression moderated by 5-HTT gene.
Source: from Caspi et al., 2003. Copyright © 2003 by Science. Adapted by permission of Science.

largest effect was evident with the co-occurrence of the susceptibility gene and the adverse environmental experience. The implication is that the two genes were not susceptibility genes for these outcomes as such but, rather, operated on susceptibility to adverse environments. Second, the genetic effects were not specific to a particular type of environmental hazard. That is, in the case of depression, they applied to both early child maltreatment and more recent acute life stressors (see Figures 9.10 and 9.11). In other words, insofar as the genes affected environmental vulnerability, it was not a vulnerability specific to one particular type of environmental hazard (nor did it apply just at one age period). Third, although neither gene could sensibly be viewed as a gene that caused a particular adverse outcome, nevertheless the effects were outcome specific. That is to say, the MAOA gene had no effect on responsivity to maltreatment in relation to the outcome of depression. Conversely, the serotonin transporter gene had no effect on responsivity to maltreatment in relation to the outcome of antisocial behavior. The implication is that both the genes and the environments were operating on a specific pathophysiological causal pathway and, moreover, that it was likely to be the same pathway for both genetic and environmental effects.

In view of the traditional behavioral genetics' reluctance to accept the reality and importance of gene–environment interactions, three further points need to be made. First, there is the methodological question of whether the finding might be an artifact of scaling with respect to either the susceptibility gene or the mental disorder outcomes (i.e., antisocial behavior and depression). Caspi, Moffitt, and colleagues[65] tackled this important issue in several different ways. They argued that if the MAOA interaction with maltreatment was a scaling artifact, it ought to be found as well with a random polymorphism (a SNP) with a similar allele frequency in their sample. The results showed that did not happen.[17] Similarly, if the scaling of the behavior created an artifact, the MAOA gene ought to interact with maltreatment in relation to other outcomes with similar scaling properties. That was found not to be the case. Also, the MAOA gene ought to interact with maltreatment in relation to depression as well as antisocial behavior, but it did not. Similarly, the serotonin transporter gene ought to interact with maltreatment in relation to antisocial behavior, but that was found not to be the case.[66] It may be concluded that it is most unlikely that the interactions were artifacts of scaling.

Second, it was important to consider the possibility that the GxE interaction was actually brought about by a more direct genetic effect on the environment. This was tested first by checking whether there were significant correlations between the susceptibility gene involved in the interaction and the environment in the interaction. None were found. The possibility of the effect of other genes on the environment was tested by checking if the GxE applied to life events occurring *after* the depressive episode. If the GxE reflected genetic effects on life events, it ought to apply to life events at any time, but that was not found. There was no GxE for life events after the depressive episode.[62]

The third point is that if the gene–environment interaction reflects an important biological mechanism, other research strategies on the biology ought to confirm the effects of the gene on physiological responses to stress. That is exactly what the research has shown in both humans and other animals.[17] Thus, Hariri et al.,[67] using a functional brain imaging strategy, showed that humans with a short copy of the 5HTT allele[68] exhibited greater amygdala neuronal activity (i.e., in the part of the brain concerned with emotional reactivity) to fearful visual stimuli compared with individuals with two copies of the long allele (see Figure 9.12). Heinz et al.[69] confirmed this effect. Monkey studies have shown, too, that the same short allele was associated with a different response to adverse rearing, as shown by 5HTT metabolites in the cerebrospinal fluid (i.e., the fluid surrounding the brain and spinal cord)[70] and by visual orientation to stimuli.[71] In addition, Murphy et al.[72] found a difference in hormonal responses to stress according to the 5HTT gene (using a gene knockout model in mice). These findings on the likely biological underpinning for the GxE with respect to the 5HTT gene mean that it is highly probable that the interaction does indeed reflect an important biological mechanism.

One further point that emerges from the 5HTT findings is that the GxE did not apply to anxiety disorders in the replication by Kendler et al.[73] The

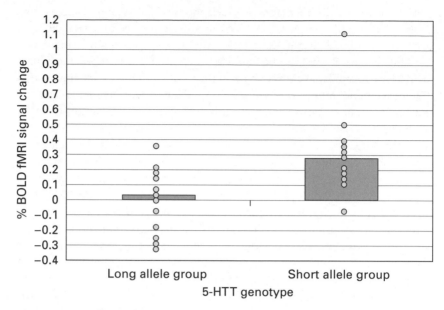

Figure 9.12   Effects of 5-HTT genotype on right amygdala activation in response to fearful stimuli.
Source: from Hariri et al., 2002. Copyright © 2002 by Science.

interest in this negative finding is that the findings from twin studies (see Chapter 4) showed that the genetic liability for depression and for generalized anxiety was largely shared. In other words, the implication was that the *same* genes provided a susceptibility for these two disorders. The GxE findings, on the other hand, suggest that although that may well be so, that does not necessarily mean that the risk operates through the same mechanism. Possibly, the genetic influences on anxiety may not involve an interaction with an environmental risk factor or, alternatively, the environmental risk involves another type of risk environment. Either way, one of the potential ways in which GxE research may be informative is the leads provided on *how* risks operate.

The third example from the Dunedin study concerned the question of why early exposure to heavy cannabis use provokes schizophrenic psychosis in some users but not others. It was hypothesized that a functional polymorphism in the catechol-O-methyltransferase (COMT) gene would moderate the risk from adolescent cannabis use for developing adult psychosis (see Figure 9.13). Cannabis users carrying the valine allele version of the COMT gene were more likely to develop psychotic symptoms and to develop a schizophreniform disorder, whereas cannabis use had no such influence on individuals with two copies of the COMT methionine allele.[74] Again, there is the implication that both the genetic susceptibility and the

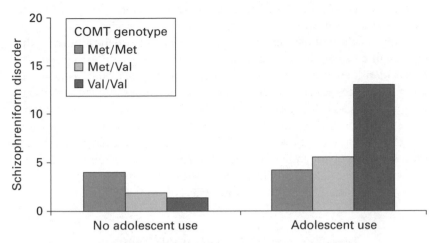

Figure 9.13 Schizophrenia spectrum disorder: Cannabis use interacts with genotype.
Source: Caspi et al., 2005.

cannabis effect operate through the same pathophysiological pathway. The evidence with respect to schizophrenia suggests that this is likely to involve dopamine and glutamate metabolism. Taken in conjunction with the epidemiological evidence,[75] there are implications for how the environmental risks might operate. What is striking is that the risks for schizophrenia derive from cannabis and not from stronger drugs such as heroin or cocaine, and that the effects are confined to heavy early use, rather than later sporadic use. Putting all of that together, it would seem to imply that the risk operates through biochemical pathways rather than through social stressors and peer group pressures or stigma, all of which would be likely to be greater with drugs other than cannabis. Nevertheless, as always, it will be essential to determine whether the GxE finding can be confirmed by other researchers investigating other samples and it will be necessary to study further the postulated biological mechanisms thought to be involved in GxE.

The history of searching for susceptibility genes for mental disorders is that, time and again, what seemed to be a promising finding could not be confirmed. As we saw in Chapter 8, to a certain extent, the tide has turned in a more positive direction with the beginnings of confirmed findings. Will the same apply in the field of GxE? It is encouraging that, although some uncertainties remain, both the MAOA and 5HTT findings have been replicated, despite all the statistical problems that surround interaction effects.[76] More than the replications, however, it is the evidence on the biological underpinning that provides some confidence in the reality of the GxE effect.

It may be concluded, therefore, that the identification of interactions be-tween specific identified genes and specific measured environments is going to be informative not only about the indirect effects of genetic influences that operate in co-action with the environment, but also it will cast light on the effects of risk environments on the organism and of the likely pathways by which such effects lead to disorder. Critics have sometimes worried that genetic research will lead to a neglect of the environment but, actually, the evidence suggests that the findings may bring renewed vigor to environmental research and cast important light on how environmental risk factors may operate. Moreover, one of the important consequences of findings on GxE is that it may enable personalized modifications of the environments (rather than the genes) to translate genetic findings into ways of improving health.[77]

Targeting genetically vulnerable individuals

Many people tend to assume that the identification of susceptibility genes for mental disorder should make it possible to target interventions on individuals most at risk. Critics, using the same expectation, worry about the possible stigma associated with any such labeling. What do the findings on gene–environment interplay have to say on this topic? The question may be approached in several different ways. First, the findings on the three genetic risk alleles involved in the GxE may be used to consider what proportion of the population would need to be targets. The Dunedin study showed that 55 percent of the general population had two copies of at least one of these three risk alleles; that is, they were homozygous and so lacked any of the alleles that did not carry risk.[78] Moreover, a staggering 80 percent had one copy of at least one of these three risk alleles (the allele leading to low levels of MAOA expression, or the short allele version of the 5HTT gene, or the valine version of the COMT gene). If targeting genetically vulnerable individuals picks up a majority of the population with one of only three susceptibility genes, then it is obvious that everyone is likely to have a susceptibility gene for some adverse outcome. The key point is that these genes are common normal allelic variations and not some rare genetic mutation. If the risk is extended to physical diseases (such as cancer, coronary artery disease, and asthma) almost no one will be without a susceptibility gene for some undesirable outcome. It would make no sense to target everyone at genetic risk because that would constitute the entire general population.

The second approach is to focus on the combinations of genetic and environmental risk involved in the GxE. The interaction between the COMT valine genotype and early cannabis use illustrates the consequences.[74] The general population prevalence of schizophrenia spectrum psychosis is about

1 in 100, in adolescent cannabis users the risk multiplies to 4 per 100, and in adolescent cannabis users with the COMT valine genotype this multiplies still further to 15 per 100 – a huge increase in relative risk. Nevertheless, coming back to the different approaches to risk discussed in Chapter 2, this also means that the vast majority (85 percent) of early cannabis users with the risk geno-type showed no psychotic manifestations, and only a tiny fraction of psychosis cases could be attributed to this particular GxE. Despite the very strong relative risk, they would be quite useless at the individual level of risk identification because there would be far too many false positives and false negatives.

The third approach picks up on this last point, by focusing on the fact that the identified risk deals with only a small proportion of the genetic and environmental risk factors. Using the genetic findings (with respect to either susceptibility genes or GxE) to target vulnerable individuals simply will not work because of the plethora of other risk factors, both genetic and environmental.

Good genes and bad genes

Commentators on the potential of genetic findings often slide into the assumption that genes can be subdivided into those that are good and those that are bad – the implication being that if we could get rid of the bad sort this would be generally beneficial for both the individual and for society. However, any such suggestion reflects a misunderstanding of how genes operate. To begin with, it is known that some important diseases are predisposed to by an absence of protective genes, rather than the presence of risky genes. At first sight, that might be thought to be just a matter of playing with words. Surely, if the absence of some allelic variation removes a protective effect, it follows that an alternative allelic variation must carry risk. In a sense, that is true but what is misleading is the assumption that the risk comes from what the gene does. Instead, however, it may come from some non-genetic risk against which the protective gene provided what was needed to resist the environmental hazard, whatever that may be in any particular case. Cancer provides the best-studied examples of this kind.[79]

The extension of the same notion implies that there are some human attributes or traits that are inherently good or bad in their effects. That probably is the case with some (for example, Huntington's disease) but it definitely is not the case for many. For example, the temperamental feature of so-called behavioral inhibition or emotional constraint or withdrawal in new or challenging situations constitutes a risk factor for anxiety disorders but it is a protective factor against antisocial behavior. Somewhat similarly, sensation seeking, or novelty seeking, is another risk factor for antisocial behavior (for reasons that are fairly obvious). On the other hand, although not systematically studied so far as I know, the same propensity to enjoy taking risks probably predisposes individuals to engage in rock climbing, exploring new and dangerous territories, motorcar racing, and playing the stock market. Those vary in their degree of desirability but it would scarcely seem sensible to view the effects as so ambiguously bad as to make it a desirable goal to get rid of the genetic effects on these traits. Indeed, major advances in science often come from creative innovators who take risks in their research.[80] Surely, it would not be desirable to get rid of that creative risk-taking propensity.

However, there are two other important reasons why the attempt to subdivide genes into those that are inherently good and those that are inherently bad is seriously mistaken. The first is that when dealing with multifactorial traits (and that applies to most human features) the resulting trait will derive from the operation of several, sometimes many, genes acting together with a range of environmental influences. Insofar as the susceptibility genes have been identified (and that applies to very few traits up to now), the effect of the individual identified genes has proved to be very small. For example, with respect to the possible genetic influence on sensation seeking, the identified susceptibility gene accounted for only some 4 percent of the variance on that trait. Not only would removal of that gene (even if that proved to be possible) make scarcely any difference, it would create an imbalance among genes, the influence of which would be totally unknown. Meddling with one tiny element of a complex system without knowing what the effects are going to be on the rest of that complex system is a hazardous enterprise.[81] The second reason is that because, with multi-factorial disorders, multiple genes are required to provide the liability to the handicapping disorder that we wish to prevent, it follows (as discussed above) that most people in the population will have at least some, perhaps many, of these susceptibility genes that carry potential risk. The reason why they do not develop the handicapping condition is that they do not have enough of the susceptibility genes, or that they do not have the right pattern of susceptibility genes, or they have not encountered the environmental hazards required to bring out the genetic effects. The situation is quite different from that in which there is just one gene with relatively direct risk effects that are not contingent on the presence of other genes or the presence of particular environmental risks.

But, even with single-gene disorders, there may still be an important mixture of good and bad effects. Undoubtedly, the best known example of this kind is provided by thalassemia, the condition giving rise to sickle-cell disease.[82] This is a serious killing disorder and obviously it would be good to be able to eliminate the suffering and death that it brings about. However, it is due to a recessive gene – meaning that an individual has got to have a copy of the gene from each of the two parents. The consequence is that there are a lot more people who carry just one of these genes but who do not have sickle-cell disease because they have only the one copy of the mutated allele. What is interesting and important is that these people with just one of the relevant alleles, heterozygotes, have an increased resistance to malaria, which is an equally serious killing disease. This is a really important protective effect in areas of the world where malaria is endemic. Obviously, however, it is of no importance in countries where there is no malaria. This situation constitutes an interesting example of how environmental conditions can influence gene frequencies in a population. The available evidence suggests that the rate of the sickle-cell gene has fallen over time in the United States among ethnic groups known to include a substantial proportion of individuals with the sickle-cell gene. By contrast, in areas of the world where protection against malaria is important there has not been the same fall.[83]

Accordingly, it is clear that the supposed subdivision of genes into good ones and bad ones is misleading and unhelpful and, moreover, leads to potentially damaging implications with respect to strategies for getting rid of genes playing a role in multifactorial conditions.

Targeting behaviorally vulnerable individuals

The gene–environment correlation findings suggest a different approach to targeting – namely, one based on either risky parent behavior or risky child behavior. The gene–environment correlation data do not help very much in identifying risky behaviors except in the limited (but important) sense of highlighting those that influence social interactions in ways that provide mental health risks for the children. The considerations in this connection parallel those on genes in emphasizing that, although there are some behaviors (such as abuse or neglect) that are unambiguously negative, there are many more that may be good or bad in their effects depending on circumstances (both genetic and environmental). That would apply, for example, to both behavioral inhibition and sensation-seeking. What is needed is not more targeting of vulnerable individuals but rather a better understanding of causal mechanisms.

Understanding causal mechanisms

The main value of genetic knowledge, and especially of gene–environment interplay, lies in its potential to delineate causal processes. Such processes include both the various pathways by which genes play a role in predisposing to mental disorder,[84] and the ways in which environmental circumstances bring about risks. The findings on gene–environment interplay also emphasize that a crucial element concerns the processes involved in the co-action between genes and environment in the production of risk and protection in relation to the development, or avoidance, of mental disorder. If we consider the broader body of evidence on gene–environment interplay as it applies to somatic, as well as mental, disorders, what general messages are evident?

First, the susceptibility genes that have been identified concern common polymorphisms that do not themselves directly cause disease, rather than rare genetic mutations with more obviously pathological consequences. The early days of psychiatric genetics rather misleadingly took single-gene Mendelian diseases as the model,[85] but it is now evident that these constitute the exception, rather than the rule.

Second, these common allelic variations have been found to affect several rather different causal pathways, as would be expected from earlier epidemiological and clinical research findings.[86] Thus, in the field of cardiovascular disease, the susceptibility genes include the hepatic lipase gene promoter,[42] the apolipoprotein E4 genotype,[45] and the angiotensin-converting enzyme gene.[47] The same must be expected in the field of mental disorders. It similarly follows that the genetic risks are probabilistic, rather than deterministic, and that they concern physiological mechanisms of a normal kind, rather than disease effects as such.

Third, the replicated findings on GxE all involved research that took as its starting point a known environmental pathogen. Thus, for cardiovascular disease these included high dietary fat intake,[42] smoking,[44] and a high salt diet.[47] The same applied to the GxE examples in the field of mental disorder discussed in this chapter; thus, they covered maltreatment, life stressors, and heavy early cannabis use.[87] The implication is that genetic research is likely to be particularly informative on environmental risk mechanisms.

Fourth, the findings on gene–environment correlations bring out two rather different points. On the one hand, they emphasize the important indirect route by which genes affect the risk of mental disorder through influences on individual differences in liability to experience risk and protective environments. All too often, discussions on risk focus only on risk effects. The genetic findings emphasize that attention must also be given to an understanding of why and how individuals differ in the environments they experience.[88] Of course, the answers will not be confined to individual features; societal factors such as racial discrimination and adverse housing policies may also be influential. On the other hand, the gene–environment correlations findings emphasize that the key causal mechanisms involve the role of people's behavior in shaping and selecting environment. This behavior will be genetically, as well as environmentally, influenced but the proximal causal mechanism involves behavior rather than genes. Accordingly, the research need is to focus on how the behavioral effects on the environment operate.

The fifth point is that the gene–environment interplay must involve thought processes and active agency concerned with what people do about the challenges and stress situations they face, as well as the neural under pinning. It is not, of course, that the workings of the mind occur outside of the brain; the very suggestion is ridiculous. Nevertheless, it is to say that neural science can be informative on the basis of the ability to think back and think ahead, and it can be informative on which parts of the brain are involved in these thought processes, and can contribute to an understanding of how this happens. That takes scientific understanding a long way, but it is not likely to be able to explain the specific details of the thinking or the mental sets that develop. Research into cognitive functioning provides a different level of enquiry that has to be considered as part of what is needed to understand how different people respond in contrasting ways to what seems to be the same objective situation. Biological reductionism, as discussed in Chapter 1, is highly desirable up to a point, but it should have its limits.[89]

Conclusions

The overall message is that the imprint of genes is evident in almost all causal pathways leading to psychopathology (see examples in Figure 2.1 and Figure 5.5) but, equally, in many cases the effects of genes are contingent upon co-action with environmental hazards. The old-fashioned split between disorders that are largely genetic and disorders that are largely environmental has become outmoded. The need is as great as ever to identify the separate measured effects of specific genes and specific environments but any adequate understanding of how all of this leads to disorder has to involve a bringing together of genes and environment. Some critics have worried that studies of genes will inevitably land up with a misleading deterministic view of disorder, but the reality is that the genetic findings actually lead in quite the opposite direction. In this chapter, gene–environment interplay has been discussed with respect to effects on some behavioral outcomes. It remains to consider the rather different form of interplay seen in relation to the effects of the environment on gene expression (see Chapter 10).

Notes

See Reference list for full details.

1   Gottlieb et al., 1998; Meaney, 2001
2   Gerlai, 1996
3   Crabbe et al., 1999
4   Cabib et al., 2000
5   See Greenland & Rothman, 1998
6   See Rutter & Pickles, 1991
7   See Moffit et al., 2005 & in press
8   Button et al., 2005; Rowe et al., 1999; Turkheimer et al., 2003
9   Fombonne et al., 1997
10   Tizard, 1964
11   Koeppen-Schomerus et al., 2000
12   Cameron et al., 2005; Meaney, 2001; Weaver et al., 2004
13   Abdolmaleky et al., 2004; Kramer, 2005
14   Plomin et al., 1977; Rutter & Silberg, 2002
15   Ge et al., 1996; O'Connor et al., 1998
16   Ge et al., 1996
17   See Moffitt et al., in press; Rutter, Caspi, & Moffitt, in press
18   Boomsma & Martin, 2002; Eaves et al., 1977; Plomin et al., 1988
19   Greenland & Rothman, 1998; Rutter & Pickles, 1991
20   Brown & Harris, 1978
21   Tennant & Bebbington, 1978
22   See Brown et al., 1991, for an example.
23   Heath & Nelson, 2002
24   Rutter, 1983; Rutter & Pickles, 1991; Yang & Khoury, 1997
25   Aidoo et al., 2002; Hill, 1998 a
26   See Scarr, 1992
27   See Plomin et al., 1977
28   Rutter & Quinton, 1984
29   Meyer et al., 2000
30   Rutter, Caspi, & Moffitt, in press
31   Robins, 1966
32   Champion et al., 1995
33   O'Connor et al., 1998
34   Riggins-Caspers et al., 2003
35   Boomsma & Martin, 2002; Plomin et al., 1988; Wachs & Plomin, 1991
36   Ridley, 2003
37   Bateson & Martin, 1999; Gottlieb, 2003
38   Rutter, in press b
39   Johnston & Edwards, 2002
40   See Kotb et al., 2002 and examples discussed below
41   Rutter, in press c
42   Ordovas et al., 2002

43   Tai et al., 2003
44   Talmud et al., 2000
45   Humphries et al., 2001
46   Talmud, 2004
47   Yamori et al., 1992
48   Wang et al., 2002
49   Mayeux et al., 1995; Nicholl et al., 1995
50   Yaffe et al., 2000
51   Meisel et al., 2002
52   Meisel et al., 2004
53   Tsuang et al., 2004
54   Kendler et al., 1999
55   Jaffee et al., 2005
56   Cadoret & Cain, 1981; Cadoret et al., 1995 b
57   Cadoret et al., 1995 b
58   Tienari, 1991, 1999; Tienari et al., 2004
59   Carter et al., 2002; van Os & Sham. 2003
60   Caspi et al., 2002
61   Foley et al., 2004
62   Caspi et al., 2003
63   See Eley et al., 2004 and more extensive list in Rutter, Caspi, & Moffitt, in
     press
64   Gillespie et al., 2005
65   Caspi et al., 2002 & 2003; Moffitt et al., in press; Rutter, Caspi, & Moffitt, in
     press
66   Caspi et al., 2002 & 2003
67   Hariri et al., 2002 & 2005
68   i.e., the one involved in the GxE in the Caspi et al., 2003 study
69   Heinz et al., 2005
70   Bennett et al., 2002
71   Champoux et al., 2002
72   Murphy et al., 2001
73   Kendler et al., 2005 c
74   Caspi et al., 2005 b
75   Arseneault et al., 2004; Henquet et al., 2005
76   McClelland & Judd, 1993
77   Guttmacher & Collins, 2003
78   Caspi, personal communication, January 2005
79   Strachan & Read, 2004
80   See Rutter, 2005 e
81   Thomas, 1979
82   Aidoo et al., 2002; Rotter & Diamond, 1987
83   Weatherall & Clegg, 2001
84   See Rutter, 2004
85   See Rutter, 1994, for critique

86   Rutter, 1997
87   Caspi et al., 2002, 2003, 2005 b
88   Rutter et al., 1995
89   Kendler, 2005 b

Further reading

Moffitt, T.E., Caspi, A., & Rutter, M. (2005). Interaction between measured genes and measured environments: A research strategy. *Archives of General Psychiatry, 62,* 473–481.

Moffitt, T.E., Caspi, A., & Rutter, M. (in press). Measured gene–environment interactions in psychopathology: Concepts, research strategies, and implications for research, intervention, and public understanding of genetics. *Perspectives on Psychological Science.*

Rutter, M., Dunn, J., Plomin, R., Simonoff, E., Pickles, A., Maughan, B., Ormel, J., Meyer, J., & Eaves, L. (1997). Integrating nature and nurture: Implications of person–environment correlations and interactions for developmental psychopathology. *Development and Psychopathology (Special issue), 9,* 335–366.

Rutter, M., Moffitt, T.E., & Caspi, A. (in press). Gene–environment interplay and psychopathology: Multiple varieties but real effects. *Journal of Child Psychology and Psychiatry.*

Rutter, M., & Silberg, J. (2002). Gene–environment interplay in relation to emotional and behavioral disturbance. *Annual Review of Psychology, 53,* 463–490.

Chapter 10

What environments do to genes

Psychosocial researchers have tended to view environmental influences as separate from genetics. Indeed, even today, many continue to seek to deny the possibility of genes having any major impact on either psychological development or the liability to suffer from the common multifactorial mental disorders (such as depression and anxiety) that blend into normality.[1] Some even extend that denial to seriously handicapping conditions such as schizophrenia, autism and bipolar affective disorder. There are several different reasons why these views are mistaken. First, as discussed in Chapter 9, genetic influences play an important role in the origin of individual differences in environmental risk exposure. This comes about through gene–environment correlations that are concerned with emotional and behavioral differences in how people select and shape their environments. Most psychologists today adopt a transactional model of development – meaning two-way influences on people's interactions with other people and with their broader social environment. Not only is there consistent evidence that there are genetic influences on the ways in which individuals shape and select their environments, but it would seem decidedly odd to think that the behaviors involved are unusual in being outside the scope of genetic influence. The proximal risk process concerns environmental mediation but whether or not people experience risk or protective environments is influenced by their genes.

Second, as discussed in Chapter 9, genes are influential in effects on individual differences in people's susceptibility to risk environments. Again the proximal risk process is environmentally mediated but the risk pathway predominantly affects individuals who are genetically susceptible. In other words, with respect to both risk exposure and risk vulnerability, the outcome is not simply an additive sum of the effects of genes plus the effects of the environment but, rather, it is the sum of both of these plus the effects of the co-action of genes and environment through gene–environment correlations and interactions.

However, there is a third reason why psychosocial researchers are mistaken in ignoring genes. If psychosocial risks have lasting effects, it is essential to consider what the experiences do to the organism in order for there to be persistent sequelae. The predominant paradigm in social development has involved a focus on mental models or cognitive/affective sets.[2] The rationale has been that people of all ages process their experiences and it has seemed reasonable to suppose that how they do so could make a difference to the long-term effects. Of course, there must be a neural basis for these mental operations, but they have been little studied in relation to psychosocial stresses and adversities. The other major focus of interest has been on the **neuroendocrine** effects with respect to both the possibility of damaging neural consequences and influences on responsivity to later environments.[3] More recently, there has been an interest in biological programming in relation to brain development.[4] The phenomenon is reasonably well established, although its extent remains quite uncertain, but its neural basis is only just beginning to be studied.

Any, or all, of these processes may involve genes in some way but there is one mechanism that does so directly, namely gene expression. There is now a growing body of evidence that a range of environmental experiences can and do affect gene expression. Thus, studies with mice have shown that variations in diets can have important effects on epigenetic gene regulation.[5] These could well be important in relation to cancer.[6] Genes constitute an important part of the body's defense mechanisms. Such mechanisms include those concerned with the suppression of tumor formation. It seems that one of the mechanisms by which diet predisposes to certain forms of cancer is through effects on **methylation** by which there is an epigenetic silencing of one or more tumor suppressor genes.

A very unusual, but nevertheless striking, example of the effects of diet on gene expression is provided by the effects of maternal diet on the coat color of the offspring of a particular species of mouse.[5] The findings showed that the mechanism lay in methylation, which altered gene expression. In essence, the research involved establishing first that hair color was associated with variations in the methylation of a promoter on a particular gene. The second step examined the effects of dietary methyl supplementation; it was found that it was associated with hair color changes and that this was a function of the increased methylation at a particular gene locus. What was extremely unusual in the findings, however, is that, in some cases, it seems that the effects were carried on to the next generation. Ordinarily, epigenetic modifications of the genome are erased during the cell division that leads to the next generation. These findings indicate that, although that is certainly ordinarily the case, there may be occasional exceptions. If so, it will be important to determine the mechanisms and also to consider whether or not the findings can be extrapolated to humans.

A quite different environmental stimulus was studied by Cancedda et al.[7] They found that raising mice in an experientially enriched environment accelerated the development of the visual system and that this was associated with altered gene expression leading to an increase in BDNF protein in the visual cortex of the brain.

Petronis[8] has suggested that prenatal/neonatal sex hormones might bring about effects on gene expression in humans. What is known is that these do have effects on later psychological functioning; these effects are modest rather than major, and there is considerable individual variation in response, but the effects are far from trivial.[9] The mechanisms remain uncertain but they could involve gene expression. If so, they might be relevant in relation to the well-established finding that most neurodevelopmental disorders are much more common in boys than in girls.[10] Baron-Cohen[11] has suggested that autism constitutes a form of extreme maleness. That seems rather implausible but the male preponderance in autism just might reflect a hormonal effect on gene expression.

Inevitably, all of this is rather speculative. Because gene expression is tissue specific, it is not usually feasible to study effects on the brain in humans during life. In addition, it is necessarily more difficult in humans to provide the experimental control that is needed to separate prenatal, postnatal, and genetic effects. That is where animal studies come into their own. The pioneering studies of Michael Meaney and his colleagues with rats[12] illustrate the power of the research strategy. The starting point was the observation that lactating mother rats varied markedly in the extent to which they licked and groomed their offspring and showed arched back nursing, and that the individual differences were stable over the first week of lactation. Crucially, however, these differences in nurturant behavior were not associated with differences in the time the mothers spent with their pups. In other words, what was being studied was the consequences for the offspring of a particular type of nurturant behavior, and not just a difference in contact. Moreover, these individual differences in nurturant behavior were associated with variations in dopamine (a neurotransmitter) in a particular part of the brain. Most striking, with respect to the implications for gene expression, was the observation that the variations in maternal behavior were associated with individual differences in the offspring's behavior and in the offspring's response to stress.

A series of research questions necessarily followed. The first that needed addressing was whether these differences in the offspring were genetic in origin. In other words, were they a consequence of the DNA inherited from the rat parents, or were they a consequence of the different patterns of rearing? This question was tackled by a cross-fostering research design in which the offspring of mothers with high licking and grooming behavior were reared by mothers with low licking and grooming behavior, and vice versa. The question, then, was whether the endocrine responses in behavior of the offspring were a function of their biological parentage or their social rearing. The results clearly showed that the effects were a consequence of the rearing environment and not biological inheritance.

A parallel study with mice contrasted prenatal and postnatal effects.[13] A single inbred mouse strain was cross-fostered prenatally by removing cells after mating for implantation in foster mice. Postnatal fostering was performed soon after birth by transferring newborn pups from these litters to two genetically different parturient females. The findings showed that the prenatal and postnatal environmental influences combined to produce marked differences in behavior thought to reflect emotionality. Because the groups being compared were genetically identical, the effects had to be environmentally mediated. Because of the combined effect of the prenatal and postnatal environment, the findings suggested that the prenatal environment may prime the developing organism to respond in a particular way to postnatal care.

Returning to the rat research, the next challenge was to determine the effects on the organism of the offspring that brought about this behavioral effect that was transmitted to the next generation in a way that resulted in consequences that persisted into adult life. In brief, what the research showed was that maternal behavior had lastingly altered the development of the endocrine response to stress through tissue-specific effects on gene expression. In particular, the effects were on a specific **glucocorticoid** receptor gene promoter in the **hippocampus** (see Figure 10.1). It should be noted that, in this instance, the effects were not on a protein-producing gene but rather on a promoter gene that affected protein production indirectly through its effects on another gene. Moreover, the effects seemed specific to what was happening in a particular part of the brain. The consequences of this effect on a promoter gene seemed to be carried through by the knock-on effects on serotonin activity. Meaney and his colleagues hypothesized that maternal care was altering the DNA methylation of this particular promoter gene and that these changes were stably maintained into adulthood and, because of that, they were associated with differences in endocrine responses to stress even at maturity. Their experimental studies demonstrated that this hypothesis was indeed correct. Interestingly, however, the results also showed that the group difference in DNA methylation occurred as a function of maternal behavior only during the first week of life. What happened later did not seem to be of the same consequence.

The next question was whether this maternally mediated epigenetic marking was actually irreversible or whether there were ways in which it could be altered in later life. The findings showed that treatment with a particular drug called trichostatin-A (TSA) did go some way to reversing the maternal effect of methylation. The detailed findings showed that it did

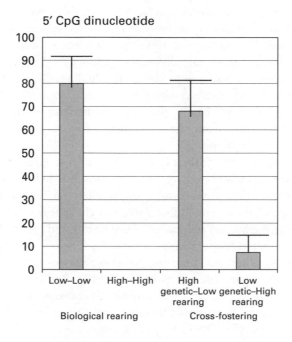

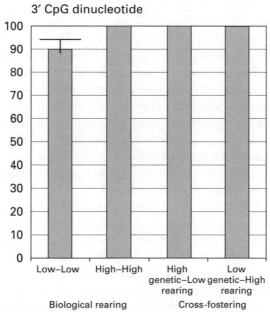

Figure 10.1 Gene expression findings from cross-fostering study. *Source*: from Weaver et al., 2004.

this through an effect on acetylation, which is a kind of balancing chemical process that counteracts methylation. The next question examined in the papers published so far was whether this reversal of the early DNA methylation actually made any difference to function. In particular, did it change the endocrine response to stress? The findings showed that it did – providing a convincing demonstration that the methylation effect truly caused the behavioral difference. Finally, the most recent research has shown that these intergenerational effects of early patterns of nurturing affect the sexual responsiveness of the offspring.[14]

These findings are compelling in being based on a series of particularly rigorous, creative, and well-controlled experiments. What we need to consider is whether the findings have broader implications for human functioning and, if they do, what they are. At first sight, it might appear as if the challenge is to determine the human equivalent of this licking and grooming behavior by mothers of their infants. However, that really is not the most appropriate way of thinking about it. There may, or there may not, be some human equivalent of this particular form of mothering. Rather, the question is whether or not the mechanisms illustrated by the Meaney research are likely to apply more generally. It would be very surprising indeed if it turned out to be a one-off specific. The history of biology in general, and genetics in particular, well illustrates that once a novel mechanism has been demonstrated, it almost always turns out to apply more broadly. The example of trinucleotide repeats discussed in Chapter 6 provides an interesting example of just that feature. Once the intergenerational expansion of trinucleotide repeats had been shown for one disorder, further research quickly demonstrated that it also applied to a broader range of disorders. That is the usual history of mechanistic research in biology and medicine. Moreover, there is research showing profound maternal effects on individual differences in offspring in species ranging from plants through insects to birds.[14] Meaney and his colleagues have suggested that it is likely that these wide-ranging phenomena probably reflect similar mechanisms on gene expression, although that has yet to be empirically demonstrated.

So, let us consider how far we should generalize the findings in humans. To begin with, the most plausible extrapolation is to effects from environments in utero and in the early postnatal period that have enduring effects that persist into adulthood. That would apply to effects of diet, toxins, drugs (including alcohol) and probably sex hormones.[9]

The area to which extrapolation seems most likely to apply is the area of so-called developmental programming.[15] Developmental-adaptive programming refers to the phenomenon whereby early experiences lastingly affect later development. For example, during the first six months of life or so, infants all over the world show much the same ability to discriminate among different sounds. But, then, from about the middle of the first year of life, this changes and it changes specifically in relation to the language environment in which the infant is reared. The best known consequence of this is the great difficulty that Japanese people have in discriminating between the sounds of "R" and "L." This differentiation has no part in the Japanese language whereas it does in the English language, and in many other languages. In other words, something about the language environment has permanently changed responses to the language environment. There are other examples within the broader field of medicine.[16] For example, it appears that diet in the first year of life lastingly alters people's responses to later diet. Interestingly, it does this in a fashion that is the reverse of what is found in adult life. In other words, it is inadequate diet and poor growth in infancy that carry risk for coronary artery disease and diabetes and hypertension in middle life whereas, of course, it is overeating and obesity that carry the risk in adulthood. The precise mechanisms have yet to be adequately delineated but the hypothesis is that the diet in infancy programs the organism to be well adapted to dealing with subnutrition but this appropriate adaptation at a time when nutrition is suboptimal means that it is maladaptive for dealing with overnutrition in later life.

Two features, both emphasized by Meaney and his colleagues,[14] are that the environmental effects apply to normal variations within the environment and not just to pathological extremes of abnormal environments. Second, the consequences cannot sensibly be viewed as either good or bad in absolute terms. Rather, the consequences are adaptive to particular environmental circumstances. It is perhaps a bit early to be sure that these inferences are correct but the evidence to date certainly suggests that they are likely to prove to be valid. If they are true, they support the human evidence that environments do have an influence within the normal range, not just at the extremes, and also they point to the need to consider effects in terms of a broader range of adaptational variations and not just in terms of patholo-gical damage.

Although it has not been studied in this way, the findings are entirely in keeping with the much earlier findings on the phenomenon of imprinting in birds.[17] That is to say, the effects on imprinting were environmentally induced, and were remarkably enduring but, in special circumstances, they were to a degree modifiable. It is tempting to suppose that somewhat similar biological mechanisms may have been involved. Research by Gabriel Horn[18] and his colleagues showed that there was a neural substrate for imprinting and the recent research on gene expression possibly provides an explanation of how the environment affected the neural substrate.

How much further should one extrapolate the findings to the effects of experiences in humans? Should it apply, for example, to influences occurring much later in the course of development? In principle, provided that the effects are indeed strongly enduring, it is possible that epigenetic effects might apply (as indicated by the Cancedda et al.[19] study) although that is less certain than with these early experiences. Could it apply to less enduring effects occurring at any age? Probably not, although that too remains to be put to the test.

The research considered in this chapter has concentrated on effects on gene expression but there may also be other, somewhat different environmental effects on genes. Thus, Epel et al.[20] found that chronic stress in humans was associated with a reduction in **telomere** length (these are DNA-protein complexes that cap the ends of chromosomes and which promote chromosomal stability). The effects of telomere shortening have been thought to relate to biological aging. The finding is too recent for any assessment of its validity but it serves as a reminder that there may be more than one type of effect of the environment on genes.

Although we are only just at the beginning of achieving an understanding of the implications of epigenetic effects, already the results show that the clean separation of nature and nurture, or of genes and the environment as more broadly conceptualized, is misleading. Genes affect the liability to experience different forms of environments and they influence susceptibility to different environments (as discussed in Chapter 9) but, equally, environments affect gene expression.

The one human example on gene expression that is relevant to possible major effects in later life concerns smoking. The requirement that gene expression must be studied in relevant tissues could be met through the use of bronchoscopy (using a tube that can be put down the main air passage) to obtain airway cells by brushings from the airway linings. Three key epidemiological findings are relevant.[21] First, there is strong evidence that smoking is implicated in the causation of lung cancer; this is evident from both the consistency of the dose–response relationship and the benefits that follow stopping smoking. Second, there is considerable individual variation in response; only some 10–20 percent of smokers actually develop lung cancer. Third, the risks for lung cancer persist a surprisingly long time after stopping smoking.

An interesting study by Spira et al.[22] compared gene expression in smokers and non-smokers and showed that cigarette smoking affected the expression of multiple genes involved with carcinogenesis and the regulation of airway inflammation. The expression level of these genes among former smokers began to resemble those of non-smokers about two years after people stopped smoking. However, there were a few genes that failed to revert to non-smoker levels even after many years of non-smoking.

Conclusions

The field of gene expression is much too new, and the findings far too sparse, for any firm conclusions on either the importance of environmental effects, or the range of effects that involve influences on gene expression. Nevertheless, what is clear is that some environmental effects do operate through influences on gene expression. Once again, the message is that it makes no sense to regard genes and environments as entirely separate in their effects, and operating through quite disparate mechanisms. That will sometimes be the case but, probably, more often (at least with respect to long-term effects) they come together in some kind of co-action on the same physiological or pathophysiological pathway.

Not only does methylation constitute a key mechanism in the persistence of environmental effects but, potentially, it may be informative in the processes involved in nature–nurture interplay.[23] The point here is that because epigenetic changes alter gene expression, and because the changes tend to be both gene specific and tissue specific, it is possible that they may be implicated in the gene–environment interactions considered in Chapter 9. At present, the suggestion is speculative, but what is clear is that research into the causal processes involving nature–nurture interplay will need to examine mechanisms at the intra-organismic neurochemical level, as well as at the psychological and societal levels.

Notes

See Reference list for full details.
1 James, 2003; Joseph, 2003
2 See, e.g., Abramson et al., 2002; Bretherton & Mulholland, 1999
3 Gunnar & Donzella, 2002; McEwen & Lasley, 2002
4 Bateson et al., 2004; Knudsen, 2004; Rutter, in press b
5 Waterland & Jirtle, 2003
6 Jaenisch & Bird, 2003
7 Cancedda et al., 2004
8 Petronis, 2001
9 Hines, 2004
10 Rutter, Caspi, & Moffitt, 2003
11 Baron-Cohen, 2002
12 Champagne et al., 2004; Cameron et al., 2005; Weaver et al., 2004
13 Francis et al., 2003
14 Cameron et al., 2005
15 Rutter, in press b; Rutter et al., 2004

16 Bateson et al., 2004
17 Bateson, 1966, 1990
18 Horn, 1990
19 Cancedda et al., 2004
20 Epel et al., 2004
21 Doll et al., 2004
22 Spira et al., 2004
23 Abdolmaleky et al., 2004

Further reading

Weaver, I.C.G., Cervoni, N., Champagne, F.A., D'Alessio, A.C., Charma, S., Seckl, J., Dymov, S., Szyf, M., & Meaney, M.J. (2004). Epigenetic programming by maternal behavior. *Nature Neuroscience*, 7, 847–854.

Jaenisch, R., & Bird, A. (2003) Epigenetic regulation of gene expression: How the genome integrates intrinsic and environmental signals. *Nature Genetics Supplement*, 33, 245–254.

Cameron, N.M., Parent, C., Champagne, F.A., Fish, E.W., Ozaki-Kuroda, K., & Meaney, M.J. (2005). The programming of individual differences in defensive responses and reproductive strategies in the rat through variations in maternal care. *Neuroscience and Biobehavioral Reviews*, 29, 843–865.

Chapter 11

Conclusions

Where does this journey through a wide range of research into the interconnections between genes and behavior leave us? I suggest that seven main conclusions stand out.

First, the general subdivision of either traits or disorders into those that are environmental in origin and those that are genetic makes little sense. Of course, there are rare examples that seem to fit into that dichotomy. Thus there are single-gene Mendelian disorders such as Rett syndrome, or early-onset autosomal dominant Alzheimer's disease, or Prader-Willi syndrome, in which the basic abnormality is entirely genetic in origin, without the need to involve any kind of environmental input. However, even in these cases, although the basic abnormality is entirely genetic in origin, it is beginning to be evident that environmental circumstances may perhaps have a contributory (albeit minor) effect on phenotypic expression. Similarly, there are disorders primarily due to overwhelming psychosocial trauma (such as some instances of post-traumatic stress disorder) that seem to require no genetic predisposition. Nevertheless, even in these instances, there is marked heterogeneity in response, and genetic influences play some part in that individual variation.

However, the great bulk of psychological traits and of mental disorders is multifactorial in origin. With these, there is good evidence of the importance of both genetic and environmental influences. It is of little value to attempt to quantify the relative influence of the two in any precise way, because it will vary by population and over time. Moreover, the precise estimates for the strength of genetic and of environmental influences have few policy or practice implications. Nevertheless, there is some interest in the possible differences associated with the small handful of disorders for which genetic factors appear to account for most of the individual variations in risk in the populations studied.

Second, a point that follows from the first, is that genetic influences operate to varying degrees with virtually all behaviors. This applies to disorders but it also applies to psychological traits operating as dimensions within the general population. Moreover, it similarly extends to attitudes and to individual differences in environmental risk exposure insofar as such environments are subject to shaping or selecting influences deriving from the individuals' own actions. The fact that behaviors may be socially defined and socially influenced (as is the case with antisocial behavior) does not alter this conclusion. Of course, there is not, and could not be, a gene for burglary or divorce; the very idea is absurd. Nevertheless, a person's propensity to steal or to have a disrupted marital relationship is likely to be influenced by temperamental and cognitive features that will be subject to genetic (as well as environmental) influences. The workings of the mind must be based on the functioning of the brain, and the brain's structure and development (as with any other bodily organ) will be shaped by both genes and environment. It is necessary that we get rid of the notion that there are some behaviors that arise from outside the body, and which have no biological substrate. The effects of genes are all-pervasive – which, of course, is not to say that the effects will usually predominate over the influences of the environment.

Third, there is no clear-cut qualitative distinction between normal psychological variations and clinically significant mental disorders. That does not mean that clinical diagnoses – such as of schizophrenia or autism or major depressive disorder – are not justified. To the contrary, diagnoses indicate that there is a degree of suffering or social impairment that warrants some form of intervention. The reason for the blurring of the normal–abnormal distinction is simply that many mental disorders both involve dimensional risk factors and involve degrees of malfunctioning that extend into normality. The situation is no different from that in the rest of medicine. Coronary artery disease arises on the basis of raised levels of cholesterol and a clotting tendency that are not in themselves pathological, but which nevertheless predispose to coronary artery disease. Moreover, such disease is based on atheroma in the blood vessels, which has been present many years before symptoms arose. However, these dimensional considerations in no way obviate the need to diagnose and treat heart attacks due to occlusion of one of the coronary arteries feeding the heart. Equally, the manifest pathological changes in the blood vessels, plus the evidence that genetic factors play a substantial role in the liability for this to occur, does not mean that we should neglect the environmental influences of cigarette smoking, over-eating and stress.

Fourth, with most multifactorial traits and disorders, genes are centrally involved in multiple aspects of the causal pathways. They play a role in influencing individual differences in exposure to risk and protective envir-onments, they influence individual differences in susceptibility or vulner-ability to risk and protective environments, and they are implicated in the intra-organismic mechanisms that provide a carry-forward in time of major environmental effects. Indeed, it is not going too far to assert that virtually all major environmental effects involve genetic mechanisms of one sort or another. Psychosocial researchers ignore these genetic effects at their peril. One of the major needs in psychosocial research concerns identification of the effects of the environment on the organism. The research findings have shown that one key mechanism concerns the effects on gene expression. Through biochemical epigenetic effects, the environment influences the functioning of genes.

Equally, however, genetic researchers need to take on board the evidence that many genetic effects are contingent upon one or other of several different forms of gene–environment co-action. Thus, some effects are operative by virtue of their role in increasing or decreasing the likelihood that a person will be exposed to risk environments. Other effects operate through influences on susceptibility to environmental hazards. The proximal risk mechanism is environmental but the vulnerability to risk environments is influenced by genes.

Fifth, the molecular genetic findings, by determining what individual susceptibility genes do, have the potential for casting much-needed light on the basic causal pathophysiological pathways. Critics of behavioral genetics have expressed concern that this shifts "responsibility" from society to the individual, and within the individual from the workings of the mind to the molecular processes within the cell. But that objection involves a return to an outdated, and wholly misleading, dualism. Biology incorporates, and has to incorporate, interactions between individuals and their environments. Because of that, it is not just meaningful, but also it is essential, to seek to understand the functional connections between brain processes and the workings of the mind. Necessarily, that involves genes and we need to understand how they operate. The study of gene–environment interactions seems likely to be especially informative in that connection. That is because their operation implies that both genes and environment operate on the same causal pathway. Accordingly, the study of such interactions carries the potential of providing a better understanding of how environmental risk and protective mechanisms operate.

Sixth, although the identification of susceptibility genes will provide an essential first step toward an understanding of basic biological mechanisms that are concerned with the causation of disorder, it is only a first step. Animal models will be required to elucidate just what it is that any individual gene does. There will next be the major challenge of undertaking the research necessary to appreciate what the proteins do – the emerging field of proteomics. But even that will only take us to the middle of the story. That is because there is the further challenge of understanding how the various protein products lead to depression or schizophrenia or autism or whatever disorder is being considered. In many instances, more than one causal pathway may be involved.

The evidence that some gene is implicated in the liability to develop depression, or to behave in antisocial ways, or even to develop a seriously handicapping condition such as schizophrenia or autism, does not mean that the gene "causes" these outcomes. Rather, the evidence indicates that, in most cases, the gene products operate via one or more biochemical pathways that only indirectly lead to the psychological outcome, normal or abnormal. The main effect may be on a specific part of the brain that is responsible for a key psychological function, on neurotransmitter functions, on some aspect of cognition or some aspect of neuroendocrine operation. Genetic research strategies can, and will, be used to delineate the modes of operation of genes but, until these have been identified, there should be avoidance of misleading shorthand statements that a gene "for," say, schizophrenia or intelligence has been found.

Genetic evangelists have been problematic in both their suggestion of a much more directly deterministic effect of genes than is warranted by the evidence, and by their earlier dismissal of environmental influences, at least insofar as they apply within the normal range. Equally, psychosocial evangelists have been problematic in their disregard of genetic influences, and their focus on the workings of the mind without attention to the functioning of the brain. Fortunately, the top exponents in both fields do not show this blinkered vision and it seems likely that the absurd polarizations of the past are just that – part of history and not of the future.

Seventh, it is becoming increasingly evident that it is a mistake to assume that the only genes that matter are those that code for some protein. As some of the examples noted in Chapters 8, 9, and 10 showed, the key genetic effects may be a consequence of genes that regulate the transcription and expression of other genes (rather than themselves specifying RNA that regulates the production of particular polypeptides, and thereby proteins).

Without reverting to an unhelpfully vague and global holistic approach, we need to appreciate that, although in a real sense genes, as represented in DNA, operate as discrete particles, nevertheless there is not a single "bit" that can be said to be "the" gene for anything. That is because multiple genes (many of which do not themselves have protein products) determine the action of each and every single gene that gives rise to a protein product. Moreover, although the gene (with its multiple elements) provides the basis for all that follows, it leads into a more complex pathway that results in some phenotype (meaning trait or disorder) only through a complicated hierarchical system that is subject to non-genetic as well as genetic influences. These pathways are in a real sense deterministic (in that they are organized and structured), rather than chaotic, but they are not inevitable and impervious to influence. An understanding of how they operate constitutes a major challenge for the future.

In the meanwhile, both policy and practice need to take on board the reality of gene–environment interplay and to seek to take account of the specifics of what is currently known on how that interplay operates.

Complete reference list

Abdolmaleky, H.M., Smith, C.L., Faraone, S.V., Shafa, R., Stone, W., Glatt, S.J., & Tsuang, M.T. (2004). Methylomics in psychiatry: Modulation of gene–environment interactions may be through DNA methylation. *American Journal of Medical Genetics (Neuropsychiatric Genetics), 1273*, 51–59.

Abramson, L.Y., Alloy, L.B., Hankin, B.L., Haeffel, G.J., MacCoon, D.G., & Gibb, B.E. (2002). Cognitive vulnerability-stress models of depression in a self-regulatory and psychobiological context. In I.H. Gotlib & C.K. Hammen (Eds.), *Handbook of depression*. New York: The Guilford Press. pp. 268–294.

Achenbach, T.M. (1985). *Assessment and taxonomy of child and adolescent psychopathology*. Beverly Hill, CA: Sage Publications.

Achenbach, T.M. (1988). Integrating assessment and taxonomy. In M. Rutter, A.H. Tuma, & I.S. Lann (Eds.), *Assessment and diagnosis in child psychopathology*. New York: The Guilford Press. pp. 300–343.

Aidoo, M., Terlouw, D.T., Kolczak, M.S., McElroy, P.D., ter Kuile, F.O., Kariuki, S., Nahlen, B.L., Lal, A.A., & Udhayakumar, V. (2002). Protective effects of the sickle cell gene against malaria morbidity and mortality. *The Lancet, 359*, 1311–1312.

Aitchison, K.J., & Gill, M. (2003). Pharmacogenetics in the postgenomic era. In R. Plomin, J.C. DeFries, I.W. Craig, & P. McGuffin (Eds.), *Behavioral genetics in the postgenomic era*. Washington, DC: American Psychological Association. pp. 335–361.

Aitken, D.A., Crossley, J.A., & Spencer, K. (2002). Prenatal screening for neural tube defects and aneuploidy. In D.L. Rimoin, J.M. Connor, R.E. Pyeritz, & B.R. Korf (Eds.). *Emery & Rimoin's principles and practice of medical genetics, 4th ed., vol. 1*. London: Churchill Livingstone. pp. 763–801.

Allanson, J.E., & Graham, G.E. (2002). Sex chromosome abnormalities. In D.L. Rimoin, J.M. Connor, R.E. Pyeritz, & B.R. Korf (Eds.), *Emery and Rimoin's principles and practice of medical genetics, vol. 2*. London & New York: Churchill Livingstone. pp. 1184–1201.

American Psychiatric Association. (2000). *Diagnostic and statistical manual of mental disorders (DSM-IV) – 4th ed*. Washington, DC: American Psychiatric Association.

Amir, R.E., van den Veyver, I.B., Wan, M., Tran, C.Q., Francke, U., & Zoghbi, H.Y. (1999). Rett syndrome is caused by mutations in X-linked MECP2, encoding methyl-CpG-binding protein 2. *Nature Genetics, 23*, 185–188.

Angst, J. (2000). Course and prognosis of mood disorders. In M.G. Gelder, J.L. López-Ibor, & N. Andreasen (Eds.), *New Oxford textbook of psychiatry, vol. 1*. Oxford: Oxford University Press. pp. 719–724.

Angst, J., Gamma, A., Benazzi, F., Ajdacic, V., Eich, S., & Rössler, W. (2003). Toward a re-definition of subthreshold bipolarity: Epidemiology and proposed criteria for bipolar-II, minor bipolar disorders and hypomania. *Journal of Affective Disorders, 73*, 133–146.

Antonuccio, D.O., Danton, W.G., & McClanahan, T.M. (2003). Psychology in the prescription era: Building a firewall between marketing and science. *American Psychologist, 58*, 1028–1043.

Ardlie, K.G., Lunetta, K.L., & Seielstad, M. (2002). Testing for population subdivision and association in four case control studies. *American Journal of Human Genetics, 71*, 304–311.

Aro, M., & Wimmer, H. (2003). Learning to read: English in comparison to six more regular orthographies. *Applied Psycholinguistics, 24*, 621–635.

Arseneault, L., Cannon, M., Witton, J., & Murray, R. (2004). Causal association between cannabis and psychosis: Examination of the evidence. *British Journal of Psychiatry, 184*, 110–117.

Asherson, P., & the IMAGE Consortium. (2004). Attention-Deficit Hyperactivity Disorder in the post-genomic era. *European Child and Adolescent Psychiatry, 13*, Supp 1, 50–70.

Badner, J.A., & Gershon, E.S. (2002). Meta-analysis of whole-genome linkage scans of bipolar disorder and schizophrenia. *Molecular Psychiatry, 7*, 405–411.

Bailey, A., Le Couteur, A., Gottesman, I., Bolton, P., Simonoff, E., Yuzda, E., & Rutter, M. (1995). Autism as a strongly genetic disorder: Evidence from a British twin study. *Psychological Medicine, 25*, 63–77.

Bailey, A., Luthert, P., Dean, A., Harding, B., Janota, I., Montgomery, M., Rutter, M., & Lantos, P. (1998). A clinicopathological study of autism. *Brain, 121*, 889–905.

Bailey, A., Palferman, S., Heavey, L., & Le Couteur, A. (1998). Autism: The phenotype in relatives. *Journal of Autism and Developmental Disorders, 28*, 381–404.

Bakermans-Kranenburg, M.J., & IJzendoorn, M. (2004). No association of the dopamine D4 receptor (DRD4) and −521 C/T promoter polymorphisms with infant attachment disorganization. *Attachment and Human Development, 6*, 211–218.

Bakker, S.C., van der Meulen, E.M., Buitelaar, J.K., Sandkuijl, L.A., Pauls, D.L., Monsuur, A.J., van 't Slot, R., Minderaa, R.B., Gunning, W.B., Pearson, P.L., & Sinke, R.J. (2003). A whole-genome scan in 164 Dutch sib pairs with Attention-Deficit/Hyperactivity Disorder: Suggestive evidence for linkage on chromosomes 7p and 15q. *American Journal of Human Genetics, 72*, 1251–1260.

Ball, D., & Collier, D. (2002). Substance misuse. In P. McGuffin, M.J. Owen, & I.I. Gottesman (Eds.), *Psychiatric genetics and genomics*. Oxford: Oxford University Press. pp. 267–302.

Bank, L., Dishion, T.J., Skinner M.L., & Patterson, G.R. (1990). Method variance in structural equation modeling: Living with "glop". In G.R. Patterson (Ed.), *Depression and aggression in family interaction.* Hillsdale, NJ: Erlbaum. pp. 247–279.

Barcellos, L.F., Klitz, W., Field, L.L., Tobias, R., Bowcock, A.M., Wilson, R., et al. (1997). Association mapping of disease loci, by use of a pooled DNA genomic screen. *American Journal of Human Genetics, 61,* 734–747.

Barkley, R.A., and 20 Co-endorsers. (2004). Critique or misrepresentation? A reply to Timimi et al. *Clinical Child and Family Psychology Review, 7,* 65–70.

Baron-Cohen, S. (2002). The extreme male brain theory of autism. *Trends in Cognitive Sciences, 6,* 248–254.

Bateson, P. (1966). The characteristics and context of imprinting. *Biological Reviews, 41,* 177–211.

Bateson, P. (1990). Is imprinting such a special case? *Philosophical Transactions of the Royal Society of London, 329,* 125–131.

Bateson, P., Barker, D., Clutton-Brock, T., Deb, D., D'Udine, B., Foley, R.A., Gluckman, P., Godfrey, K., Kirkwood, T., Lahr, M.M., McNamara, J., Metcalfe, N.B., Monaghan, P., Spencer, H.G., & Sultan, S.E. (2004). Developmental plasticity and human health. *Nature, 430,* 419–421.

Bateson, P., & Martin, P. (1999). *Design for a life: How behaviour develops.* London: Jonathan Cape.

Baumrind, D. (1993). The average expectable environment is not good enough: A response to Scarr. *Child Development, 64,* 1299–1317.

Baxter, L.R. Jr., Schwartz, J.M., Bergman, K.S., Szuba, M.P., Guze, B.H., Maziotta, J.C., Alazraki, A., Selin, C.E., Ferng, H.K., & Munford, P. (1992). Caudate glucose metabolic rate changes with both drug and behavior therapy for obsessive–compulsive disorder. *Archives of General Psychiatry, 49,* 681–689.

Bekelman, J.E., Li, Y., & Gross, C.P. (2003). Scope and impact of financial conflicts of interest in biomedical research: A systematic review. *Journal of the American Medical Association, 289,* 454–465.

Bennett, A.J., Lesch, K.P., Heils, A., Long, J.D., Lorenz, J.G., Shoaf, S.E., Champoux, M., Suomi, S.J., Linnoila, M.V., & Higley, J.D. (2002). Early experience and serotonin transporter gene variation interact to influence primate CNS function. *Molecular Psychiatry, 7,* 118–122.

Berger, M., Yule, W., & Rutter, M. (1975). Attainment and adjustment in two geographical areas: II. The prevalence of specific reading retardation. *British Journal of Psychiatry, 126,* 510–519.

Berk, R.A. (1983). An introduction to sample selection bias in sociological data. *American Sociological Review, 48,* 386–398.

Berkson, J. (1946). Limitations of the application of four-fold table analysis to hospital data. *Biometrics, 2,* 47–53.

Bishop, D.V.M. (2001). Genetic and environmental risks for specific language impairment in children. *Philosophical Transactions of the Royal Society, Series B, 356,* 369–380.

Bishop, D.V.M. (2002 a). The role of genes in the etiology of specific language impairment. *Journal of Communication Disorders, 35,* 311–328.

Bishop, D.V.M. (2002 b). Speech and language difficulties. In M. Rutter & E. Taylor (Eds.), *Child and adolescent psychiatry, 4th ed.* Oxford: Blackwell Science. pp. 664–681.

Bishop, D.V.M. (2003). Genetic and environmental risks for specific language impairment in children. *International Journal of Pediatric Otorhinolaryngology, 67S1,* S143–S157.

Bishop, D.V.M., Bishop, S.J., Bright, P., James, C., Delaney, T., & Tallal, P. (1999). Different origin of auditory and phonological processing problems in children with language impairment: Evidence from a twin study. *Journal of Speech, Language, and Hearing Research, 42,* 155–168.

Bishop, D.V.M., North, T., & Donlan, C. (1995). Genetic basis of specific language impairment: Evidence from a twin study. *Developmental Medicine and Child Neurology, 37,* 56–71.

Black, E. (2003). *War against the weak: Eugenics and America's campaign to create a master race.* New York: Thunder Mount Press.

Blair, R.J.R., Jones, L., Clark, F., & Smith, M. (1997). The psychopathic individual: A lack of responsiveness to distress cues? *Psychophysiology, 34,* 192–198.

Blair, R.J.R., Mitchell, D.G., Richell, R.A., Kelly, S., Leonard, A., Newman, C., & Scott, S.K. (2002). Turning a deaf ear to fear: Impaired recognition of vocal affect in psychopathic individuals. *Journal of Abnormal Psychology, 11,* 682–686.

Blumenthal, D. (2003). Academic–industrial relationships in the life sciences. *The New England Journal of Medicine, 349,* 2452–2459.

Bock, G., & Goode, J.A. (Eds.). (1998). *The limits of reductionism in biology.* Novartis Foundation Symposium 213. Chichester, West Sussex: John Wiley & Sons Ltd.

Bock, G., & Goode, J.A. (2003). *Autism: Neural basis and treatment possibilities.* Novartis Foundation Symposium 251. Chichester, West Sussex: John Wiley & Sons Ltd.

Bolton, P., Macdonald, H., Pickles, A., Rios, P., Goode, S., Crowson, M., et al. (1994). A case–control family history study of autism. *Journal of Child and Adolescent Psychiatry, 35,* 877–900.

Bolton, P.F., Park, R.J., Higgins, J.N., Griffiths, P.D., & Pickles, A. (2002). Neuro-epileptic determinants of autism spectrum disorders in tuberous sclerosis complex. *Brain, 125,* 1247–1255.

Boomsma, D.I., & Martin, N.G. (2002). Gene–environment interactions. In H. D'haenen, J.A. den Boer, & P. Willner (Eds.), *Biological psychiatry.* New York: Wiley. pp. 181–187.

Booth, A., Shelley, G., Mazur, A., Tharp, G., & Kittok, R. (1989). Testosterone, and winning and losing in human competition. *Hormones and Behavior, 23,* 556–571.

Borge, A.I.H., Rutter, M., Côté, S., & Tremblay, R.E. (2004). Early childcare and physical aggression: Differentiating social selection and social causation. *Journal of Child Psychology and Psychiatry, 45,* 367–376.

Bouchard, T.J. (1997). IQ similarity in twins reared apart: Findings and responses to critics. In R.J. Sternberg & E. Grigorenko (Eds.), *Intelligence, heredity and environment.* New York: Cambridge University Press. pp. 126–160.

Bouchard, T.J. Jr., & Loehlin, R.C. (2001). Genes, evolution, and personality. *Behavior Genetics, 31,* 243–73.

Boydell, J., van Os, J., & Murray, R. (2004). Is there a role for social factors in a comprehensive development model for schizophrenia? In M.S. Keshavan, J.L. Kennedy, & R.M. Murray (Eds.), *Neurodevelopment and schizophrenia.* London & New York: Cambridge University Press. pp. 224–247.

Bremner, J.D. (1999). Does stress damage the brain? *Biological Psychiatry, 45,* 797–805.

Brent, D.A., Gaynor, S.T., & Weersing, V.R. (2002). Cognitive behavioural approaches to the treatment of depression and anxiety. In M. Rutter & E. Taylor (Eds.), *Child and adolescent psychiatry, 4th ed.,* Oxford: Blackwell Scientific. pp. 921–937.

Bretherton, I., & Mulholland, K.A. (1999). Internal working models in attachment relationships: A construct revisited. In J. Cassidy & P.R. Shaver (Eds.), *Handbook of attachment: Theory, research and critical applications.* New York & London: The Guilford Press. pp. 89–111.

Bretsky, P., Guralnik, J.M., Launer, L., Albert, M., & Seeman, T.E. (2003). The role of *APOE*-E4 in longitudinal cognitive decline. *Neurology, 60,* 1077–1081.

Brody, G.H., Murry, V.M., Gerrard, M., Gibbons, F.X., Molgaard, V., McNair, L., Brown, A.C., Wills, T.A., Spoth, R.L., Luo, Z., Chen, Y-f., & Neubaum-Carlan, E. (2004). The Strong African American Families Program: Translating research into prevention programming. *Child Development, 75,* 900–917.

Brown, G.W. (1996). Genetics of depression: A social science perspective. *International Review of Psychiatry, 8,* 387–401.

Brown, G.W., & Harris, T.O. (1978). *The social origins of depression: A study of psychiatric disorder in women.* London: Tavistock.

Brown, G.W., Harris, T.O., & Eales, M.J. (1996). Social factors and comorbidity of depressive and anxiety disorders. *British Journal of Psychiatry, 168,* Supp. 30, 50–57.

Brown, G.W., Harris, T.O., & Lemyre, L. (1991). Now you see it, now you don't – some considerations on multiple regression. In D. Magnusson, L.R. Bergman, G. Rudinger, & B. Törestad (Eds.), *Problems and methods in longitudinal research: Stability and change.* Cambridge: Cambridge University Press. pp. 67–94.

Brown, G.W., & Rutter, M. (1966). The measurement of family activities and relationships: A methodological study. *Human Relations, 19,* 241–263.

Bryant, P. (1990). Empirical evidence for causes in development. In G. Butterworth & P. Bryant (Eds.), *Causes of development: Interdisciplinary perspectives.* Hemel Hempstead: Harvester Wheatsheaf. pp. 33–45.

Bryson, B. (2003). *A short history of nearly everything.* London: Transworld/Doubleday.

Buss, A.H., & Plomin, R. (1984). *Temperament: Early developing personality traits.* Hillsdale, NJ: Erlbaum.

Button, T.M.M., Scourfield, J., Martin, N., Purcell, S., & McGuffin, P. (2005). Family dysfunction interacts with genes in the causation of antisocial symptoms. *Behavior Genetics, 35,* 115–120.

Cabib, S., Orsini, C., Le Moal, M., & Piazza, P.V. (2000). Abolition and reversal of strain differences in behavioral responses to drugs of abuse after a brief experience. *Science, 289,* 463–465.

Cadoret, R., & Cain, R.A. (1981). Environmental and genetic factors in predicting antisocial behavior in adoptees. *Psychiatric Journal of the University of Ottawa, 6,* 220–225.

Cadoret, R.J., Yates, W.R., Troughton, E., Woodworth, G., & Stewart, M.A. (1995 a). Adoption study demonstrating two genetic pathways to drug abuse. *Archives of General Psychiatry*, 52, 42–52.

Cadoret, R.J., Yates, W.R., Troughton, E. Woodworth, G., & Stewart, M.A.S. (1995 b). Genetic–environmental interaction in the genesis of aggressivity and conduct disorders. *Archives of General Psychiatry*, 52, 916–924.

Cameron, N.M., Parent, C., Champagne, F.A., Fish, E.W., Ozaki-Kuroda, K., & Meaney, M.J. (2005). The programming of individual differences in defensive responses and reproductive strategies in the rat through variations in maternal care. *Neuroscience and Biobehavioral Reviews*, 29, 843–865.

Cancedda, L., Putignano, E., Sale, A., Viegi, A., Berardi, N., & Maffei, L. (2004). Acceleration of visual system development by environmental enrichment. *Journal of Neuroscience*, 24, 4840–4848.

Cannon, M., Caspi, A., Moffitt, T.E., Harrington, H.L., Taylor, A., Murray, R.M., & Poulton, R. (2002). Evidence for early-childhood, pan-developmental impairment specific to schizophreniform disorder. *Archives of General Psychiatry*, 59, 449–456.

Cannon, M., Dean, K., & Jones, P.B. (2004). Early environmental risk factors for schizophrenia. In M.S. Keshavan, J.L. Kennedy, & R.M. Murray (Eds.), *Neurodevelopment and schizophrenia*. London & New York: Cambridge University Press. pp. 191–209.

Cannon, T.D., Kaprio, J., Lonnqvist, J., Huttunen, M., & Koskenvuo, M. (1998). The genetic epidemiology of schizophrenia in a Finnish twin cohort: A population-based modeling study. *Archives of General Psychiatry*, 55, 67–74.

Cardno, A.G., & Gottesman, I.I. (2000). Twin studies of schizophrenia: From bow-and-arrow concordances to star wars Mx and functional genomics. *American Journal of Medical Genetics*, 97, 12–17.

Cardno, A.G., Marshall, E.J., Coid, B., Macdonald, A.M., Ribchester, T.R., Davies, N.J., Venturi, P., Jones, L.A., Lewis, S.W., Sham, P.C., Gottesman, I.I., Farmer A.E., McGuffin, P., Reveley, A.M., & Murray, R.M. (1999). Heritability estimates for psychotic disorders: The Maudsley twin psychosis series. *Archives of General Psychiatry*, 56, 162–168.

Cardno, A.G., Rijsdijk, F.V., Sham, P.C., Murray, R.M., & McGuffin, P. (2002). A twin study of genetic relationships between psychotic symptoms. *American Journal of Psychiatry*, 159, 539–545.

Cardon, L.R. (2003). Practical barriers to identifying complex trait loci. In R. Plomin, J.C. DeFries, I. Craig, & P. McGuffin (Eds.), *Behavioural genetics in the postgenomic era*. Washington, DC: American Psychological Association. pp. 55–69.

Cardon, L.R., & Palmer, L.J. (2003). Population stratification and spurious allelic association. *The Lancet*, 361, 598–604.

Carter, J.W., Schulsinger, F., Parnas, J., Cannon, T., & Mednick, S.A. (2002). A multivariate prediction model of schizophrenia. *Schizophrenia Bulletin*, 28, 649–682.

Caspi, A., McClay, J., Moffitt, T.E., Mill, J., Martin, J., Craig, I.W., Taylor, A., & Poulton, R. (2002). Role of genotype in the cycle of violence in maltreated children. *Science*, 297, 851–854.

Caspi, A., Moffitt, T.E., Cannon, M., McClay, J., Murray, R., Harrington, H., Taylor, A., Arseneault, L., Williams, B., Braithwaite, A., Poulton, R., & Craig, I.W. (2005 b). Moderation of the effect of adolescent-onset cannabis use on adult psychosis by a functional polymorphism in the COMT gene: Longitudinal evidence of a gene X environment interaction. *Biological Psychiatry, 57,* 1117–1127.

Caspi, A., Moffitt, T.E., Morgan, J., et al. (2004). Maternal expressed emotion predicts children's externalizing behavior problems: Using MZ-twin differences to identify environmental effects on behavioral development. *Developmental Psychology, 40,* 149–161.

Caspi, A., Roberts, B.W., & Shiner, R.L. (2005 a). Personality development: Stability and change. *Annual Review of Psychology, 56,* 17.1–17.32.

Caspi, A., Sugden, K., Moffitt, T.E., et al. (2003). Influence of life stress on depression: Moderation by a polymorphism in the 5-HTT gene. *Science, 301,* 386–389.

Caspi, A., Taylor, A., Moffitt, T.E., & Plomin, R. (2000). Neighborhood deprivation affects children's mental health: Environmental risks identified in a genetic design. *Psychological Science, 11,* 338–342.

Castellanos, F.X., & Tannock, R. (2002). Neuroscience of attention-deficit/ hyperactivity disorder: The search for endophenotypes. *Nature Reviews: Neuroscience, 3,* 617–628.

Ceci, S.J., & Papierno, P.B. (2005). Psychoeconomic consequences of resource allocation: What happens when an intervention works for those it was intended for, but works even better for others? *American Psychologist, 60,* 140–160.

Champagne, F., Chretien, P., Stevenson, C.W., Zhang, T.Y., Gratton, A., & Meaney, M.J. (2004). Variations in nucleus accumbens dopamine associated with individual differences in maternal behavior in the rat. *Journal of Neuroscience, 24,* 4113–4123.

Champion, L.A., Goodall, G.M., & Rutter, M. (1995). Behaviour problems in childhood and stressors in early adult life. I. A 20 year follow-up of London school children. *Psychological Medicine, 25,* 231–246.

Champoux, M., Bennett, A., Shannon, C., Higley, J.D., Lesch, K.P., & Suomi, S.J. (2002). Serotonin transporter gene polymorphism, differential early rearing, and behavior in rhesus monkey neonates. *Molecular Psychiatry, 7,* 1058–1063.

Chang, E.F., & Merzenich, M.M. (2003). Environmental noise retards auditory cortical development. *Science, 300,* 498–502.

Cherny, S.S., Fulker, D.W., & Hewitt, J.K. (1997). Cognitive development from infancy to middle childhood. In R.J. Sternberg & E.L. Grigorenko (Eds.), *Intelligence, heredity and environment.* Cambridge: Cambridge University Press. pp. 463–482.

Cleckley, H.C. (1941). *The mask of sanity: An attempt to reinterpret the so-called psychopathic personality.* St Louis, MO: Mosby.

Clegg, J., Hollis, C., Mawhood, L., & Rutter, M. (2005). Developmental language disorder – a follow-up in later adult life. Cognitive, language, and psychosocial outcomes. *Journal of Child Psychology and Psychiatry, 46,* 128–149.

Cohen, S., Tyrrell, D.A.J., & Smith, A.P. (1991). Psychological stress and susceptibility to the common cold. *New England Journal of Medicine, 325,* 606–612.

Collins, F.S. (1996). BRCA1: Lots of mutations, lots of dilemmas. *New England Journal of Medicine, 334,* 186–188.

Collishaw, S., Maughan, B., Goodman, R., & Pickles, A. (2004). Time trends in adolescent mental health. *Journal of Child Psychology and Psychiatry, 45*, 1350–1362.

Compas, B.E., Benson, M., Boyer, M. Hicks, T.V., & Konik, B. (2002). Problem-solving and problem-solving therapies. In M. Rutter and E. Taylor (Eds.), *Child and adolescent psychiatry, 4th ed.* Oxford: Blackwell Science. pp. 938–948.

Conger, R.D., Rueter, M.A., & Elder, G.H. (1999). Couple resilience to economic pressure. *Journal of Personality and Social Psychology, 76*, 54–71.

Conger, R., Ge, X., Elder, G.H., Lorenz, F.O., & Simons, R. (1994). Economic stress, coercive family processes and developmental problems of adolescents. *Child Development, 65*, 541–561.

Cordell, H.J. (2002). Epistasis: What it means, what it doesn't mean, and statistical methods to detect it in humans. *Human Molecular Genetics, 11*, 2463–2468.

Costello, E.J., Compton, F.N., Keeler, G., & Angold, A. (2003). Relationships between poverty and psychopathology: A natural experiment. *Journal of American Medical Association, 290*, 2023–2029.

Côté, S., Borge, A.I.H., Rutter, M., & Tremblay, R. (submitted). *Associations between nonmaternal care in infancy and emotional/behavioral difficulties at school entry: Moderation by family and infant characteristics.*

Courchesne, E., Carper, R., & Akshoomoff, N. (2003). Evidence of brain overgrowth in the first year of life in autism. *Journal of the American Medical Association, 290*, 337–344.

Cox, A., Rutter, M., Yule, B., & Quinton, D. (1977). Bias resulting from missing information: Some epidemiological findings. *British Journal of Preventive and Social Medicine, 31*, 131–136.

Crabbe, J.C. (2003). Finding genes for complex behaviors: Progress in mouse models of the addictions. In R. Plomin, J.C. DeFries, I.W. Craig, & P. McGuffin (Eds.), *Behavioral genetics in the postgenomic era*. Washington, DC: American Psychological Association. pp. 291–308.

Crabbe, J.C., Wahlsten, D., & Dudek, B.C. (1999). Genetics of mouse behavior: Interactions with laboratory environment. *Science, 284*, 1670–1672.

Curtis, W.J., & Nelson, C.A. (2003). Toward building a better brain: Neurobehavioral outcomes, mechanisms, and processes of environmental enrichment. In S.S. Luthar (Ed.), *Resilience and vulnerability: Adaptation in the context of childhood adversities*. Cambridge: Cambridge University Press. pp. 463–488.

Cutting, G.R. (2002). Cystic fibrosis. In D.L. Rimoin, J.M. Connor, R.E. Pyeritz, & B.R. Korf (Eds.), *Emery and Rimoin's principles and practice of medical genetics, vol. 2.* London & New York: Churchill Livingstone. pp. 1561–1606.

Dale, P.S., Simonoff, E., Bishop, D.V.M., Eley, T.C., Oliver, B., Price, T.S., et al. (1998). Genetic influence on language delay in two-year-old children. *Nature Neuroscience, 1*, 324–328.

Daniels, J., Holmans, J., Williams, N., Turic, D., McGuffin, P., Plomin, R., & Owen, M.J. (1998). A simple method for analyzing microsatellite allele image patterns generated from DNA pools and its application to allelic association studies. *American Journal of Human Genetics, 62*, 1189–1197.

Davis, S., Schroeder, M., Goldin, L.R., & Weeks, D.E. (1996). Nonparametric simulation-based statistics for detecting linkage in general pedigrees. *American Journal of Human Genetics, 58*, 867–880.

De Fries, J.C., & Fulker, D.W. (1988). Multiple regression analysis of twin data: Aetiology of deviant scores versus individual differences. *Acta Geneticae Medicae et Gemellogiae, 37*, 205–216.

DeFries, J.C., Plomin, R., & Fulker, D.W. (1994). *Nature and nurture during middle childhood*. Oxford: Blackwell.

Démonet, J.F., Taylor, M.J., & Chaix, Y. (2004). Developmental dyslexia. *Lancet, 363*, 1451–1460.

Dennett, D.C. (2003). *Freedom evolves*. London: Allen Lane, The Penguin Press.

Devlin, B. Fienberg, S. Resnick, D., & Roeder, K. (Eds.) (1997). *Intelligence, genes and success: Scientists respond to The Bell Curve*. New York: Copernicus.

Diamond, M.J., Miner, J.N., Yoshinaga, S.K., & Yamamoto, K.R. (1990). Transcription factor interactions: Selectors of positive or negative regulation from a single DNA element. *Science, 249*, 1266–1272.

Dickens, W.T., & Flynn, J.R. (2001). Heritability estimates vs. large environmental effects: The IQ paradox resolved. *Psychological Review, 108*, 346–369.

Dodge, K.A., Bates, J.E., & Pettit, G.S. (1990). Mechanisms in the cycle of violence. *Science, 250*, 1678–1683.

Dodge, K.A., Pettit, G.S., Bates, J.E., & Valente, E. (1995). Social information-processing patterns partially mediate the effect of early physical abuse on later conduct problems. *Journal of Abnormal Psychology, 104*, 632–643.

Doll, R., Peto, R., Boreham, J., & Sutherland, I. (2004). Mortality in relation to smoking: 50 years' observations on male British doctors. *British Medical Journal, 328*, 1519.

Doll, R., & Crofton, J. (1999). *Tobacco and health*, London: British Council/Royal Society of Medicine Press.

D'Onofrio, B., Turkheimer, E., Eaves, L., Corey, L.A., Berg, K., Solaas, M.H., & Emery, R.E. (2003). The role of the children of twins design in elucidating causal relations between parent characteristics and child outcomes. *Journal of Child Psychology and Psychiatry, 44*, 1130–1144.

Duyme, M., Arseneault, L., & Dumaret, A-C. (2004). Environmental influences on intellectual abilities in childhood: Findings from a longitudinal adoption study. In P.L. Chase-Lansdale, K. Kiernan, & R. Friedman (Eds.), *Human development across lives and generations: The potential for change*. New York & Cambridge: Cambridge University Press. pp. 278–292.

Duyme, M., Dumaret, A-C., & Tomkiewicz, S. (1999). How can we boost IQs of "dull children"? A late adoption study. *Proceedings of the National Academy of Sciences of the United States of America, 96*, 8790–8794.

Eaves, L.J., Last, K.S., Martin, N.G., & Jinks, J.L. (1977). A progressive approach to non-additivity and genotype–environmental covariance in the analysis of human differences. *British Journal of Mathematical and Statistical Psychology, 30*, 1–42.

Eaves, L.J., & Meyer, J. (1994). Locating human quantitative trait loci: Guidelines for the selection of sibling pairs for genotyping. *Behavior Genetics, 24*, 443–455.

Eaves, L., Silberg, J., & Erkanli, A. (2003). Resolving multiple epigenetic pathways to adolescent depression. *Journal of Child Psychology and Psychiatry, 44*, 1006–1014.

Eaves, L.J., Silberg, J.L., Meyer, J.M., Maes, H.H., Simonoff, E., Pickles, A., Rutter, M., Neale, M.C., Reynolds, C.A., Erikson, M.T., Heath, A.C., Loeber, R., Truett, T.R., & Hewitt, J.K. (1997). Genetics and developmental psychopathology: 2. The main effects of genes and environment on behavioral problems in the Virginia Twin Study of Adolescent Behavioral Development. *Journal of Child Psychology and Psychiatry, 38*, 965–980.

Ebstein, R.P., Benjamin, J., & Belmaker, R.H. (2003). Behavioral genetics, genomics, and personality. In R. Plomin, J.C. DeFries, I.W. Craig, & P. McGuffin (Eds.), *Behavioral genetics in the postgenomic era*. Washington, DC: American Psychological Association. pp. 365–388.

Eddy, S.R. (2001). Non-coding RNA genes and the modern RNA world. *Nature Reviews: Genetics, 2*, 919–929.

Ehrlich, P., & Feldman, M. (2003). Genes and culture: What creates our behavioral phenome? *Current Anthropology, 44*, 87–107.

Elder, Jr. G.H. (1986). Military times and turning points in men's lives. *Developmental Psychology, 22*, 233–245.

Eley, T., & Stevenson, J. (1999). Exploring the covariation between anxiety and depression symptoms: A genetic analysis of the effects of age and sex. *Journal of Child Psychology and Psychiatry, 40*, 1273–1282.

Eley, T.C., & Stevenson, J. (2000). Specific life events and chronic experiences differentially associated with depression and anxiety in young twins. *Journal of Abnormal Child Psychology, 28*, 383–394.

Eley, T.C., Sugden, K., Corsico, A. Gregory, A.M., Sham, P., McGuffin, P., Plomin, R., & Craig, I.W. (2004). Gene–environment interaction analysis of serotonin system markers with adolescent depression. *Molecular Psychiatry, 9*, 908–915.

Elkin, A., Kalidindi, S., & McGuffin, P. (2004). Have schizophrenia genes been found? *Current Opinion in Psychiatry, 17*, 107–113.

Epel, E.S., Blackburn, E.H., Lin, J., Dhabhar, F.S., Adler, N.E., Morrow, J.D., & Cawthon, R.M. (2004). Accelerated telomere shortening in response to life stress. *Proceedings of the National Academy of Science, 101*, 17312–17315.

Eysenck, H.J. (1965). *Smoking, health and personality*. London: Weidenfeld.

Eysenck, H.J. (1971). *The IQ argument: Race, intelligence, and education*. New York: Library Press.

Eysenck, H.J., with contributions by Eaves, L.J. (1980). *The causes and effects of smoking*. London: Temple Smith.

Falconer, D.S., & Mackay, T.F.C. (1996). *Introduction to quantitative genetics*. Longman: Harlow.

Falk, C.T., & Rubinstein, P. (1987). Haplotype relative risks: An easy reliable way to construct a proper control sample for risk calculations. *Annals of Human Genetics, 1*, 227–233.

Faraone, S.V., Biederman, J., Mennin, D., Russell, R., & Tsuang, M.T. (1998). Familial subtypes of attention deficit hyperactivity disorder: A 4-year follow-up study of children from antisocial-ADHD families. *Journal of Child Psychology and Psychiatry, 39*, 1045–1053.

Faraone, S.V., Doyle, A.E., Mick, E., & Biederman, J. (2001). Meta-analysis of the association between the 7-repeat allele of the Dopamine D4 receptor gene and Attention Deficit Hyperactivity Disorder. *American Journal of Psychiatry, 158*, 1052–1057.

Farrer, L.A., Cupples, L.A., Haines, J.L., Hyman, B., Kukull, W.A., Mayeux, R., Myers. R.H., Pericak-Vance, M.A., Risch, N., & van Duijn, C.M. (1997). Effects of age, sex, and ethnicity on the association between apolipoprotein E genotype and Alzheimer disease. A meta-analysis. APOE and Alzheimer Disease Meta Analysis Consortium. *Journal of the American Medical Association, 278*, 1349–56.

Felsenfeld, G., & Groudine, M. (2003). Controlling the double helix. *Nature, 421*, 448–453.

Fergusson, D.M., Horwood, L.J., & Lynskey, M.T. (1992). Family change, parental discord and early offending. *Journal of Child Psychology and Psychiatry, 33*, 1059–1075.

Fergusson, D.M., Horwood, L.J., Caspi, A., Moffitt, T.E., & Silva, P.A. (1996). The (artefactual) remission of reading disability: Psychometric lessons in the study of stability and change in behavioral development. *Developmental Psychology, 32*, 132–140.

Finlay-Jones, R., & Brown, G.W. (1981). Types of stressful life event and the onset of anxiety and depressive disorders. *Psychological Medicine, 11*, 803–815.

Firkowska-Mankiewicz, A. (2002). *Intelligence and success in life*. Warsaw: IFiS Publishers.

Fisher, R.E. (1918). The correlation between relatives under the supposition of mendelian inheritance. *Transactions of the Royal Society, 52*, 399–433.

Fisher, S.E. (2003). Isolation of the genetic factors underlying speech and language disorders. In R. Plomin, J.C. DeFries, I.W. Craig, & P. McGuffin (Eds.), *Behavioral genetics in the postgenomic era*. Washington, DC: American Psychological Association. pp. 205–226.

Fisher, S.E., & DeFries, J.C. (2002). Developmental dyslexia: Genetic dissection of a complex cognitive trait. *Nature Reviews Neuroscience, 3*, 767–780.

Fisher, S.E., Francks, C., McCracken, J.T., et al. (2002). A genomewide scan for loci involved in attention-deficit/hyperactivity disorder. *American Journal of Human Genetics, 70*, 1183–1196.

Flynn, J.R. (1987). Massive IQ gains in 14 nations: What IQ tests really measure. *Psychological Bulletin, 101*, 171–191.

Flynn, J.R. (2000). IQ gains, WISC subtests and fluid g: g theory and the relevance of Spearman's hypothesis to race. In G.R. Bock, J.A. Goode, & K. Webb (Eds.), *The nature of intelligence. Novartis Foundation Symposium 233*. Chichester: Wiley. pp. 202–216.

Foley, D.L., Eaves, L.J., Wormley, B., Silberg, J.L., Maes, H.H., Kuhn, J., & Riley, B. (2004). Childhood adversity, monoamine oxidase A genotype, and risk for conduct disorder. *Archives of General Psychiatry, 61*, 738–744.

Folstein, S., & Rutter, M. (1977 a). Genetic influences and infantile autism. *Nature, 265*, 726–728.

Folstein, S., & Rutter, M. (1977 b). Infantile autism: A genetic study of 21 twin pairs. *Journal of Child Psychology and Psychiatry, 18*, 297–321.

Folstein, S.E., & Rosen-Sheidley, B. (2001). Genetics of autism: Complex aetiology for a heterogeneous disorder. *Nature Reviews: Genetics, 2*, 943–955.

Fombonne, E., Bolton, P., Prior, J., Jordan, H., & Rutter, M. (1997). A family study of autism: Cognitive patterns and levels in parents and siblings. *Journal of Child Psychology and Psychiatry, 38*, 667–683.

Francis, D., Insel, T., Szegda, K., Campbell, G., & Martin, W.D. (2003). Epigenetic sources of behavioural differences in mice. *Nature Neuroscience, 6*, 445–446.

Francks, C., Paracchini, S., Smith, S.D., Richardson, A.J., Scerri, T.S., Cardon, L.R., Marlow, A.J., MacPhie, I.L., Walter, J., Pennington, B.F., Fisher, S.E., Olson, R.K., DeFries, J.C., Stein, J.F., & Monaco, A.P. (2004). A 77-kilobase region of chromosome 6p22.2 is associated with dyslexia in families from the United Kingdom and from the United States. *American Journal of Human Genetics, 75*, 1046–1058.

Freimer, N., & Sabatti, C. (2004). The use of pedigree, sib-pair and association studies of common diseases for genetic mapping and epidemiology. *Nature Genetics, 36*, 1045–1051.

Frith, C. (2003). What do imaging studies tell us about the neural basis of autism? In G. Bock and J. Goode (Eds.). *Autism: Neural basis and treatment possibilities.* Chichester: John Wiley & Sons Ltd. pp. 149–176.

Frith, U. (2003). *Autism: Explaining the enigma, 2nd ed.* Oxford: Blackwell.

Fulker, D.W., & Cherny, S.S. (1996). An improved multipoint sib-pair analysis of quantitative traits. *Behavior Genetics, 26*, 527–532.

Furmark, T., Tillfors, M., Marteinsdottir, I., Fischer, H., Pissiota, A., Langstrom, B., & Fredrikson, M. (2002). Common changes in cerebral blood flow in patients with social phobia treated with citalopram or cognitive-behavioral therapy. *Archives of General Psychiatry, 59*, 425–433.

Ge, X., Conger, R.D., Cadoret, R.J., Neiderhiser, J.M., Yates, W., Troughton, E., & Stewart, M.A. (1996). The developmental interface between nature and nurture: A mutual influence model of child antisocial behavior and parent behaviors. *Developmental Psychology, 32*, 574–589.

Gerlai, R. (1996). Gene-targeting studies of mammalian behavior: Is it the mutation or the background genotype? *Trends in Neuroscience, 19*, 177–181.

Gervai, J., Nemoda, Z., Lakatos, K., Ronai, Z., Toth, I., Ney, K., & Sasvari-Szekely, M. (2005). Transmission disequilibrium tests confirm the link between DRD4 gene polymorphism and infant attachment. *American Journal of Medical Genetics B: Neuropsychiatric Genetics, 132*, 126–130.

Gharani, N., Benayed, R., Mancuso, V., Brzustowicz, L.M., & Millonig, J.H. (2004). Association of the homeobox transcription factor, *ENGRAILED 2*, with autism spectrum disorder. *Molecular Psychiatry, 9*, 474–484.

Gibbs, W.W. (2003a). The unseen genome: Beyond DNA. *American Scientist, 289*, 78–85.

Gibbs, W.W. (2003b). The unseen genome: Gems among the junk. *American Scientist, 289*, 27–33.

Gillespie, N.A., Whitfield, J.B., Williams, B., Heath, A.C., & Martin, N. (2005). The relationship between stressful life events, the serotonin transporter (5-HTTLPR) genotype and major depression. *Psychological Medicine, 35*, 101–111.

Glantz, S.A., Barnes, D.E., Bero, L., Hanauer, P., & Slade, J. (1995). Looking through a keyhole at the tobacco industry. The Brown and Williamson documents. *Journal of the American Medical Association, 274,* 219–24.

Glatt, S.J., Faraone, S.V., & Tsuang, M.T. (2003). Association between a functional catechol O-methyltransferase gene polymorphism and schizophrenia: Meta-analysis of case–control and family-based studies. *American Journal of Psychiatry, 160,* 469–476.

Goldapple, K., Segal, Z., Garson, C., Lau, M., Bieling, P., Kennedy, S., & Mayberg, H. (2004). Treatment-specific effects of Cognitive Behavior Therapy. *Archives of General Psychiatry, 61,* 34–41.

Goodman, R., & Stevenson, J. (1989). A twin study of hyperactivity: II. The aetiological role of genes, family relationships and perinatal adversity. *Journal of Child Psychology and Psychiatry, 30,* 691–709.

Gottesman, I.I. (1991). *Schizophrenia genesis: The origins of madness.* New York: W.H. Freeman & Company.

Gottesman, I.I., & Gould, T.D. (2003). The endophenotype concept in psychiatry: Etymology and strategic intentions. *American Journal of Psychiatry, 160,* 636–645.

Gottlieb, G., Wahlsten, D., & Lickliter, R. (1998). The significance of biology for human development: A developmental psychobiological systems view. In W. Damon and R.M. Lerner (Eds.), *Handbook of child psychology.* Toronto: Wiley. pp. 233–273.

Gottlieb, G. (2003). On making behavioral genetics truly developmental. *Human Development, 46,* 337–355.

Greenland, S., & Rothman, K.J. (1998). Concepts of interaction. In R. Winters & E. O'Connor (Eds.), *Modern epidemiology, 2nd ed.* Lippincott-Raven: Philadelphia. pp. 329–342.

Greenough, W.T., Black, J.E., & Wallace, C.S. (1987). Experience and brain development. *Child Development, 58,* 539–559.

Greenough, W.T., & Black, J.E. (1992). Induction of brain structure by experience: Substrates for cognitive development. In M.R. Gunnar and C.A. Nelson (Eds.), *Developmental behavior neuroscience.* Hillsdale, NJ: Erlbaum. pp. 155–200.

Grigorenko, E.L. (2003). Epistasis and the genetics of complex traits. In R. Plomin, J.C. DeFries, I.W. Craig, & P. McGuffin (Eds.), *Behavioral genetics in the postgenomic era.* Washington: American Psychological Association.

Gunnar, M.R., & Donzella, B. (2002). Social regulation of the cortisol levels in early human development. *Psychoneuroendocrinology, 27,* 199–220.

Guttmacher, A.E., & Collins, F.S. (2003). Welcome to the genomic era. *The New England Journal of Medicine, 349,* 996–998.

Guy, J., Hendrich, B., Holmes, M., Martin, J.E., & Bird, A. (2001). A mouse Mecp2-null mutation causes neurological symptoms that mimic Rett syndrome. *Nature Genetics, 27,* 322–326.

Hagberg, B., Aicardi, J., Dias, K., & Ramos, O. (1983). A progressive syndrome of autism, dementia, ataxia and loss of purposeful hand use in girls: Rett's syndrome: report of 35 cases. *Annals of Neurology, 14,* 471–479.

Hariri, A.R., Mattay, V.S., Tessitore, A., Kolachana, B., Fera, F., Goldman, D., Egan, M.F., & Weinberger, D. (2002). Serotonin transporter genetic variation and the response of the human amygdala. *Science, 297,* 400–403.

Hariri, A.R., Drabant, E.M., Munoz, K.E., Kolachana, B.S., Mattay, V.S., Egan, M.F., & Weinberger, D.R. (2005). A susceptibility gene for affective disorders and the response of the human amygdala. *Archives of General Psychiatry, 62*, 146–152.

Harper, P.S. (1998). *Practical genetic counselling*. London: Butterworth Heinemann.

Harper, P.S. (2001). *Practical genetic counselling*. London: Hodder Arnold.

Harris, J.R. (1998). *The nurture assumption: Why children turn out the way they do*. London: Bloomsbury.

Harris, T. (Ed.) (2000). *Where inner and outer worlds meet: Psychosocial research in the tradition of George W. Brown*. London: Routledge/Taylor & Francis.

Harris, T., Brown, G.W., & Bifulco, A. (1986). Loss of parent in childhood and adult psychiatric disorder: The role of lack of adequate parental care. *Psychological Medicine, 16*, 641–659.

Harrison, J.E., & Bolton, P.F. (1997). Annotation: Tuberous sclerosis. *Journal of Child Psychology and Psychiatry, 38*, 603–614.

Harrison, P., & Owen, M. (2003). Genes for schizophrenia: Recent findings and their pathophysiological implications. *The Lancet, 361*, 417–419.

Hart, J., Gunnar, M., & Cicchetti, D. (1996). Altered neuroendocrine activity in maltreated children related to symptoms of depression. *Development and Psychopathology, 8*, 201–214.

Hattori, E., Liu, C., Badner, J.A., Bonner, T.I., Christian, S.L., Maheshwari, M., Detera-Wadleigh, S.D., Gibbs, R.A., & Gershon, E.S. (2003). Polymorphisms at the G72/G30 gene locus, on 13q33, are associated with bipolar disorder in two independent pedigree series. *American Journal of Human Genetics, 72*, 1131–1140.

Heath, A.C., Madden, P.A.F., Bucholz, K.K., Nelson, E.C., Todorov, A., Price, R.K., Whitfield, J.B., & Martin, N.G. (2003). Genetic and environmental risks of dependence on alcohol, tobacco, and other drugs. In R. Plomin, J.C. DeFries, G.E. McClearn, & P. McGuffin (Eds.), (2001), *Behavioral genetics*, 4th ed. New York: Worth. pp. 309–334.

Heath, A.C., & Nelson, E.C. (2002). Effects of the interaction between genotype and environment: Research into the genetic epidemiology of alcohol dependence. *Alcohol Research and Health, 26*, 193–201.

Heinz, A., Braus, D.F., Smolka, M.N., Wrase, J., Puls, I., Hermann, D., Klein, S., Grüsser, S.N., Flor, H., Schumann, G., Mann, K., & Bücher, C. (2005). Amygdala-prefrontal coupling depends on a genetic variation of the serotonin transporter. *Nature Neuroscience, 8*, 20–21.

Hennessey, J.W., & Levine, S. (1979). Stress, arousal, and the pituitary-adrenal system: a psychoendocrine hypothesis. In J.M. Sprague & A.N. Epstein (Eds.), *Progress in psychobiology and physiological psychology*. New York: Academic Press. pp. 133–178.

Henquet, C., Krabbendam, L., Spauwen, J., Kaplan, C., Lieb, R., Wittchen, H-U., & van Os, J. (2005). Prospective cohort study of cannabis use, predisposition for psychosis, and psychotic symptoms in young people. *British Medical Journal, 330*, 11–15.

Herrnstein, R.J., & Murray, C. (1994). *The bell curve: Intelligence and class structure in American life*. New York: Free Press.

Hetherington, E.M., Reiss, D., & Plomin, R. (1994). *Separate social worlds of siblings: Impact of nonshared environment on development*. Hillsdale, NJ: Lawrence Erlbaum.

Hettema, J.M., Neale, M.C., & Kendler, K.S. (1995). Physical similarity and the equal-environment assumption in twin studies of psychiatric disorders. *Behavior Genetics, 25*, 327–335.

Hewison, J., & Tizard, J. (1980). Parental involvement and reading attainment. *British Journal of Educational Psychology, 50*, 209–215.

Higley, J.D., & Suomi, S.J. (1989). Temperamental reactivity in non-human primates. In G.A. Kohnstamm, J.E. Bates, & M.K. Rothbart (Eds.), *Temperament in childhood.* Chichester: John Wiley & Sons. pp. 153–167.

Hill, A.V.S. (1998 a). Genetics and genomics of infectious disease susceptibility. *British Medical Bulletin, 55*, 401–413.

Hill, A.V.S. (1998 b). The immunogenetics of human infectious diseases. *Annual Review of Immunology, 16*, 593–617.

Hilts, P.J. (1996). *Smokescreen: The truth behind the tobacco industry cover-up.* Reading, MA: Addison-Wesley.

Hines, M. (2004). *Brain gender.* New York: Oxford University Press.

Hirotsune, S., Yoshida, N., Chen, A., Garrett, L., Sugiyama, F., Takahashi, S., et al. (2003). An expressed pseudogene regulates the messenger-RNA stability of its homologous coding gene. *Nature, 423*, 91–96.

Hirschorn, J.N., & Daly, M.J. (2005). Genome-wide association studies for common diseases and complex traits. *Nature Reviews – Genetics, 6*, 95–118.

Honda, H., Shimizu, Y., & Rutter, M. (2005). No effect of MMR withdrawal on the incidence of autism: A total population study. *Journal of Child Psychology and Psychiatry, 46*, 572–579.

Horn, G. (1990). Neural bases of recognition memory investigated through an analysis of imprinting. *Philosophical Transactions of the Royal Society of London, 329*, 133–142.

Hornig, M., Chian, D., & Lipkin, W.I. (2004). Neurotoxic effects of postnatal thimerosal are mouse strain-dependent. *Molecular Psychiatry, 9*, 833–845.

Howlin, P., Mawhood, L., & Rutter, M. (2000). Autism and developmental receptive language disorder – a follow-up comparison in early adult life. II: Social, behavioural, and psychiatric outcomes. *Journal of Child Psychology and Psychiatry, 41*, 561–578.

Humphries, S.E., Talmud, P.J., Hawe, E., Bolla, M., Day, I.N.M., & Miller, G.J. (2001). Apolipoprotein E4 and coronary heart disease in middle-aged men who smoke: A prospective study. *Lancet, 358*, 115–119.

Huson, S.M., & Korf, B. (2002). The phakomatoses. In D.L. Rimoin, J.M. Connor, R.E. Pyeritz, & B.R. Korf (Eds.), *Emery and Rimoin's principles and practice of medical genetics, vol. 3.* London & New York: Churchill Livingstone. pp. 3162–3202.

Huttenlocher, P.R. (2002). *Neural plasticity: The effects of environment on the development of the cerebral cortex.* Cambridge, MA: Harvard University Press.

Insel, T.R., & Young, L.J. (2001). The neurobiology of attachment. *Nature Reviews: Neuroscience, 2*, 129–136.

International Human Genome Sequencing Consortium. (2001). Initial sequencing and analysis of the human genome. *Nature, 409*, 860–921.

International Human Genome Sequencing Consortium. (2004). Finishing the euchromatic sequence of the human genome. *Nature, 431*, 931–945.

Jablensky, A. (2000). Epidemiology of schizophrenia. In M.G. Gelder, J.L. López-Ibor, & N. Andreasen (Eds.), *New Oxford textbook of psychiatry, vol. 1.* Oxford: Oxford University Press. pp. 585–599.

Jackson, J.F. (1993). Human behavioral genetics, Scarr's theory, and her views on interventions: A critical review and commentary on their implications for African American Children. *Child Development, 64,* 1318–1332.

Jacob, T., Waterman, B., Heath, A., True, W., Bucholz, K.K., Haber, R., Scherrer, J., & Fu, Q. (2003). Genetic and environmental effects on offspring alcoholism. *Archives of General Psychiatry, 60,* 1265–1272.

Jaenisch, R., & Bird, A. (2003). Epigenetic regulation of gene expression: How the genome integrates intrinsic and environmental signals. *Nature Genetics Supplement, 33,* 245–254.

Jaffee, S.R., Caspi, A., Moffitt, T.E., Dodge, K.A., Rutter, M., Taylor, A., & Tully, L. (2005). Nature x nurture: Genetic vulnerabilities interact with child maltreatment to promote behavior problems. *Development and Psychopathology, 17,* 67–84.

James, O. (2003). *They f*** you up: How to survive family life.* London: Bloomsbury.

Jensen, A.R. (1969). How much can we boost IQ and scholastic achievement? *Harvard Educational Review, 39,* 1–123.

Jensen, A.R. (1998). *The g factor: The science of mental abilities.* Westport, CN: Praeger.

Johnston, T.D., & Edwards, L. (2002). Genes, interaction, and the development of behavior. *Psychological Review, 109,* 26–34.

Johnstone, E.C., Ebmeier, K.P., Miller, P., Owens, D.G.C., & Lawrie, S.M. (2005). Predicting schizophrenia: Findings from the Edinburgh High-Risk study. *British Journal of Psychiatry, 186,* 18–25.

Johnstone, E.C., Lawrie, S.M., & Cosway, R. (2002). What does the Edinburgh High-Risk Study tell us about schizophrenia? *American Journal of Medical Genetics, 114,* 906–912.

Jones, I., Kent, L., & Craddock, N. (2002). Genetics of affective disorders. In P. McGuffin, M.J. Owen, & I.I. Gottesman (Eds.), *Psychiatric genetics and genomics.* Oxford: Oxford University Press. pp. 211–245.

Jones, P.B., & Fung, W.L.A. (2005). Ethnicity and mental health: The example of schizophrenia in the African-Caribbean population in Europe. In M. Rutter & M. Tienda (Eds.), *Ethnicity and causal mechanisms.* New York: Cambridge University Press. pp. 227–261.

Joseph, J. (2003). *The gene illusion: Genetic research in psychiatry and psychology under the microscope.* Ross on Wye: PCCS Books.

Kagan, J. (1994). *Galen's prophecy.* London: Free Association Books Ltd.

Kagan, J., & Snidman, N. (2004). *The long shadow of temperament.* Cambridge, MA: The Belknap Press.

Kamin, L.J. (1974). *The science and politics of IQ.* Potomac: Erlbaum.

Kamin, L.J., & Goldberger, A.S. (2002). Twin studies in behavioral research: A skeptical view. *Theoretical Population Biology, 61,* 83–95.

Kendell, R.E. (1975). *The role of diagnosis in psychiatry.* Oxford: Blackwell Scientific.

Kendler, K.S. (1996). Major depression and generalised anxiety disorder. Same genes, (partly) different environments – revisited. *British Journal of Psychiatry, 168* (suppl. 30), 68–75.

Kendler, K.S. (1998). Major depression and the environment: A psychiatric genetic perspective. *Pharmacopsychiatry, 31,* 5–9.

Kendler, K.S. (2005 a). Psychiatric genetics: A methodological critique. *American Journal of Psychiatry, 162,* 3–11.

Kendler, K.S. (2005 b). Towards a philosophical structure for psychiatry. *American Journal of Psychiatry, 162,* 433–440.

Kendler, K.S. (2005 c). "A gene for. . . ." The nature of gene action in psychiatric disorders. *American Journal of Psychiatry, 162,* 1243–1252.

Kendler, K.S., Gardner, C.O., & Prescott, C.A. (2002). Toward a comprehensive developmental model for major depression in women. *American Journal of Psychiatry, 159,* 1133–1145.

Kendler, K.S., Gruenberg, A.M., & Kinney, D.K. (1994). Independent diagnoses of adoptees and relatives as defined by DSM-III in the provincial and national samples of the Danish Adoption Study of Schizophrenia. *Archives of General Psychiatry, 51,* 436–468.

Kendler, K.S., Karkowski, L.M., & Prescott, C.A. (1999). Causal relationship between stressful life events and the onset of major depression. *American Journal of Psychiatry, 156,* 837–841.

Kendler, K.S., Kuhn, J.W., Vittum, J., Prescott, C.A., & Riley, B. (in press). The interaction of stressful life events and a serotonin transporter polymorphism in the prediction of episodes of major depression: A replication. *Archives of General Psychiatry.*

Kendler, K.S., Myers, J.M., & Neale, M.C. (2000a). A multidemensional twin study of mental health in women. *American Journal of Psychiatry, 157,* 506–513.

Kendler, K.S., Neale, M.C., Kessler, R.C., Heath, A.C., & Eaves, L.J. (1993 a). The lifetime history of major depression in women: Reliability of diagnosis and heritability. *Archives of General Psychiatry, 50,* 863–870.

Kendler, K.S., Neale, M., Kessler, R., Heath, A., & Eaves, L. (1993 b). A twin study of recent life events and difficulties. *Archives of General Psychiatry, 50,* 789–796.

Kendler, K.S., Neale, M.C., Kessler, R.C., Heath, A.C., & Eaves, L.J. (1994). Parental treatment and the equal environment assumption in twin studies of psychiatric illness. *Psychological Medicine, 24,* 579–590.

Kendler, K.S., Neale, M.C., Prescott, C.A., Heath, A.C., Corey, L.A., & Eaves, L.J. (1996). Childhood parental loss and alcoholism in women: A causal analysis using a twin-family design. *Psychological Medicine, 26,* 79–95.

Kendler, K.S., Neale, M.C., & Walsh, D. (1995). Evaluating the spectrum concept of schizophrenia in the Roscommon Family Study. *American Journal of Psychiatry, 152,* 749–754.

Kendler, K.S., Thornton, L.M., & Gardner, C.O. (2000 b). Stressful life events and previous episodes in the etiology of major depression in women: An evaluation of the "kindling" hypothesis. *American Journal of Psychiatry, 157,* 1243–1251.

Kendler, K.S., Thornton, L.M., & Gardner, C.O. (2001). Genetic risk, number of previous depressive episodes, and stressful life events in predicting onset of major depression. *American Journal of Psychiatry, 158,* 582–586.

Kerwin, R.W., & Arranz, M.J. (2002). Psychopharmacogenetics. In P. McGuffin, M.J. Owen, & I.I. Gottesman (Eds.), *Psychiatric genetics and genomics*. Oxford: Oxford University Press. pp. 397–413.

Keshavan, M.S., Kennedy, J.L., & Murray, R.M. (Eds.) (2004). *Neurodevelopment and schizophrenia*. London, & New York: Cambridge University Press.

Kidd, K.K., Castiglione, C.M., Kidd, J.R., Speed, W.C., Goldman, D., Knowler, W.C., Lu, R.B., & Bonne-Tamir, B. (1996). DRD2 halotypes containing the TaqI A1 allele: Implications for alcoholism research. *Alcoholism, Clinical and Experimental Research, 20*, 697–705.

Kimmelman, J. (2005). Recent developments in gene transfer: risk and ethics. *British Medical Journal, 330*, 79–82.

Knapp, M., & Becker, T. (2004). Impact of genotyping errors on type I error rate of the haplotype-sharing transmission/disequilibrium test (HS-TDT). *American Journal of Human Genetics, 74*, 589–591; author reply 591–593.

Knopik, V.S., Smith, S.D., Cardon, L., Pennington, B., Gayan, J., Olson, R.K., & DeFries, J.C. (2002). Differential genetic etiology of reading component processes as a function of IQ. *Behavior Genetics, 32*, 181–198.

Knudsen, E.I. (2004). Sensitive periods on the development of the brain and behavior. *Journal of Cognitive Neuroscience, 16*, 1412–1425.

Koeppen-Schomerus, G., Eley, T.C., Wolke, D., Gringras, P., & Plomin, R. (2000). The interaction of prematurity with genetic and environmental influences on cognitive development in twins. *Journal of Pediatrics, 137*, 527–533.

Kohnstamm, G.A., Bates, J.E., & Rothbart, M.K. (Eds.) (1989). *Temperament in childhood*. Chichester: John Wiley, & Sons.

Kotb, M., Norrby-Teglund, A., McGeer, A., El-Sherbini, H., Dorak, M.T., Khurshid, A., Green, K., Peeples, J., Wade, J., Thomson, G., Schwartz, B., & Low, D.E. (2002). An immunogenetic and molecular basis for differences in outcomes of invasive group A streptococcal infections. *Nature Medicine, 8*, 1398–1404.

Kotimaa, A.J., Moilanen, I., Taanila, A., et al. (2003). Maternal smoking and hyperactivity in 8-year-old children. *Journal of the American Academy of Child and Adolescent Psychiatry, 42*, 826–833.

Kraemer, H.C. (2003). Current concepts of risk in psychiatric disorders. *Current Opinion in Psychiatry, 16*, 421–430.

Kramer, D.A. (2005). Commentary: Gene–environment interplay in the context of genetics, epigenetics, and gene expression. *Journal of the American Academy of Child and Adolescent Psychiatry, 44*, 19–27.

Kuntsi, J., Eley, T.C., Taylor, A., Hughes, C., Asherson, P., Caspi, A., & Moffitt, T.E. (2004). Co-occurrence of ADHD and low IQ has genetic origins. *American Journal of Medical Genetics B (Neuropsychiatric Genetics), 124B*, 41–47.

Kupfer, D.J., First, M.B., & Regier, D.A. (2002). *A research agenda for DSM-V*. Washington, DC: American Psychiatric Association.

Lakatos, K., Nemoda, Z., Toth, I., Ronai, Z., Ney, K., Sasvari-Szekely, M., & Gervai, J. (2002). Further evidence for the role of the dopamine D4 receptor (DRD4) gene in attachment disorganization: Interaction of the exon III 48-bp repeat and the -521 C/T promoter polymorphisms. *Molecular Psychiatry, 7*, 27–31.

Laub, J.H., Nagin, D.S., & Sampson, R.J. (1998). Trajectories of change in criminal offending: Good marriages and the desistance process. *American Sociological Review, 63*, 225–238.

Laub, J.H., & Sampson, R.J. (2003). *Shared beginnings, divergent lives: Delinquent boys to age 70.* Cambridge, Massachusetts: Harvard University Press.

Leckman, J.F., & Cohen, D.J. (2002). Tic disorders. In M. Rutter & E. Taylor (Eds.), *Child and adolescent psychiatry, 4th ed.* Oxford: Blackwell Scientific. pp. 593–611.

Lee, A.S., & Murray, R.M. (1988). The long-term outcome of Maudsley depressives. *British Journal of Psychiatry, 153*, 741–751.

Le Fanu, J. (1999). *The rise and fall of modern medicine.* London: Abacus.

Lesch, K.P., Bengel, D., Heils, A., et al. (1996). A gene regulatory region polymorphism alters serotonin transporter expression and is associated with anxiety-related personality traits. *Science, 274*, 1527–1531.

Levine, S. (1982). Comparative and psychobiological perspectives on development. In W.A. Collins (Ed.), *Minnesota Symposia on Child Psychology: Vol. 15. The concept of development.* Hillsdale, NJ: Lawrence Erlbaum Associates. pp. 29–53.

Levinson, D.F., Levinson, M.D., Segurado, R., & Lewis, C.M. (2003). Genome scan meta-analysis of schizophrenia and bipolar disorder, part I: Methods and power analysis. *American Journal of Human Genetics, 73*, 17–33.

Levy, F., & Hay, D. (Eds.) (2001). *Attention, genes and ADHD.* Hove, Sussex: Brunner-Routledge.

Lewin, B. (2004). *Genes VIII.* Upper Saddle River, NJ: Pearson Prentice Hall.

Lewontin, R. (2000). *The triple helix: Gene, organism and environment,* Cambridge MA, & London: Harvard University Press.

Liddell, M.B., Williams, J., & Owen, M.J. (2002). The dementias. In P. McGuffin, M.J. Owen, & I.I. Gottesman (Eds.), *Psychiatric genetics and genomics.* Oxford: Oxford University Press. pp. 341–393.

Liddle, P.F. (2000). Descriptive clinical features of schizophrenia. In M.G. Gelder, J.L. López-Ibor, & N. Andreasen (Eds.), *New Oxford textbook of psychiatry, vol. 1.* Oxford: Oxford University Press. pp. 571–576.

Liu, D., Diorio, J., Tannenbaum, B., Caldji, C., Francis, D., Freedman, A., Sharma, S., Pearson, D., Plotsky, P., & Meaney, M.J. (1997). Maternal care, hippocampal glucocorticoid receptors, and hypothalamic-pituitary-adrenal responses to stress. *Science, 277*, 1659–1662.

Loehlin, J.C. (1989). Partitioning environmental and genetic contributions to behavioral development. *The American Psychologist, 44*, 1285–1292.

Lord, C., & Bailey, A. (2002). Autism spectrum disorders. In M. Rutter & E. Taylor (Eds.), *Child and adolescent psychiatry, 4th ed.* Oxford: Blackwell Scientific. pp. 636–663.

Lyytinen, H., Ahonen, T., Eklund, K., Guttorm, T., Kulju, P., Laakso, M-L., Leiwo, M., Leppänen, P., Lyytinen, P., Poikkeus, A-M., Richardson, U., Torppa, M., & Viholainen, H. (2004). Early development of children at familial risk for dyslexia – follow-up from birth to school age. *Dyslexia, 10*, 146–178.

Mackintosh, N.J. (1995). *Cyril Burt: Fraud or framed?* Oxford: Oxford University Press.

Maes, H.H., Woodard, C.E., Murrelle, L., Meyer, J.M., Silberg, J.L., Hewitt, J.K., Rutter, M., Simonoff, E., Pickles, A., Carbonneau, R., Neale, M.C., & Eaves, L.J.

(1999). Tobacco, alcohol and drug use in eight- to sixteen-year-old twins: The Virginia Twin Study of Adolescent Behavioral Development. *Journal of Studies on Alcohol, 60,* 293–305.

Marcus, G. (2004). *The birth of the mind: How a tiny number of genes creates the complexities of human thought.* New York: Basic Books.

Margolis, R.L., McInnis, M.G., Rosenblatt, A., & Ross, C.A. (1999). Trinucleotide repeat expansion and neuropsychiatric disease. *Archives of General Psychiatry, 56,* 1019–1031.

Marks, J. (2002). *What it means to be 98% chimpanzee: Apes, people, and their genes.* Berkeley & Los Angeles: University of California Press.

Marlow, N. (2004). Neurocognitive outcome after very preterm birth. *Archives of Disease in Childhood, 89,* F224–F228.

Marlow, N., Wolke, D., Bracewell, M.A., & Samara, M., for the EPICure Study Group (2005). Neurologic and developmental disability at six years of age after extremely preterm birth. *New England Journal of Medicine, 352,* 9–19.

Marmot, M., & Wilkinson, R.G. (1999). *Social determinants of health.* Oxford: Oxford University Press.

Marshall, E. (1995 a). Less hype, more biology needed for gene therapy. *Science, 270,* 1751.

Marshall, E. (1995 b). Gene therapy's growing pains. *Science, 269,* 1050–1055.

Maughan, B., Collishaw, S., & Pickles, A. (1998). School achievement and adult qualifications among adoptees: A longitudinal study. *Journal of Child Psychology and Psychiatry, 39,* 669–685.

Maughan, B., & Pickles, A. (1990). Adopted and illegitimate children growing up. In L. Robins, & M. Rutter (Eds.), *Straight and devious pathways from childhood to adulthood.* New York: Cambridge University Press. pp. 36–61.

Maughan, B., Pickles, A., Collishaw, S., Messer, J., Shearer, C., & Rutter, M. (to be submitted). *Age at onset and recurrence of depression: Developmental variations in risk.*

Maughan, B., Taylor, A., Caspi, A., & Moffitt, T.E. (2004). Prenatal smoking and child antisocial behavior: Testing genetic and environmental confounds. *Archives of General Psychiatry, 61,* 836–843.

Mayes, L.C. (1999). Developing brain and in-utero cocaine exposure: Effects on neural ontogeny. *Development and Psychopathology, 11,* 685–714.

Mayeux, R.M., Ottman, R.P., Maestre, G.M., Ngai, C.B., Tang, M.-X.P., & Ginsberg, H.M. (1995). Synergistic effects of traumatic head injury and apolipoprotein-epsilon4 in patients with Alzheimer's disease. *Neurology, 45,* 555–557.

Mazur, A. Booth, A., & Dabbs, J.M. (1992). Testosterone and chess competition. *Social Psychology Quarterly, 55,* 70–77.

McClelland, G.H., & Judd, C.M. (1993). Statistical difficulties of detecting interactions and moderator effects. *Psychological Bulletin, 114,* 376–390.

McDonald, C., Bullmore, E.T., Sham, P.C., Chitnis, X., Wickham, H., Bramon, E., & Murray, R.M. (2004). Association of genetic risks for schizophrenia and bipolar disorder with specific and generic brain structural endophenotypes. *Archives of General Psychiatry, 61,* 974–984.

McEwen, B., & Lasley, E.N. (2002). *The end of stress.* Washington, DC: Joseph Henry Press.

McGuffin, P., Asherson, P., Owen, M., & Farmer, A. (1994). The strength of the genetic effect. Is there room for an environmental influence in the aetiology of schizophrenia? *British Journal of Psychiatry, 164,* 593–599.

McGuffin, P., Katz, R., Watkins, S., & Rutherford, J. (1996). A hospital-based twin register of the heritability of DSM-IV unipolar depression. *Archives of General Psychiatry, 53,* 129–136.

McGuffin, P., Owen, M.J., & Gottesman, I.I. (Eds.) (2002). *Psychiatric genetics and genomics.* Oxford: Oxford University Press.

McGuffin, P., & Rutter, M. (2002). Genetics of normal and abnormal development. In M. Rutter & E. Taylor. *Child and adolescent psychiatry, 4th ed.* Oxford: Blackwell Science. pp. 185–204.

McKeown, T. (1976). *The role of medicine: Dream, mirage or nemesis?* London: Nuffield Provincial Hospitals Trust.

McKusick, V.A. (2002). History of medical genetics. In D.L. Rimoin, J.M. Connor, R.E. Pyeritz, & B.E. Korf (Eds.), *Emery and Rimoin's principles of medical genetics, 4th ed.* London, & New York: Churchill Livingstone. pp. 3–36.

Meaney, M.J. (2001). Maternal care, gene expression, and the transmission of individual differences in stress reactivity across generations. *Annual Review of Neuroscience, 24,* 1161–1192.

Mednick, S.A. (1978). Berkson's fallacy and high-risk research. In L.C. Wynne & S.S. Matthysee (Eds.). *The nature of schizophrenia: New approaches to research and treatment.* New York: Wiley. pp. 442–452.

Meisel, P., Siegemund, A., Dombrowa, S., Sawaf, H., Fanghaenel, J., & Kocher, T. (2002). Smoking and polymorphisms of the interleukin-1 gene cluster (IL – 1α, IL – 1β, and IL – 1RN) in patients with periodontal disease. *Journal of Periodontology, 73,* 27–32.

Meisel, P., Schwahn, C., Gesch, D., Bernhardt, O., John, U., & Kocher, T. (2004). Dose–effect relation of smoking and the interleukin-1 gene polymorphism in periodontal disease. *Journal of Periodontology, 75,* 236–242.

Meyer, J.M., Rutter, M., Silberg, J.L., Maes, H.H., Simonoff, E., Shillady, L.L., Pickles, A., Hewitt, J.K., & Eaves, L.J. (2000). Familial aggregation for conduct disorder symptomatology: The role of genes, marital discord and family adaptability. *Psychological Medicine, 30,* 759–774.

Miele, F. (2002). *Intelligence, race and genetics: Conversations with Arthur R. Jensen.* Cambridge, MA: Westview Press.

Moffitt, T.E. (2005). The new look of behavioral genetics in developmental psychopathology: Gene–environment interplay in antisocial behaviors. *Psychological Bulletin, 131,* 533–554.

Moffitt, T.E., Caspi, A., & Rutter, M. (2005). Interaction between measured genes and measured environments: A research strategy. *Archives of General Psychiatry, 62,* 473–481.

Moffitt, T.E., Caspi, A., & Rutter, M. (in press). Measured gene–environment interactions in psychopathology: Concepts, research strategies, and implications for research, intervention, and public understanding of genetics. *Perspectives on Psychological Science.*

Moffitt, T.E., Caspi, A., Rutter, M., & Silva, P.A. (2001). *Sex differences in antisocial behaviour: Conduct disorder, delinquency, and violence in the Dunedin Longitudinal Study.* Cambridge: Cambridge University Press.

Moffitt, T.E., & the E-Risk Study Team. (2002). Teen-aged mothers in contemporary Britain. *Journal of Child Psychology and Psychiatry, 43,* 727–742.

Molenaar, P.C.M., Boomsma, D.I., & Dolan, C.V. (1993). A third source of developmental differences. *Behavior Genetics, 23,* 519–524.

Morange, M. (2001). *The misunderstood gene.* Cambridge, MA, & London: Harvard University Press.

MTA Cooperative Group. (1999 a). A 14-month randomized clinical trial of treatment strategies for attention-deficit/hyperactivity disorder. *Archives of General Psychiatry, 56,* 1073–1086.

MTA Cooperative Group. (1999 b). Moderators and mediators of treatment response for children with attention-deficit/hyperactivity disorder. *Archives of General Psychiatry, 56,* 1088–1096.

MTA Cooperative Group. (2004 a). National Institute of Mental Health Multimodal Treatment Study of ADHD follow-up: 24-month outcomes of treatment strategies for attention-deficit/hyperactivity disorder. *Pediatrics, 113,* 754–761.

MTA Cooperative Group. (2004 b). National Institute of Mental Health Multimodal Treatment Study of ADHD follow-up: Changes in effectiveness and growth after the end of treatment. *Pediatrics, 113,* 762–769.

Müller-Hill, B. (1993). The shadow of genetic injustice. *Nature, 362,* 491–492.

Munafò, M.R., Clark, T.G., Moore, L.R., Payne, E., & Flint, J. (2003). Genetic polymorphisms and personality in healthy adults: A systematic review and meta-analysis. *Molecular Psychiatry, 8,* 471–484.

Murphy, D.L., Li, Q., Wichems, C., Andrews, A., Lesch, K-P., & Uhi, G. (2001). Genetic perspectives on the serotonin transporter. *Brain Research Bulletin, 56,* 487–494.

Nadder, T.S., Silberg, J.L., Rutter, M., Maes, H.H., & Eaves, L.J. (2001). Comparison of multiple measures of adhd symptomatology: A multivariate genetic analysis. *Journal of Child Psychology and Psychiatry, 42,* 475–486.

Nadder, T.S., Silberg, J.L., Rutter, M., Maes, H.H., & Eaves, L.J. (2002). Genetic effects on the variation and covariation of attention deficit-hyperactivity disorder (ADHD) and oppositional-defiant/conduct disorder (ODD/CD) symptomatologies across informant and occasion of measurement. *Psychological Medicine, 32,* 39–53.

Nance, W.E., & Corey, L.A. (1976). Genetic models for the analysis of data from families of identical twins. *Genetics, 83,* 811–826.

Nicholl, J.A.R., Roberts, G.W., & Graham, D.I. (1995). Apolipoprotein E e4 allele is associated with deposition of amyloid-B protein following head injury. *Nature Medicine, 1,* 135–137.

Nigg, J.T., & Goldsmith, H.H. (1998). Developmental psychopathology, personality, and temperament: Reflections on recent behavioral genetics research. *Human Biology, 70,* 387–412.

Nnadi, C.U., Goldberg, J.F., & Malhotra, A.K. (2005). Pharmacogenetics in mood disorder. *Current Opinion in Psychiatry, 18,* 33–39.

Nóbrega, M.A., Zhu, Y., Plajzer-Frick, I., Afzal, V., & Rubin, E.M. (2004). Megabase deletions of gene deserts result in viable mice. *Nature, 431*, 988–993.

Nuffield Council on Bioethics. (2002). *Genetics and human behaviour: The ethical context.* London: Nuffield Council on Bioethics.

O'Brien, J.T. (1997). The "glucocorticoid cascade" hypothesis in man: Prolonged stress may cause permanent brain damage. *British Journal of Psychiatry, 170*, 199–201.

O'Connor, T.G., Bredenkamp, D., Rutter, M., & the English and Romanian Adoptees (ERA) Study Team. (1999). Attachment disturbances and disorders in children exposed to early severe deprivation. *Infant Mental Health Journal, 20*, 10–29.

O'Connor, T.G., Deater-Deckard, K., Fulker, D., Rutter, M., & Plomin, R. (1998). Genotype–environment correlations in late childhood and early adolescence: Antisocial behavioral problems and coercive parenting. *Developmental Psychology, 34*, 970–981.

O'Connor, T.G., Marvin, R.S., Rutter, M., Olrick, J.T., Britner, P.A., & the English and Romanian Adoptees Study Team. (2003). Child–parent attachment following early institutional deprivation. *Development and Psychopathology, 15*, 19–38.

O'Connor, T., Rutter, M., Beckett, C., Keaveney, L., Kreppner, J.M., & the English and Romanian Adoptees (ERA) Study Team. (2000). The effects of global severe privation on cognitive competence: Extension and longitudinal follow-up. *Child Development, 71*, 376–390.

O'Donovan, M.C., Williams, N.M., & Owen, M.J. (2003). Recent advances in the genetics of schizophrenia. *Human Molecular Genetics, 12*, R125–R133.

Office for National Statistics. (2002). *Social Trends 32.* London: Her Majesty's Stationery Office.

Ogdie, M.N., Macphie, I.L., Minassian, S.L., Yang, M., Fisher, S.E., Francks, C., Cantor, R.M., McCracken, J.T., McGough, J.J., Nelson, S.F., Monaco, A.P., & Smalley, S.L. (2003). A genomewide scan for Attention-Deficit/Hyperactivity disorder in an extended sample: Suggestive linkage on 17p11. *American Journal of Human Genetics, 72*, 1268–1279.

Ong, E.K., & Glantz, S.A. (2000). Tobacco industry efforts subverting International Agency for Research on Cancer's second-hand smoke study. *Lancet, 355*, 1253–1259.

Ordovas, J.M., Corella, D., Demissie, S., Cupples, L.A., Couture, P., Coltell, O., Wilson, P.W.F., Schaefer, E.J., & Tucker, K.L. (2002). Dietary fat intake determines the effect of a common polymorphism in the hepatic lipase gene promoter on high-density lipoprotein metabolism: Evidence of a strong dose effect in this gene–nutrient interaction in the Framingham study. *Circulation, 106*, 2315–2321.

Passarge, E. (2002). Gastrointestinal tract and hepatobiliary duct system. In D.L. Rimoin, J.M. Connor, R.E. Pyeritz, & B.R. Korf (Eds.), *Emery and Rimoin's principles and practice of medical genetics, vol. 2.* London, & New York: Churchill Livingstone. pp. 1747–1759.

Patrick, C.J., Zempolich, K.A., & Levenston, G.K. (1997). Emotionality and violent behavior in psychopaths: A biosocial analysis. In A. Raine, P. Brennan, D.P. Farrington, & S.A. Mednick (Eds.), *Biosocial bases of violence*. New York: Plenum. pp. 145–163.

Paulesu, E., Démonet, J., Fazio, F., McCrory, E., Chanoine, V., Brunswick, N., Cappa, S., Cossu, G., Habib, M., Frith, C., & Frith, U. (2001). Dyslexia: Cultural diversity and biological unity. *Science, 291,* 2165–2167.

Pedersen, N.L., Ripatti, S., Berg, S., Reynolds, C., Hofer, S.M., Finkel, D., Gatz, M., & Palmgren, J. (2003). The influence of mortality on twin models of change: Addressing missingness through multiple imputation. *Behavior Genetics, 33,* 161–169.

Pelosi, A.J., & Appleby, L. (1992). Psychological influences on cancer and ischaemic heart disease. *British Medical Journal, 304,* 1295–1298.

Petitto, J.M., & Evans, D.L., (1999). Clinical neuroimmunology: Understanding the development and pathogenesis of neuropsychiatric and psychosomatic illnesses. In D.S. Charney, E.J. Nestler, & B.S. Bunney (Eds.), *Neurobiology of mental illness.* New York, & Oxford: Oxford University Press. pp. 162–169.

Petronis, A. (2001). Human morbid genetics revisited: Relevance of epigenetics. *Trends in Genetics, 17,* 142–146.

Petronis, A., Gottesman, I.I., Kan, P., Kennedy, J.C., Basile, V.S., Paterson, A.D., & Popendikyte V. (2003). Monozygotic twins exhibit numerous epigenetic differences: clues to twin discordance? *Schizophrenia Bulletin, 29,* 169–78.

Pickles, A. (1993). Stages, precursors and causes in development. In D.F. Hay & A. Angold (Eds.), *Precursors and causes in development and psychopathology.* Chichester: Wiley. pp. 23–49.

Pickles, A., & Angold, A. (2003). Natural categories or fundamental dimensions: On carving nature at the joints and the re-articulation of psychopathology. *Development and Psychopathology, 15,* 529–551.

Pickles, A., Bolton, P., Macdonald, H., Bailey, A., Le Couteur, A., Sim, L., & Rutter, M. (1995). Latent class analysis of recurrence risk for complex phenotypes with selection and measurement error: A twin and family history study of autism. *American Journal of Human Genetics, 57,* 717–726.

Pickles, A., Starr, E., Kazak, S., Bolton, P., Papanikolau, K., Bailey, A.J., Goodman, R., & Rutter, M. (2000). Variable expression of the autism broader phenotype: Findings from extended pedigrees. *Journal of Child Psychology and Psychiatry, 41,* 491–502.

Pike, A., McGuire, S., Hetherington, E.M., Reiss, D., & Plomin, R. (1996). Family environment and adolescent depression and antisocial behavior: A multivariate genetic analysis. *Developmental Psychology, 32,* 590–603.

Pinker, S. (2002). *The blank slate: The modern denial of human nature.* New York: Viking Penguin.

Plomin, R. (1994). *Genetics and experience: The interplay between nature and nurture.* Thousand Oaks, CA: Sage Publications.

Plomin, R., & Crabbe, J. (2000). DNA. *Psychological Bulletin, 126,* 806–828.

Plomin, R., & Daniels, D. (1987). Why are children in the same family so different from one another? *The Behavioral and Brain Sciences, 10,* 1–15.

Plomin, R., DeFries, J.C., Craig, I.W., & McGuffin, P. (Eds.). (2003). *Behavioral genetics in the postgenomic era.* Washington, DC: American Psychological Association.

Plomin, R., DeFries, J.C., & Fulker, D.W. (1988). *Nature and nurture during infancy and early childhood.* New York: Cambridge University Press.

Plomin, R., DeFries, J.C., & Loehlin, J.C. (1977). Genotype–environment interaction and correlation in the analysis of human behavior. *Psychological Bulletin, 84*, 309–322.

Plomin, R., DeFries, J., McClearn, G.E., & McGuffin, P. (Eds.) (2001). *Behavioral genetics, 4th ed.* New York: Worth Publishers.

Plomin, R., & Kovas, Y. (2005). Generalist genes and learning disabilities. *Psychological Bulletin, 131*, 592–617.

Plomin, R., Owen, M.J., & McGuffin, P. (1994). The genetic basis of complex human behaviours. *Science, 264*, 1733–1739.

Poeggel, G., Helmeke, C., Abraham, A., Schwabe, T., Friedrich, P., & Braun, K. (2003). Juvenile emotional experience alters synaptic composition in the rodent cortex, hippocampus, and lateral amygdala. *Proceedings of the National Academy of Sciences, 100*, 16137–16142.

Poulton, R.P., Caspi, A., Moffitt, T.E., Cannon, M., Murray, R., & Harrington, H.L. (2000). Children's self-reported psychotic symptoms predict adult schizophreniform disorders: A 15-year longitudinal study. *Archives of General Psychiatry, 57*, 1053–1058.

Quinton, D., Pickles, A., Maughan, B., & Rutter, M. (1993). Partners, peers, and pathways: Assortative pairing and continuities in conduct disorder. *Development and Psychopathology, 5*, 763–783.

Quinton, D., & Rutter, M. (1976). Early hospital admissions and later disturbances of behaviour: An attempted replication of Douglas' findings. *Developmental Medicine and Child Neurology, 18*, 447–459.

Radke-Yarrow, M. (1998). *Children of depressed mothers.* New York: Cambridge University Press.

Ramoz, N., Reichert, J.G., Smith, C.J., Silverman, J.M., Bespalova, I.N., Davis, K.L. et al. (2004). Linkage and association of the mitochondrial aspartate/glutamate carrier SLC25A12 gene with autism. *American Journal of Psychiatry, 161*, 662–669.

Rapoport, J., & Swedo, S. (2002). Obsessive–compulsive disorder. In M. Rutter & E. Taylor (Eds.), *Child and adolescent psychiatry, 4th ed.* Oxford: Blackwell Science. pp. 571–592.

Reif, A., & Lesch, K-P. (2003). Toward a molecular architecture of personality. *Behavioural Brain Research, 139*, 1–20.

Relph, K., Harrington, K., & Pandha, H. (2004). Recent developments and current status of gene therapy using viral vectors in the United Kingdom. *British Medical Journal, 329*, 839–842.

Rhee, S.H., & Waldman, I.D. (2002). Genetic and environmental influences on antisocial behavior: A meta-analysis of twin and adoption studies. *Psychological Bulletin, 128*, 490–529.

Ridley, M. (2003). *Nature via nurture: Genes, experience and what makes us human.* London: Fourth Estate.

Riggins-Caspers, K.M., Cadoret, R.J., Knutson, J.F., & Langbehn, D. (2003). Biology–environment interaction and evocative biology–environment correlation: Contributions of harsh discipline and parental psychopathology to problem adolescent behaviors. *Behavior Genetics, 33*, 205–220.

Rimoin, D.L., Connor, J.M., Pyeritz, R.E., & Korf, B.R. (Eds.) (2002). *Emery and Rimoin's principles and practice of medical genetics, 4th ed., vols. 1–3.* London: Churchill Livingstone.

Risch, N., & Merikangas, K. (1996). The future of genetic studies of complex human diseases. *Science, 273,* 1516–1517.

Risch, N., & Zhang, H. (1995). Extreme discordant sib pairs for mapping quantitative trait loci in humans. *Science, 268,* 1584–1589.

Robins, L. (1966). *Deviant children grown up: A sociological and psychiatric study of sociopathic personality.* Baltimore: Williams, & Wilkins.

Rose, R.J., Viken, R.J., Dick, D.M., Bates, J.E., Pulkkinen, L., & Kaprio, J. (2003). It *does* take a village: Non-familial environments and children's behavior. *Psychological Science, 14,* 273–277.

Rose, S. (1995). The rise of neurogenetic determinism. *Nature, 373,* 380–382.

Rose, S. (1998). *Lifelines: Biology, freedom, determinism.* Harmondsworth: The Penguin Press.

Rose, S., Lewontin, R.C., & Kamin, L.J. (1984). *Not in our genes: Biology, ideology and human nature.* London: Penguin.

Rosenweig, M.R., & Bennett, E.L. (1996). Psychobiology of plasticity: Effects of training and experience on brain and behavior. *Behavioural Brain Research, 78,* 57–65.

Rothman, K.J. (1981). Induction and latent periods. *American Journal of Epidemiology, 104,* 587–592.

Rothman, K.J., & Greenland, S. (1998). Causation and causal inference. In K.J. Rothman, & S. Greenland (Eds.), *Modern epidemiology.* Philadelphia, PA: Lippcott-Raven. pp. 7–28.

Rotter, J.I., & Diamond, J.M. (1987). What maintains the frequencies of human genetic diseases? *Nature, 329,* 289–290.

Rowe, D.C. (1994). *The limits of family influence: Genes, experience, and behavior.* New York: The Guilford Press.

Rowe, D.C., Jacobson, K.C., & van den Oord, E.J.C.G. (1999). Genetic and environmental influences on vocabulary IQ: Parental education level as moderator. *Child Development, 70,* 1151–1162.

Rowe, R., Maughan, B., Worthman, C.M., Costello, E.J., & Angold, A. (2004). Testosterone, antisocial behavior, and social dominance in boys: Pubertal development and biosocial interaction. *Biological Psychiatry, 55,* 546–552.

Royal College of Psychiatrists' Working Party. (2001). *Guidelines for researchers and for research ethics committees on psychiatric research involving human participants* (Council Report No: CR82). London: Gaskell.

Rutter, M. (1965). Classification and categorization in child psychiatry. *Journal of Child Psychology and Psychiatry, 6,* 71–83.

Rutter, M. (1971). Parent–child separation: Psychological effects on the children. *Journal of Child Psychology and Psychiatry, 12,* 233–260.

Rutter, M. (1972). *Maternal deprivation reassessed.* Harmondsworth, Middlesex: Penguin.

Rutter, M. (1978). Diagnostic validity in child psychiatry. *Advances in Biological Psychiatry, 2,* 2–22.

Rutter, M. (1983). Statistical and personal interactions: facets and perspectives. In D. Magnusson & V. Allen (Eds.), *Human development: An interactional perspective.* New York: Academic Press. pp. 295–319.

Rutter, M. (1987). Continuities and discontinuities from infancy. In J. Osofsky (Ed.), *Handbook of infant development, 2nd ed.* New York: Wiley. pp. 1256–1296.

Rutter, M. (1989). Pathways from childhood to adult life. *Journal of Child Psychology and Psychiatry, 30,* 23–51.

Rutter, M. (1994). Psychiatric genetics: Research challenges and pathways forward. *American Journal of Medical Genetics (Neuropsychiatric Genetics), 54,* 185–198.

Rutter, M. (1997). Comorbidity: Concepts, claims and choices. *Criminal Behaviour and Mental Health, 7,* 265–286.

Rutter, M. (1999 a). Genes and behaviour: Health potential and ethical concerns. In A. Carroll, & C. Skidmore (Eds.), *Inventing heaven? Quakers confront the challenges of genetic engineering.* Reading, Berks: Sowle Press. pp. 66–88.

Rutter, M. (1999 b). Social context: Meanings, measures and mechanisms. *European Review, 7,* 139–149.

Rutter, M. (2000 a). Genetic studies of autism: From the 1970s into the millennium. *Journal of Abnormal Child Psychology, 28,* 3–14.

Rutter, M. (2000 b). Negative life events and family negativity: Accomplishments and challenges. In T. Harris (Ed.), *Where inner and outer worlds meet: Psychosocial research in the tradition of George W. Brown.* London: Routledge/Taylor & Francis. pp. 123–149.

Rutter, M. (2000 c). Resilience reconsidered: Conceptual considerations, empirical findings, and policy implications. In J.P. Shonkoff & S.J. Meisels (Eds.), *Handbook of early childhood intervention, 2nd ed.* New York: Cambridge University Press. pp. 651–682.

Rutter, M. (2002 a). Maternal deprivation. In M.H. Bornstein (Ed.), *Handbook of parenting: vol. 4. Social conditions and applied parenting, 2nd ed.* Mahwah, NJ: Lawrence Erlbaum. pp. 181–202.

Rutter, M. (2002 b). Nature, nurture, and development: From evangelism through science toward policy and practice. *Child Development, 73,* 1–21.

Rutter, M. (2002 c). Substance use and abuse: Causal pathways considerations. In M. Rutter & E. Taylor (Eds.), *Child and adolescent psychiatry, 4th ed.* Oxford: Blackwell Scientific. pp. 455–462.

Rutter, M. (2003 a). Categories, dimensions, and the mental health of children and adolescents. In J.A. King, C.F. Ferris, & I.I. Lederhendler (Eds.), *Roots of mental illness in children.* New York: The New York Academy of Sciences. pp. 11–21.

Rutter, M. (2003 b). Crucial paths from risk indicator to causal mechanism. In B. Lahey, T. Moffitt, & A. Caspi (Eds.), *The causes of conduct disorder and serious juvenile delinquency.* New York: The Guilford Press. pp. 3–24.

Rutter, M. (2003 c). Genetic influences on risk and protection: Implications for understanding resilience. In S. Luthar (Ed.), *Resilience and vulnerability: Adaptation in the context of childhood adversities.* New York: Cambridge University Press. pp. 489–509.

Rutter, M. (2004). Pathways of genetic influences on psychopathology. *European Review, 12,* 19–33.

Rutter, M. (2005 a). Incidence of autism spectrum disorders: Changes over time and their meaning. *Acta Paediatrica, 94*, 2–15.

Rutter, M. (2005 b). Environmentally mediated risks for psychopathology: Research strategies and findings. *Journal of the American Academy of Child and Adolescent Psychiatry, 44*, 3–18.

Rutter, M. (2005 c). Adverse pre-adoption experiences and psychological outcomes. In D.M. Brodzinsky & J. Palacios (Eds.), *Psychological issues in adoption: Theory, research, and application.* Westport, CT: Greenwood Publishing. pp. 67–92.

Rutter, M. (2005 d). Genetic influences in autism. In F. Volkmar, R. Paul, A. Klin, & D. Cohen (Eds.), *Handbook of Autism and Pervasive Developmental Disorders (3rd ed.).* New York: Wiley. pp. 425–452.

Rutter, M. (2005 e). Autism research: Lessons from the past and prospects for the future. *Journal of Autism and Developmental Disorders, 35*, 241–257.

Rutter, M. (2005 f). What is the meaning and utility of the psychopathy concept? *Journal of Abnormal Child Psychology, 33*, 499–503.

Rutter, M. (in press a). Multiple meanings of a developmental perspective in psychopathology. *European Journal of Developmental Psychology.*

Rutter, M. (in press b). The psychological effects of institutional rearing. In P. Marshall & N. Fox (Eds.). *The development of social engagement.* New York: Oxford University Press.

Rutter, M. (in press c). *The promotion of resilience in the face of adversity.* In A. Clarke-Stewart & J. Dunn (Eds.). *Families count: Effects on child and adolescent development.* New York & Cambridge: Cambridge University Press.

Rutter, M., Bolton, P., Harrington, R., Le Couteur, A., Macdonald, H., & Simonoff, E. (1990a). Genetic factors in child psychiatric disorders – I. A review of research strategies. *Journal of Child Psychology and Psychiatry, 31*, 3–37.

Rutter, M., & Brown, G.W. (1966). The reliability and validity of measures of family life and relationships in families containing a psychiatric patient. *Social Psychiatry, 1*, 38–53.

Rutter, M., Caspi, A., Fergusson, D., Horwood, L.J., Goodman, R., Maughan, B., Moffitt, T.E., Meltzer, H., & Carroll, J. (2004). Sex differences in developmental reading disability: New findings from 4 epidemiological studies. *Journal of American Medical Association, 291*, 2007–2012.

Rutter, M., Caspi, A., & Moffitt, T.E. (2003). Using sex differences in psychopathology to study causal mechanisms: Unifying issues and research strategies. *Journal of Child Psychology and Psychiatry, 44*, 1092–1115.

Rutter, M., Champion, L., Quinton, D., Maughan, B., & Pickles, A. (1995). Understanding individual differences in environmental risk exposure. In P. Moen, G.H. Elder, Jr., & K. Lüscher. (Eds.), *Examining lives in context: Perspectives on the ecology of human development.* Washington, DC: American Psychological Association. pp. 61–93.

Rutter, M., Cox, A., Tupling, C., Berger, M., & Yule, W. (1975 a). Attainment and adjustment in two geographical areas: I. The prevalence of psychiatric disorder. *British Journal of Psychiatry, 126*, 493–509.

Rutter, M., Dunn, J., Plomin, R., Simonoff, E., Pickles, A., Maughan, B., Ormel, J., Meyer, J., & Eaves, L. (1997). Integrating nature and nurture: Implications of person–environment correlations and interactions for developmental psychology. *Development and Psychopathology, 9,* 335–364.

Rutter, M., & the English and Romanian Adoptees (E.R.A.) Study Team. (1998 a). Developmental catch-up, and deficit, following adoption after severe global early privation. *Journal of Child Psychology and Psychiatry, 39,* 465–476.

Rutter, M., Giller, H., & Hagell, A. (1998). *Antisocial behavior by young people.* New York: Cambridge University Press.

Rutter, M., Kreppner, J., O'Connor, T.G., & the English and Romanian Adoptees (ERA) Study Team. (2001). Specificity and heterogeneity in children's responses to profound institutional privation. *British Journal of Psychiatry, 179,* 97–103.

Rutter, M., Macdonald, H., Le Couteur, A., Harrington, R., Bolton, P., & Bailey, A. (1990). Genetic factors in child psychiatric disorders. II. Empirical findings. *Journal of Child Psychology and Psychiatry, 31,* 39–83.

Rutter, M., & Madge, N. (1976). *Cycles of disadvantage: A review of research.* London: Heinemann Educational.

Rutter, M., & Maughan, B. (2002). School effectiveness findings 1979–2002. *Journal of School Psychology, 40,* 451–475.

Rutter, M., Maughan, B., Mortimore, P., Ouston, J., & Smith, A. (1979). *Fifteen thousand hours: Secondary schools and their effects on children.* London: Open Books.

Rutter, M., & McGuffin, P. (2004). The Social, Genetic Developmental Psychiatry Research Centre: Its origins, conception, and initial accomplishments. *Psychological Medicine, 34,* 933–947.

Rutter, M., Moffitt, T.E., & Caspi, A. (in press). Gene–environment interplay and psychopathology: Multiple varieties but real effects. *Journal of Child Psychology and Psychiatry.*

Rutter, M., O'Connor, T., Beckett, C., et al. (2000). Recovery and deficit following profound early deprivation. In P. Selman (Ed.), *Intercountry adoption: Developments, trends and perspectives.* London: British Association for Adoption and Fostering. pp. 107–125.

Rutter, M., O'Connor, T., & the English and Romanian Adoptees Research Team. (2004). Are there biological programming effects for psychological development? Findings from a study of Romanian adoptees. *Developmental Psychology, 40,* 81–94.

Rutter, M., & Pickles, A. (1991). Person–environment interactions: Concepts, mechanisms, and implications for data analysis. In T.D. Wachs & R. Plomin (Eds.), *Conceptualization and measurement of organism–environment interaction.* Washington, DC: American Psychological Association. pp. 105–141.

Rutter, M., Pickles, A., Murray, R., & Eaves, L. (2001 a). Testing hypotheses on specific environmental causal effects on behavior. *Psychological Bulletin, 127,* 291–324.

Rutter, M., & Plomin, R. (1997). Opportunities for psychiatry from genetic findings. *British Journal of Psychiatry, 171,* 209–219.

Rutter, M., & Quinton, D. (1977). Psychiatric disorder – ecological factors and concepts of causation. In H. McGurk (Ed.), *Ecological factors in human development.* Amsterdam: North-Holland. pp. 173–187.

Rutter, M., & Quinton, D. (1984). Parental psychiatric disorder: Effects on children. *Psychological Medicine, 14,* 853–880.

Rutter, M., & Quinton, D. (1987). Parental mental illness as a risk factor for psychiatric disorders in childhood. In D. Magnusson & A. Ohman (Eds.), *Psychopathology: An interactional perspective*. New York: Academic Press. pp. 199–219.

Rutter, M., & Redshaw, J. (1991). Annotation: Growing up as a twin: Twin–singleton differences in psychological development. *Journal of Child Psychology and Psychiatry, 32*, 885–895.

Rutter, M., & Silberg, J. (2002). Gene–environment interplay in relation to emotional and behavioral disturbance. *Annual Review of Psychology, 53*, 463–490.

Rutter, M., Silberg, J., O'Connor, T., & Simonoff, E. (1999a). Genetics and child psychiatry: I. Advances in quantitative and molecular genetics. *Journal of Child Psychology and Psychiatry, 40*, 3–18.

Rutter, M., Silberg, J., & Simonoff, E. (1993). Whither behavioral genetics? A developmental psychopathological perspective. In R. Plomin & G.E. McClearn (Eds.), *Nature, nurture, and psychology*. Washington, DC: APA Books. pp. 433–456.

Rutter, M., & Smith, D. (1995). *Psychosocial disorders in young people: Time trends and their causes*. Chichester: Wiley.

Rutter, M., Thorpe, K., Greenwood, R., Northstone, K., & Golding, J. (2003). Twins as a natural experiment to study the causes of mild language delay: I. Design; twin–singleton differences in language, and obstetric risks. *Journal of Child Psychology and Psychiatry, 44*, 326–334.

Rutter, M., & Tienda, M. (2005). The multiple facets of ethnicity. In M. Rutter & M. Tienda (Eds.), *Ethnicity and causal mechanisms*. New York: Cambridge University Press. pp. 50–79.

Rutter, M., Yule, B., Quinton, D., Rowlands, O., Yule, W., & Berger, M. (1975 b). Attainment and adjustment in two geographical areas: III Some factors accounting for area differences. *British Journal of Psychiatry, 126*, 520–533.

Sampson, R.J., & Laub, J.H. (1993). *Crime in the making: Pathways and turning points through life*. Cambridge, MA: Harvard University Press.

Sampson, R.J., & Laub, J.H. (1996). Socioeconomic achievement in the life course of disadvantaged men: Military service as a turning point, circa 1940–1965. *American Sociological Review, 61*, 347–367.

Sampson, R.J., Raudenbush, S.W., & Earls, F. (1997). Neighborhoods and violent crime: A multilevel study of collective efficacy. *Science, 277*, 918–924.

Sandberg, S., McGuinness, D., Hillary, C., & Rutter, M. (1998). Independence of childhood life events and chronic adversities: A comparison of two patient groups and controls. *Journal of the American Academy of Child and Adolescent Psychiatry, 37*, 728–735.

Sapolsky, R.M. (1993). Endocrinology alfresco: Psychoendocrine studies of wild baboons. *Recent Progress in Hormone Research, 48*, 437–468.

Sapolsky, R.M. (1998). *Why zebras don't get ulcers: An updated guide to stress, stress-related diseases, and coping*. New York: W.H. Freeman, & Co.

Sargant, W., & Slater, E. (1954). *An introduction to physical methods of treatment in psychiatry, 3rd ed.* Edinburgh: Livingstone.

Saunders, A.M. (2000). Apolipoprotein E and Alzheimer disease: An update on genetic and functional analyses. *Journal of Neuropathology and Experimental Neurology, 59*, 751–758.

Scarr, S. (1992). Developmental theories for the 1990s: Development and individual differences. *Child Development, 63*, 1–19.

Scarr, S., & McCartney, K. (1983). How people make their own environment: A theory of genotype-environmental effects. *Child Development, 54*, 424–435.

Schachar, R., & Tannock, R. (2002). Syndromes of hyperactivity and attention deficit. In M. Rutter & E. Taylor (Eds.), *Child and adolescent psychiatry, 4th ed.* Oxford: Blackwell Scientific. pp. 399–418.

Scourfield, J., & Owen, M.J. (2002). Genetic counseling. In P. McGuffin, M.J. Owen, & I.I. Gottesman (Eds.), *Psychiatric genetics and genomics.* Oxford: Oxford University Press. pp. 415–423.

Segal, N.L. (1999). *Entwined lives: Twins and what they tell us about human behavior.* New York: Dutton.

Seglow, J., Pringle, M.K., & Wedge, L. (1972). *Growing up adopted.* Windsor, UK: National Foundation for Educational Research.

Shahbazian, M.D., Young, J.I., Yuva-Paylor, L.A., Spencer, C.M., Antalffy, B.A., Noebels, J.L., Armstrong, D.L., Paylor, R., & Zoghbi, H.Y. (2002). Mice with truncated MeCP2 recapitulate many Rett syndrome features and display hyper-acetylation of histone H3. *Neuron, 35*, 243–254.

Shahbazian, M.D., & Zoghbi, H.Y. (2001). Molecular genetics of Rett syndrome and clinical spectrum of MECP2 mutations. *Current Opinion in Neurology, 14*, 171–176.

Sham, P. (2003). Recent developments in quantitative trait loci analysis. In R. Plomin, J.C. DeFries, I. Craig, & P. McGuffin (Eds.), *Behavioural genetics in the postgenomic era.* Washington, DC: American Psychological Association. pp. 41–54.

Shaywitz, S.E., Shaywitz, B.A., Fulbright, R.K. Skudlarski, P., Mencl, W.E., Constable, R.T., Pugh, K.R., Holahan, J.M., Marchione, K.E., Fletcher, J.M., Lyon, G.R., & Gore, J.C. (2003). Neural systems for compensation and persistence: Young adult outcome of childhood reading disability. *Biological Psychiatry, 54*, 25–33.

Shields, J. (1962). *Monozygotic twins brought up apart and brought up together.* London: Oxford University Press.

Shiner, R., & Caspi, A. (2003). Personality differences in childhood and adolescence: Measurement, development, and consequences. *Journal of Child Psychology and Psychiatry, 44*, 2–32.

Shonkoff, J.P., & Phillips, D.A. (2000). *From neurons to neighborhoods: The science of early childhood development.* Washington, DC: National Academy Press.

Siever, K.J., Kalus, O.F., & Keefe, R.S. (1993). The boundaries of schizophrenia. *Psychiatric Clinics of North America, 16*, 217–244.

Silberg, J.L., & Eaves, L.J. (2004). Analysing the contributions of genes and parent–child interaction to childhood behavioural and emotional problems: A model for the children of twins. *Psychological Medicine, 34*, 347–356.

Silberg, J.L., Parr, T., Neale, M.C., Rutter, M., Angold, A., & Eaves, L.J. (2003). Maternal smoking during pregnancy and risk to boys' conduct disturbance: An examination of the causal hypothesis. *Biological Psychiatry, 53*, 130–135.

Silberg, J., Pickles, A., Rutter, M., Hewitt, J., Simonoff, E., Maes, H., et al. (1999). The influence of genetic factors and life stress on depression among adolescent girls. *Archives of General Psychiatry, 56*, 225–232.

Silberg, J., Rutter, M., D'Onofrio, B., & Eaves, L. (2003). Genetic and environmental risk factors in adolescent substance use. *Journal of Child Psychology and Psychiatry, 44*, 664–676.

Silberg, J.L., Rutter, M., & Eaves, L. (2001 a). Genetic and environmental influences on the temporal association between earlier anxiety and later depression in girls. *Biological Psychiatry, 49*, 1040–1049.

Silberg, J., Rutter, M., Neale, M., & Eaves, L. (2001 b). Genetic moderation of environmental risk for depression and anxiety in adolescent girls. *British Journal of Psychiatry, 179*, 116–121.

Simonoff, E., Pickles, A., Hervas, A., Silberg, J.L., Rutter, M., & Eaves, L. (1998 a). Genetic influences on childhood hyperactivity: Contrast effects imply parental rating bias, not sibling interaction. *Psychological Medicine, 28*, 825–837.

Simonoff, E., Pickles, A., Meyer, J., Silberg, J., & Maes, H. (1998 b). Genetic and environmental influences on subtypes of conduct disorder behavior in boys. *Journal of Abnormal Child Psychology, 27*, 497–511.

Skuse, D., & Kuntsi, J. (2002). Molecular genetic and chromosomal anomalies: Cognitive and behavioural consequences. In M. Rutter & E. Taylor (Eds.), *Child and adolescent psychiatry, 4th ed.* Oxford: Blackwell Scientific. pp. 205–240.

SLI Consortium. (2004). Highly significant linkage to the SLI1 locus in an expanded sample of individuals affected by Specific Language Impairment. *American Journal of Human Genetics, 74*, 1225–1238.

Slutske, W.S., Heath, A.C., Dinwiddie, S.H., Madden, P.A.F., Bucholz, K.K., Dunne, M.P., Statham, D.J., & Martin, N.G. (1997). Modeling genetic and environmental influences in the etiology of conduct disorder: A study of 2,682 adult twin pairs. *Journal of Abnormal Psychology, 106*, 266–279.

Small, G.W., Ercoli, L., Silverman, D.H.S., Huang, S-C., Komo, S., Bookheimer, S.Y., Lavretsky, H. Miller, K., Siddharth, P, Rasgon, N.L., Mazziotta, J.C., Saxena, S., Wu, H.M., Mega, M.S., Cummings, J.L., Saunders, A.M, Pericak-Vance, M.A., Roses, A.D., Barrio, J.R., & Phelps, M.E. (2000). Cerebral metabolic and cognitive decline in persons at genetic risk for Alzheimer's disease. *Proceedings of the National Academy of Sciences of the USA, 11*, 6037–6042.

Smalley, S.L. (1998). Autism and tuberous sclerosis. *Journal of Autism and Developmental Disorders, 28*, 419–426.

Smith, S.D., Kimberling, W.J., Pennington, B.F., & Lubs, H.A. (1983). Specific reading disability: Identification of an inherited form through linkage analysis. *Science, 219*, 1345.

Snowling, M.J., Gallagher, A., & Frith, U. (2003). Family risk of dyslexia is continuous: Individual differences in the precursors of reading skill. *Child Development, 74*, 358–373.

Snyder, J., Reid, J., & Patterson, G. (2003). A social learning model of child and adolescent antisocial behavior. In B.B. Lahey, T.E. Moffitt, & A. Caspi (Eds.), *Causes of conduct disorder and juvenile delinquency.* New York & London: The Guilford Press. pp. 27–48.

Sonuga-Barke, E.J.S. (1998). Categorical models of childhood disorder: A conceptual and empirical analysis. *Journal of Child Psychology and Psychiatry, 39*, 115–133.

Spence, M.A., Greenberg, D.A., Hodge, S.E., & Vieland, V.J. (2003). The Emperor's new methods. *American Journal of Human Genetics, 72*, 1084–1087.

Spielman, R.S., & Ewens, W.J. (1996). Invited Editorial: The TDT and other family-based tests for linkage disequilibrium and association. *American Journal of Human Genetics, 59*, 983–989.

Spira, A., Beane, J., Shah, V., Liu, G., Schembri, F., Yang, X., Palma, J., & Brody, J.S. (2004). Effects of cigarette smoke on the human airway epithelial cell transcriptome. *Proceedings of the National Academy of Sciences of the United States of America, 101*, 10143–10148.

Starfield, B. (1998). *Primary care: Balancing health needs, services, and technology.* Oxford: Oxford University Press.

Steffenburg, S., Gillberg, C., Hellgren, L., Andersson, L., Gillberg, I., Jakobsson, G., & Bohman, M. (1989). A twin study of autism in Denmark, Finland, Iceland, Norway and Sweden. *Journal of Child Psychology and Psychiatry, 30*, 405–416.

Stehr-Green, P., Tull, P., Stellfeld, M., Mortenson, P-B., & Simpson, D. (2003). Autism and Thimerosal-containing vaccines: Lack of consistent evidence for an association. *American Journal of Preventive Medicine, 25*, 101–106.

Stevenson, J. (2001). Comorbidity of reading/spelling diability and ADHD. In F. Levy, & D. Hay (Eds.), *Attention, genes and ADHD.* Hove, Sussex: Brunner-Routledge. pp. 9–114.

Stevenson, L., Graham, P., Fredman, G., & McLoughlin, V. (1987). A twin study of genetic influences on reading and spelling ability and disability. *Journal of Child Psychology and Psychiatry, 28*, 229–247.

Stone, A.A., Bovbjerg, D.H., Neale, J.M., Napoli, A., Valdimarsdottir, H., Cox, D., Hayden, F.G., & Gwaltney, J.M. Jr. (1992). Development of common cold symptoms following experimental rhinovirus infection is related to prior stressful life events. *Behavioral Medicine, 18*, 115–120.

Stoolmiller, M. (1999). Implications of the restricted range of family environments for estimates of heritability and nonshared environment in behavior-genetic adoption studies. *Psychological Bulletin, 125*, 392–409.

Storms, L.H., & Sigal, J.J. (1958). Eysenck's personality theory with special reference to 'The Dynamics of Anxiety and Hysteria'. *British Journal of Medical Psychology, 31*, 228–246.

Strachan, T., & Read, A.P. (2004). *Human molecular genetics 3.* New York, & Abingdon, Oxon: Garland Science, Taylor, & Francis.

Stratton, K., Howe, C., & Battaglia, F. (1996). *Fetal alcohol syndrome: Diagnosis, epidemiology, prevention, and treatment.* Washington, DC: National Academy Press.

Streissguth, A.P., Barr, H.M., Bookstein, F.L., Sampson, P.D., & Olson, H.C. (1999). The long term neurocognitive consequences of prenatal alcohol exposure: A 14 year study. *Psychological Science, 10*, 186–190.

Strittmatter, W.J., Saunders, A.M., Schmechel, D., Pericak-Vance, M., Enghild, J., Salvesen, G.S., & Roses, A.D. (1993). Apolipoprotein E: high-avidity binding to beta-amyloid and increased frequency of type 4 allele in late-onset familial Alzheimer disease. *Proceedings of the National Academy of Sciences of the USA, 90*, 1977–1981.

Suarez, B.K., Hampe, C.L., & Van Eerdewegh, P. (1994). Problems of replicating linkage claims in psychiatry. In E.S. Gershon, D.R. Cloninger, & J.E. Barrett

(Eds.), *Genetic approaches to mental disorders*. Washington, DC: American Psychiatric Press. pp. 23–46.

Sutherland, G.R., Gecz, J., & Mulley, J.C. (2002). Fragile X syndrome and other causes of X-linked mental handicap. In D.L. Rimoin, J.M. Connor, R.E. Pyeritz, & B.R. Korf (Eds.), *Emery and Rimoin's principles and practice of medical genetics, vol. 3*. London & New York: Churchill Livingstone. pp. 2801–2826.

Sullivan, P.F., & Eaves, L.J. (2002). Evaluation of analyses of univariate discrete twin data. *Behavior Genetics, 32*, 221–227.

Sullivan, P.F., Neale, M.C., & Kendler, K.S. (2000). Genetic epidemiology of major depression: Review and meta-analysis. *American Journal of Psychiatry, 157*, 1552–1562.

Sulston, J., & Ferry, G. (2002). *The common thread: A story of science, politics, ethics and the Human Genome*. Bantam: London, & New York.

Tai, E.S., Corella, D., Deurenberg-Yap, M., Cutter, J., Chew, S.K., Tan, C.E., & Ordovas, J.M. (2003). Dietary fat interacts with the −514C>T polymorphism in the hepatic lipase gene promoter on plasma lipid profiles in multiethnic Asian population: The 1998 Singapore National Health Survey. *The Journal of Nutrition, 133*, 3399–3408.

Talmud, P.J., Bujac, S., & Hall, S. (2000). Substitution of asparagine for aspartic acid at residue 9 (D9N) of lipoprotein lipase markedly augments risk of coronary heart disease in male smokers. *Atherosclerosis, 149*, 75–81.

Talmud, P.J. (2004). How to identify gene–environment interactions in a multifactorial disease: CHD as an example. *Proceedings of the Nutrition Society, 63*, 5–10.

Tawney, R.H. (1952). *Equity*. London: Allen and Unwin.

Taylor, A. (2004). The consequences of selective participation on behaviour-genetic findings: Evidence from simulated and real data. *Twin Research, 7*, 485–504.

Taylor, E., & Rutter, M. (2002). Classification: Conceptual issues and substantive findings. In M. Rutter & E. Taylor (Eds.), *Child and adolescent psychiatry, 4th ed.* Oxford: Blackwell Scientific. pp. 3–17.

Tennant, C., & Bebbington, P. (1978). The social causation of depression: A critique of the work of Brown and his colleagues. *Psychological Medicine, 8*, 565–576.

Teasdale, J.D., & Barnard, P.J. (1993). *Affect, cognition, and change: Re-modelling depressive thought*. Hove, England: Erlbaum.

Thapar, A. (2002). Attention Deficit Hyperactivity Disorder: New genetic findings, new directions. In R. Plomin, J.C. DeFries, I. Craig, & P. McGuffin (Eds.), *Behavioural genetics in the postgenomic era*. Washington, DC: American Psychological Association. pp. 445–462.

Thapar, A., Fowler, T., Rice, F., et al. (2003). Maternal smoking during pregnancy and Attention Deficit/Hyperactivity Disorder symptoms in offspring. *American Journal of Psychiatry, 160*, 1985–1989.

Thapar, A., Hervas, A., & McGuffin, P. (1995). Childhood hyperactivity scores are highly heritable and show sibling competition effects: Twin study evidence. *Behavior Genetics, 25*, 537–544.

Thapar, A., & McGuffin, P. (1994). A twin study of depressive symptoms in childhood. *British Journal of Psychiatry, 165*, 259–265.

Thapar, A., & McGuffin, P. (1996). A twin study of antisocial and neurotic symptoms in childhood. *Psychological Medicine, 26*, 1111–1118.

Thomas, A., & Chess, S. (1977). *Temperament and development.* New York: Brunner Mazel.

Thomas, A., Chess, S., & Birch, H. (1968). *Temperament and behavior disorders in childhood.* New York: New York University Press.

Thomas, A., Chess, S., Birch, H., Hertzig, M., & Korn, S. (1963). *Behavioral individuality in early childhood.* New York: New York University Press.

Thomas, L. (1979). *The Medusa and the Snail: More notes of a biology watcher.* New York: Viking Press.

Thorpe, K., Rutter, M., & Greenwood, R. (2003). Twins as a natural experiment to study the causes of mild language delay: II. Family interaction risk factors. *Journal of Child Psychology and Psychiatry, 44*, 342–355.

Tienari, P. (1999). Genotype–environment interactions and schizophrenia. *Acta Neuropsychiatrica, 11*, 48–49.

Tienari, P. (1991). Interaction between genetic vulnerability and family environment: The Finnish adoptive family study of schizophrenia. *Acta Psychiatrica Scandinavica, 84*, 460–465.

Tienari, P., Wynne, L.C., Moring, J., Läsky, K., Nieminen, P., Sorri, A., Lahti, I., Wahlberg, K-E., Naarala, M., Kurki-Suonio, K., Saarento, O., Koistinen, P., Tarvainen, T., Hakko, H., & Miettunen, J. (2000). Finnish adoptive family study: Sample selection and adoptee DSM-III-R diagnoses. *Acta Psychiatrica Scandinavica, 101*, 433–443.

Tienari, P., Wynne, L.C., Sorri, A., Lahti, I., Laksy, K., Moring, J., Naarala, M., Nieminen, P., & Wahlberg, K.E. (2004). Genotype–environment interaction in schizophrenia-spectrum disorder. Long-term follow-up study of Finnish adoptees. *British Journal of Psychiatry, 184*, 216–222.

Tizard, J. (1964). *Community services for the mentally handicapped.* Oxford: Oxford University Press.

Tizard, J. (1975). Race and IQ: The limits of probability. *New Behaviour, 1*, 6–9.

Townsend, P., Phillimore, P., & Beattie, A. (1988). *Health and deprivation: inequality and the North.* London: Croom Helm.

Tsuang, M.T., Bar, J.L., Stone, W.S., & Faraone, S.V. (2004). Gene–environment interactions in mental disorders. *World Psychiatry, 3*, 73–83.

Turkeltaub, P.E., Gareau, L., Flowers, D.L., Zeffiro, T.A., & Eden, G.F. (2003). Development of neural mechanisms for reading. *Nature Neuroscience, 6*, 767–773.

Turkheimer, E., Haley, A., Waldron, M., D'Onofrio, B., & Gottesman, I.I. (2003). Socioeconomic status modifies heritability of IQ in young children. *Psychological Science, 14*, 623–628.

Uchiyama, T., Kurosawa, M., & Inaba, Y. (in press). Does MMR vaccine cause so-called "regressive autism"? *Journal of Autism and Developmental Disorders.*

Valentine, G.H. (1986). *The chromosomes and their disorders: An introduction for clinicians.* London: Heinemann.

van den Oord, E.J.C.G., Pickles, A., & Waldman, I.D. (2003). Normal variation and abnormality: An empirical study of the liability distributions underlying depression and delinquency. *Journal of Child Psychology and Psychiatry, 44*, 180–192.

van Os, J., & Sham, P. (2003). Gene–environment correlation and interaction in schizophrenia. In R.M. Murray, P.B. Jones, E. Susser, J. van Os, & M. Cannon (Eds.), *The epidemiology of schizophrenia.* Cambridge: Cambridge University Press. pp. 235–253.

van Wieringen, J.C. (1986). Secular growth changes. In F. Falkner & J.M. Tanner (Eds.), *Human growth, vol. 3, Methodology, 2nd ed.* New York: Plenum Press. pp. 307–331.

Venter J.C., et al. (2001). The sequence of the human genome. *Science, 291,* 1304–1351.

Viding, E., Blair, R.J., Moffitt, T.E., & Plomin, R. (2005). Evidence for substantial genetic risk for psychopathy in 7-year-olds. *Journal of Child Psychology and Psychiatry, 46,* 592–597.

Viding, E., Spinath, F., Price, T.S., Bishop, D.V.M., Dale, P.S., & Plomin, R. (2004). Genetic and environmental influence on language impairment in 4-year old same-sex and opposite-sex twins. *Journal of Child Psychology and Psychiatry, 45,* 315–325.

Volkmar, F., & Dykens, E. (2002). Mental retardation. In M. Rutter & E. Taylor (Eds.), *Child and adolescent psychiatry, 4th ed.* Oxford, England: Blackwell Scientific Publications. pp. 697–710.

Volkmar, F.R., Lord, C., Bailey, A., Schultz, R.T., Klin, A., & Wadsworth, S.J. (2004). Autism and pervasive developmental disorders. *Journal of Child Psychology and Psychiatry, 41,* 135–170.

Wachs, T.D., & Plomin, R. (1991). *Conceptualization and measurement of organism–environment interaction.* Washington, DC: American Psychological Association.

Wadsworth, S.J., Knopik, V.S., & DeFries, J.C. (2000). Reading disability in boys and girls: No evidence for a differential genetic etiology. *Reading and Writing: An Interdisciplinary Journal, 13,* 133–145.

Wahlberg, K-E., Wynne, L.C., Oja, H., Keskitalo, P., Pykalainen, L., Lahti, I., Moring, J., Naarala, M., Sorri, A., Seitarnaa, M., Laksy, K., Kolassa, J., & Tienari, P. (1997). Gene–environment interaction in vulnerability to schizophrenia: Findings from the Finnish Adoptive Family Study of Schizophrenia. *American Journal of Psychiatry 154,* 355–362.

Waldman, I.D., & Rhee, S.H. (2002). Behavioural and molecular genetic studies. In S. Sandberg (Ed.), *Hyperactivity and attention disorders of childhood, 2nd ed.* Cambridge; Cambridge University Press. pp. 290–335.

Waldman, I.D., Rhee, S.H., Levy, F., & Hay, D.A. (2001). Causes of the overlap among symptoms of ADHD, oppositional defiant disorder, and conduct disorder. In F. Levy & D. Hay (Eds.), *Attention, genes and ADHD.* Hove, East Sussex: Brunner-Routledge. pp. 115–138.

Wang, W.Y., Barratt, B.J., Clayton, D.G., & Todd, J.A. (2005). Genome-wide association studies: Theoretical and practical concerns. *Nature Reviews – Genetics, 6,* 109–118.

Wang, X., Zuckerman, B., Pearson, C., Kaufman, G., Chen, C., Wang, G., Niu, T., Wise, P.H., Bauchner, H., & Xu, X. (2002). Maternal cigarette smoking, metabolic gene polymorphism, and infant birth weight. *Journal of the American Medical Association, 287,* 195–202.

Waterland, R.A., & Jirtle, R.L. (2003). Transposable elements: Targets for early nutritional effects on epigenetic gene regulation. *Molecular and Cellular Biology, 23,* 5293–5300.

Watson, J.D., & Crick, F.H. (1953). Genetical implications of the structure of deoxyribonucleic acid. *Nature, 171,* 964–967.

Weatherall, D. (1995). *Science and the quiet art; Medical research and patient care.* Oxford: Oxford University Press.

Weatherall, D.J., & Clegg, J.B. (2001). *The thalassaemia syndromes.* Oxford: Blackwell Scientific.

Weaver, I.C.G., Cervoni, N., Champagne, F.A., D'Alessio, A.C., Charma, S., Seckl, J., Dymov, S., Szyf, M., & Meaney, M.J. (2004). Epigenetic programming by maternal behavior. *Nature Neuroscience, 7,* 847–854.

Weir, J.B. (1952). The assessment of the growth of schoolchildren with special reference to secular changes. *British Journal of Nutrition, 6,* 19–33.

Whalley, H.C., Simonotto, E., Flett, S., Marshall, I., Ebmeier, K.P., Owens, D.G.C., Goddard, N.H., Johnstone, E.C., & Lawrie, S.M. (2004). fMRI correlates of state and trait effects in subjects at genetically enhanced risk of schizophrenia. *Brain, 127,* 478–490.

Williams, J. (2002). Reading and language disorders. In P. McGuffin, M.J. Owen, & I.I. Gottesman (Eds.), *Psychiatric genetics and genomics.* Oxford: Oxford University Press. pp. 129–145.

Wimmer, H., & Goswami, U. (1994). The influence of orthographic consistency on reading development: Word recognition in English and German children. *Cognition, 51,* 91–103.

World Health Organization. (1993). *The ICD-10 classification of mental and behavioural disorders: Diagnostic criteria for research.* Geneva: World Health Organization.

Wüst, S., Van Rossum, F.C.E., Federenko, I.S., Koper, J.W., Kumsta, R., & Hellhammer, D.H. (2004). Common polymorphisms in the glucocorticoid receptor gene are associated with adrenocortical responses to psychosocial stress. *The Journal of Clinical Endocrinology and Metabolism, 89,* 565–573.

Yaffe, K., Haan, M., Byers, A., Tangen, C., & Kuller, L. (2000). Estrogen use, APOE, and cognitive decline: Evidence of gene–environment interaction. *Neurology, 54,* 1949–1953.

Yamori, Y., Nara, Y., Mizushima, S., Murakami, S., Ikeda, K., Sawamura, M., Nabika, T., & Horie, R. (1992). Gene–environment interaction in hypertension, stroke and atherosclerosis in experimental models and supportive findings from a world-wide cross-sectional epidemiologial survey: A WHO-cardiac study. *Clinical and Experimental Pharmacology and Physiology, 19,* 43–52.

Yang, Q., & Khoury, M.J. (1997). Evolving methods in genetic epidemiology III. Gene–environment interaction in epidemiological research. *Epidemiologic Reviews, 19,* 33–43.

Young, L.J. (2003). The neural basis of pair bonding in a monogamous species: A model for understanding the biological basis of human behavior. In K.W. Wachter & R.A. Bulatao (Eds.), *Offspring: Human fertility behavior in biodemographic perspective.* Washington, DC: National Academies Press. pp. 91–103.

Young, L.J., Nilsen, R., Waymire, K.G., MacGregor, G.R., & Insel, T.R. (1999). Increased affiliative response to vasopressin in mice expressing the V_{1a} receptor from a monogamous vole. *Nature, 400,* 766–768.

Zoccolillo, M., Pickles, A., Quinton, D., & Rutter, M. (1992). The outcome of childhood conduct disorder: Implications for defining adult personality disorder and conduct disorder. *Psychological Medicine, 22,* 971–986.

Zoghbi, H.Y. (2003). Postnatal neurodevelopmental disorders: Meeting at the synapse? *Science, 302,* 826–830.

Glossary

Acetylation   A chemical process that plays a role in transcription

Additive genetic effects   Those caused by the non-synergistic cumulative effect of multiple genes (see non-additive genetic effects for the contrasting alternative)

Adenine   One of the four chemicals that make up base pairs

ADHD   Attention deficit disorder with hyperactivity. A disorder usually first manifest in the preschool years and characterized by inattention, overactivity, and impulsiveness (see Chapter 4)

Adoption studies   A range of strategies that use the separation of biological and social parentage brought about by adoption to assess the relative effects of genetic and environmental influences on population variance for a particular trait or disorder

Affected sib-pair (ASP) linkage design   A linkage design that uses the study of many pairs of sibs, both of whom have the trait or disorder being studied, in order to determine the likelihood that the trait or disorder is co-inherited with a particular gene locus

Allele   An alternative form of a gene at a particular locus – such as the A, B, and O variations for the ABO blood group marker

Allelic heterogeneity   The existence of many different disease-influencing alleles at a locus

Alternative splicing   The natural occurrence of different sets of splice junction sequences that serve to allow a single gene to give rise to more than one protein product

Alzheimer's disease   A particular form of degenerative brain disease that typically begins in late life (see Chapter 4)

Amino acid   One of the building blocks of proteins

Angelman syndrome   A disorder associated with both characteristic physical features and cognitive impairment, due to a deletion of a segment of chromosome 15 that has been inherited from the mother

Animal models   These comprise the use of nonhuman animals that have been manipulated in order to produce an organism with the same genetic mutation as one causing a particular phenotype in humans, or manipulated to manifest a form of behavior that is thought to mimic some phenotype in humans. Such models, as used in genetic research, provide an important means of investigating gene action

Anticipation   The circumstance in which the severity of a disorder gets greater, or the age of onset gets younger, in subsequent generations. An identified cause of this phenomenon is the intergenerational expression of unstable trinucleotide repeats, gibing rise to a dynamic mutation (see Chapter 8)

Antisocial behavior   A general term that incorporates a range of socially disapproved and socially disruptive behavior. It includes overt delinquency/crime but also it includes oppositional/defiance behavior of marked degree (see Chapter 4)

Association strategy   The method used to test whether the particular alleles associated with a trait or disorder differ from those in appropriate control populations

Assortative mating   Mating that is non-random because of a tendency for it to be between people who are similar in their characteristics, or opposite, or who are similar in having a disorder but the disorders in the two partners being different

Autism   A neurodevelopmental disorder first manifest in the early preschool years that is characterized by deficits in social reciprocity and communication together with stereotyped and repetitive patterns of behavior (see Chapter 4)

Autosome   Any chromosome other than the X or Y chromosomes. Humans have 22 pairs of autosomal chromosomes and one pair of sex chromosomes (XX in females and XY in males)

Base   One of four chemicals: adenine, cytosine, guanine, and thymine

Base pair   One step in the spiral staircase of the double helix of DNA comprising the bonding of two of the four bases

Bipolar disorder   A recurrent disorder involving episodes of mania and hypomania, usually also with episodes of depression. It used to be referred to as manic-depressive disorder (see Chapter 4)

Carrier   An individual who has a particular genetic allele in a heterozygous form with both the mutant recessive version and the normal version. Because the relevant disorder is recessively inherited the individual will be phenotypically normal

Chromosome   A structure mainly made up of chromatin that is present in the nucleus of cells and which contains DNA. Humans have 23 pairs of chromosomes

Codon   A sequence of three base pairs (defined above) that codes for a particular amino acid

Concordance   Presence of a particular trait or disorder in two family members, usually used in relation to twin pairs

Correlation   A statistical measure of association, or resemblance, that ranges from +1.0 (indicating perfect association), through 0.0 (no association) to −1.0 (meaning complete disagreement or negative association)

Cytosine   One of the four chemicals that make up base pairs

Depressive disorder   A disorder, often recurrent, that is characterized by low mood, feelings of guilt and hopelessness, disturbances of sleep and appetite, and often by either agitation or retardation of movement (see Chapter 4)

Dizygotic   A twin pair that is non-identical (or fraternal) and therefore equivalent genetically to a pair of siblings

DNA   Deoxyribonucleic acid; the double-stranded molecule, in the form of a double helix that codes for genetic information

DNA sequence   The order of base pairs that specifies what is inherited

Dominant inheritance   A pattern of inheritance in which the possession of just one particular mutant allele (i.e., heterozygote) is sufficient to cause the disorder

Down syndrome   A syndrome associated with a range of characteristic physical features and substantial cognitive impairment that is due to chromosome 21 trisomy (i.e., an extra chromosome)

Dyslexia   A specific disability in reading skills that is discrepant with a person's general level of intelligence (sometimes referred to as specific reading retardation)

Environmental mediation   Causal mechanisms that are due to the operation of environmental influences

Epigenetic   Changes that are heritable but that do not involve any change in DNA sequence

Epistasis   Synergistic interaction among two or more genes at different loci

Equal environments assumption   The assumption that constitutes the basis of the twin strategy that specifies that the environmental variance with identical and fraternal twin pairs will be the same with respect to the environments that influence the trait or disorder being studied (see Chapter 3)

Eugenics   The topic concerning factors that could improve the hereditary qualities of either individuals or groups, including the possibility of modifying the fertility of different categories of people (see Chapter 1)

Exon   DNA sequences that are transcribed into messenger RNA and then translated into polypeptides that combine to form proteins

Familial loading   The extent to which a trait tends to be found in multiple family members

Full sibling   Siblings who are born to the same mother and have the same biological father

Gene   The basic unit of inheritance

Gene–environment correlation   Genetic influence on individual differences in exposure to particular environments (see Chapter 9)

Gene–environment interaction   Genetic influence on individual differences in susceptibility to particular environments (see Chapter 9)

Gene expression   The process by which the effects of a gene have functional effects. Most genes are expressed in only some body tissues and may be expressed only at certain phases of development. Gene expression is influenced by both other genes and by environmental factors (see Chapter 7)

Gene locus   The place on a chromosome that includes a particular gene

Genetic (genomic) imprinting   The process by which an allele at a given locus is expressed differently according to whether it is inherited from the mother or father

Genetic mediation   Causal mechanisms that are due to the operation of genes

Genetic relatedness   The degree to which relatives have genes in common. First-degree relatives of the proband (parents, siblings, and children) are 50 percent similar genetically. Second-degree relatives of the proband (grandparents, aunts, and uncles) are 25 percent similar genetically. Third-degree relatives of the proband (first cousins) are 12.5 percent similar genetically

Genome   The entire DNA of an organism as represented in one member of each chromosome pair

Genotype   The genetic make-up of an individual; usually, however, a term restricted to the combination of alleles at a particular genetic locus

Glucocorticoid   A type of steroid that is concerned with cortisol-related functions

Guanine   One of the four chemicals that make up base pairs

Half siblings   Siblings who share only one biological parent

Haplotype   A set of closely linked genetic markers that tend to be inherited together, rather than being separated during recombination

Heritability   The proportion of variation in a particular population that is attributable to genetic influences, but note that this will include co-action with the environment (see Chapter 3). Broad heritability includes both additive and non-additive effects whereas narrow heritability concerns only additive effects

Heterozygote   A person who has different alleles at a given locus on the two members of a chromosome pair

Hippocampus   A specific part of the brain that is particularly concerned with memory functions

Huntington's disease   An autosomal-dominant disease, usually having an onset in middle age or later, that leads to dementia and death

Incidence   The rate of new cases of a disorder arising in a specified population during a particular period of time (see Chapter 2)

Intron   DNA sequence that is spliced out during the process of transcription

Lambda   The statistic that quantifies the extent to which a particular genetic relationship (typically a sibling) is associated with an increase in risk for some disorder as compared with the general population

Locus   The site of a specific gene on a chromosome

LOD score   Log of the odds, a statistical term that quantifies the likelihood that two loci are linked (meaning co-inherited). By convention, a LOD score of at least +3 is accepted as showing the likelihood of significant linkage

Mendelian   Inheritance of a single-gene condition that requires no particular environment for its causation and which follows a particular pattern of inheritance (see Chapter 6)

Methylation   A chemical process that is crucially involved in epigenetic mechanisms

Mitochondrial inheritance   Inheritance through the mitochondria, which are situated in the cytoplasm (the part of the cell outside the nucleus). Mitochondrial inheritance is entirely through the mother

Monochorionic   The circumstance of monozygotic twinning in which the two twins share the same placenta and surrounding chorionic sac

Monozygotic   A twin pair that is genetically identical

mRNA (messenger RNA)   Processed RNA that leaves the nucleus of the cell and which serves as a template for the synthesis of polypeptides in the cell body

Mutation   A heritable change in the DNA base sequence of a gene

Neuroendocrine system   Involves hormones that have effects on brain functioning

Neurone   Nerve cells that are involved in the transmission of information (as distinct from the provision of support)

Non-additive genetic effects   Those involving synergism either among different alleles at the same locus (dominance) or different genes at some other locus (epistasis)

Non-shared environmental effect   Environmental influences that have the net effect of making siblings less alike. Compare with shared environmental effect. Note that the non-shared environmental effect also includes measurement error

Nucleotide   One of the building blocks of DNA and RNA, made up of a base plus a molecule of sugar and one of phosphoric acid

Oligogenic   A trait influenced by the cumulative effect of a relatively small number of genes with major effects

Pedigree   A family tree or diagram showing the genealogical history of a family and, thereby, pointing to particular patterns of inheritance (see Chapter 6)

Penetrance   The proportion of individuals with a specific genotype who manifest it in the form of the phenotype to which it gives rise

Personality   Based on temperament, but a higher-order concept involving a coherence that includes attitudinal features, patterns of thought, and motivational consideration, as well as dispositional attributes

Phenotype   The manifestation of a trait or disorder that results from the effects of genes, either with or without environmental influences

Phenylketonuria (PKU)   An autosomal recessive metabolic disorder that involves an inability to handle the phenylalanine present in all normal human diets. If untreated, the condition results in mental retardation

Pleiotropy   Genetic effects that are multiple and different

Polygenic   A trait influenced by the cumulative effect of many genes with only small effects

Polymerase chain reaction (PCR)   A method used to amplify a particular DNA sequence

Polymorphism   A locus with two or more alleles

Polypeptide   The structure composed of amino-acids that goes on to constitute proteins

Population stratification   The situation in which alleles that are associated with ethnicity (or some other genetically influenced feature) lead to an artifactual association between some trait or disorder and the allele being studied because the cases (i.e., the individuals with the disorder) and the control group differ with respect to the allele. The association with the trait is spurious because the allelic difference arises from the genetic make-up of the population studied and not from the trait or disorder (see Chapter 8)

Prader-Willi syndrome   A syndrome associated with a range of physical features, excessive appetite leading to obesity, and substantial cognitive impairment. It is due to a deletion of a portion of chromosome 15 inherited from the father

Proband   The index individual used to identify families including someone with a particular trait or disorder

Promoter region   The regulatory region that includes some of the factors involved in transcription

Protein   The ultimate products of genes, made up of polypeptides

Proteomics The analysis of protein expression, protein structure, and protein interactions. This relatively new science is fundamental for an understanding of how proteins bring about their effects and, hence, how these consequences of gene action may influence human behavior

Pseudogene A defective copy of a polypeptide-encoding gene

Quantitative trait loci (QTL) Genes that contribute (along with other genes and environmental influences) to quantitative variation in some dimensional trait

Receptor gene Genes involved with the proteins that control the response to some transmission feature

Relative risk The degree to which the presence of some factor increases the risk of some outcome as compared with the situation when the factor is absent (see Chapter 2)

Rett syndrome A rare dominant sex-linked condition that occurs almost entirely in girls, is usually first manifest at age 6 to 18 months, and which is associated with mental retardation, a loss of purposive hand movements, and a failure of head growth (see Chapter 8)

Ribosome Large RNA-protein complexes in the cytoplasm of cells (outside the nucleus) that is involved in translation

Risk factor Something that causally increases the likelihood that a person will develop a particular trait or disorder, but which does not determine the disorder or trait on its own (see Chapter 2)

Risk indicator Something that is statistically associated with an increased likelihood that someone will develop a particular trait or disorder, but which is not itself directly involved in the causal process (see Chapter 2)

RNA Ribonucleic acid (see mRNA)

Schizophrenia A serious, usually chronic, mental disorder with precursors in childhood but with psychotic manifestations (including delusions, hallucination, and thought disorders) usually first manifest only in late adolescence or adult life (see Chapter 4)

Sex chromosome One of the two chromosomes (X and Y) that specify genetic sex (XX in females, XY in males)

Shared environmental effect Environmental influences that have the net effect of making siblings more alike. The term is often referred to as the "common family environment" but this is misleading because it has no necessary connection with either the family or whether the environmental influence is family-wide (see Chapters 3 and 5)

Siblings Brothers and sisters

Specific language impairment (SLI) A specific impairment in the development of language (sometimes referred to in the past as a developmental language disorder or developmental dysphasia)

Stratification *See* population stratification

Substance use disorder A disorder in which there is social, psychological, or somatic malfunction resulting from the use of substances (drugs) that are taken for recreational reasons or from medical reasons that have become harmful in their effects. The term includes the use of alcohol or tobacco as well as illegal substances.

The malfunction includes, but is not restricted to, dependence. In the past often referred to as drug addiction

Susceptibility gene   A gene that increases the likelihood that a person will develop a particular trait or disorder, but which does not determine the disorder on its own

Telomere   A specialized structure made up of DNA and protein that caps the ends of chromosomes

Temperament   Basic traits first evident in the preschool years, concerned with behavioral tendencies often involving reactivity to the environment, and which have an important biological underpinning

Thymine   One of the four chemicals that make up base pairs

Trait   A characteristic or phenotype, which may take the form of either a dimensional attribute or a categorical condition

Transcription   The process by which DNA specifies RNA

Translation   The process whereby mRNA specifies the production of particular polypeptides (see Chapter 7)

Trinucleotide   A repetitive DNA sequence. Unstable varieties are important because the process of expansion over the course of intergenerational transmission constitutes a form of dynamic mutation that gives rise to disease (see Chapter 6)

Tuberous sclerosis   A condition, inherited in an autosomal-dominant fashion (but frequently arising as a spontaneous new mutation), due to one of two genes (on chromosomes 9 and 16). It is manifest in a very variable manner but with the most characteristic feature being the growths in the brain that give the condition its name. In its most severe forms it is associated with mental retardation and epilepsy. It is accompanied by an increased risk for autism spectrum disorders

Variable expression   The occurrence of the effect of a simple gene that is variable in its manifestations across individuals (see Chapter 6)

X inactivation   The process by which one of the two X chromosomes possessed by females is rendered inactive

X-linked trait   A phenotype that is controlled by a locus on the X chromosome

Zygosity   Whether a twin pair is monozygotic (identical) or dizygotic (fraternal)

Index